OF CELL AND CLOISTER

OF CELL AND CLOISTER

CATHOLIC RELIGIOUS ORDERS THROUGH THE AGES

Doley C. Moss

Illustrated by VIRGINIA BRODERICK

THE BRUCE PUBLISHING COMPANY
MILWAUKEE

NIHIL OBSTAT:

JOANNES A. SCHULIEN, S.T.D.
Censor librorum

IMPRIMATUR:

✠ ALBERTUS G. MEYER
Archiepiscopus Milwauchiensis
February 16, 1957

Rosary College Dewey Classification Number: 271

Library of Congress Catalog Card Number: 57–8941

© 1957 BY THE BRUCE PUBLISHING COMPANY
MADE IN THE UNITED STATES OF AMERICA

AUTHOR'S NOTE

This brief story of religious orders is told for laymen, by a layman. It makes no attempt to be historically complete, or to be exhaustive of the subject in any sense. In order to condense so much material into one book, it has been necessary to omit many orders, as well as the development of religious life in many areas. Only those orders and areas considered salient points in the story have been elaborated upon. When it is remembered that such renowned historians of monasticism as De Montalembert and Helyot left their works uncompleted in six and seven volumes, respectively, it may be realized how constricting were the limitations imposed here.

The author wishes to express her sincere gratitude for the co-operation of all the religious and clerics who so graciously contributed the information and prayers asked of them. A special debt of gratitude, for their patient assistance and advice, is owed to the Reverend James McVann, C.S.P., of St. Paul's College, Washington, D. C.; Professor Riley Hughes, of Georgetown University; and the Reverend Joseph Gallen, S.J., of Woodstock College, Woodstock, Maryland; also to Mrs. Doley T. Crawford, the author's mother, who made possible the entire project.

D. C. M.

April 1, 1957

CONTENTS

OF CELL AND CLOISTER

CHAPTER ONE

THE SEED AND THE GARDEN

It was not so long ago that religious orders were considered a last vestige of medievalism, their members victims of an outmoded notion — facing sure extinction. But instead of declining into oblivion, religious community life in the Catholic Church has steadily increased, and its members are making valuable contributions to our society as writers, scientists, nurses, educators. Aware at last of this, indifference has lately turned to interest, and even to admiration. Indeed, that interest presently amounts to almost a vogue: plays, books, motion pictures, and articles in magazines

3

or newspapers constantly feature religious of all types; the drama of their odd garb and their admitted zeal and virtue are enjoyed by a heretofore apathetic – or antipathetic – public.

Despite this new-found interest in members of religious orders, few laymen know very much about the numerous communities of monks, nuns, priests, Sisters, and Brothers, that so abound in our country, or understand the origins and motives which have created that mode of life. Many misconceptions still prevail; bewildered heads shake, suspicions are murmured, arguments ensue. The terms "frustration" and "fear of life" are still heard – but with less and less conviction. Obviously, such easy answers are not the solution to the mystery that our psychology-conscious layman once thought they were; the mystery of that compelling force which makes such a "strange" manner of life continue to thrive so tenaciously. Nor are the answers usually to be found in the crowded pages of secular histories or the dramatized lives of religious found in novels or plays. But perhaps they may be found in a record of those motives and origins of which the layman knows so little; in the lives of some of its founders and in the adventures and events which have engaged community life for the past nineteen hundred years. It is a romantic, a colorful, story – and vastly important to our civilization. If that story were better known, many remaining misconceptions and prejudices would disappear.

*   *   *

Members of religious orders are religious ascetics, their mode of life often referred to by social scientists as "organized asceticism." Whether practiced in community or individually, religious asceticism is not peculiar to the Catholic Church, or even to the Christian religion. Almost every civilization and culture has produced some forms of it. Yet the origin of religious asceticism is unknown; it seems to have come into existence with man's first awareness of God, and of good and evil – an awareness which He created in His human creatures from the very beginning. Man's desire to know God, to love Him, and to be worthy of God's love, has ever caused him to seek spiritual perfection; but to find such perfection he soon realized that he must discipline his mind and body, overcoming their weaknesses and the world's distractions. This, in essence, is religious asceticism, as distinct from natural asceticism, or self-discipline for natural ends — such as athletic or technical skill, knowledge, or even an orderly and prudent life.

However expressed, the desire to find God and to please Him in some special way extends as far back as history goes. Earliest voyagers to the Orient found nunneries and monasteries, or lamaseries, long established; yogis, fakirs, Sadhus, and various other kinds of "holy men" were as prevalent then as they are now. In the Near East, the priests of the ancient pre-Roman religions were ascetics, and moral goodness was associated with religious belief. In the pre-Roman West the Druid priests are thought to have been ascetics who lived in some sort of communities; as learned teachers and judges, they were held in great respect, much as are the lama scholars of the Orient. In Hellenic culture, however, religious asceticism was rare; the Greek and Roman mythologies were not related to personal morality, containing no god who loved or was to be loved by mortals — or who took any sympathetic interest in their lives at all. Morality was related only to ethics and philosophy, not to religion. Ascetical societies, such as the Stoics, fostered only a natural asceticism based on discipline of the senses for its own sake, with no spiritual value whatsoever. Yet there were exceptions. The six nunlike Vestal Virgins of the Romans might be considered a community of religious ascetics, and Greek drama depicts a type of aged sage — undoubtedly based on actuality — whose wisdom is semispiritual. He is a kind of hermit or eremite — another product of religious asceticism found in every age and culture. Devotee of many a religion, or of some personal persuasion, the hermit of the desert and the mountain is a traditional figure in all history.

Of all the various pre-Christian brands of it, religious asceticism in the Catholic Church descends from only one; this is the Hebraic, whose spiritual traditions are also Christianity's. The history of Judaism reveals not only many hermit-ascetics — as were the Prophets — but many ascetical communities, societies, and sects, some of which are known to have existed hundreds of years before Christ. Ascetical life in the Church but carries on Judaic spiritual values and practices to an ultimate fruition, as the Old Law is brought to fruition in the New.

Members of the oldest known and most renowned Jewish ascetical society, or "sect," were called the Essenes, or "Healers." The Essenes were large colonies of men who lived in the deserts, or on the outskirts of towns, and who practiced a very austere form of Judaism. They owned no property, abjured marriage, and devoted themselves to the healing of the sick. They also cultivated medicinal herbs, studied the curative properties of minerals, tilled the soil, and made farm implements. Despite their intense austerity, they were noted for their kindness and hospitality, especially toward the aged. At their zenith, about a hundred years before Christ, the Essenes numbered about four thousand. Legend holds that they were the "Children of the Prophet" — or their successors — spoken of in the Old Testament; that is, disciples of the Prophets Elias and Elisius, who lived as hermits in the vicinity of Mount Carmel, a mountain ridge in Palestine. The legend tells of remnants of the "Children of the Prophet" who continued as Christianized communities of hermit-monks — becoming the first Christian religious community, or "order," in the Church. This legend of the hermits of Mount Carmel is claimed by the Carmelite Order as the story of its origin, a much-disputed claim which will be examined in greater detail later. Other opinion holds that the Essenes became extinct in about the first century A.D.

Members of a similar Jewish community or society were the Therapeutae, also known as the "Healers." The Therapeutae were made up of both men and women who also specialized in healing remedies and care of the sick, living in voluntary poverty and chastity, and devoting much of their time to prayer and manual labor. The Rechabites, Sadducees, Pharisees, and Nazarites were four other such societies. The Nazarites were vowed to certain ascetical practices, such as abstinence from wine and from cutting the hair, and to scrupulous observance of the Jewish ceremonial laws. Samson was a Nazarite and St. John the Baptist was thought to be one.

So many ascetical groups and practices flourished in Judaic history that we may well see how the spiritual values and customs of the Old Testament were carried over into the New, to be re-emphasized and clarified by the teachings of Christ. Among the first and most important of these were the ascetical practices of poverty, chastity, and obedience, advocated by Christ and His Apostles in the Gospels. For this reason did the very first ascetics of the Church, the Apostles, divide their goods among one another and the first members of the faithful, separate from their wives, and live every moment in obedience to those advocations which came to be known as the Evangelical Counsels. And for the same reason did the two next kinds of Christian ascetics come into being: the consecrated virgins and the *continentes*. Aside from the Apostles and the martyrs, they were the most honored members of the early Church.

Exhorted by our Lord, preached by the Apostles, and marveled at by the pagans, continence was one of the most highly esteemed practices of the "new religion." Those who had sacrificed the consolations of marriage for the love of God — although they never considered marriage an evil in itself — were revered as a special class from the first century onward. Among these were the wives of men in Holy Orders who, by mutual consent, had separated themselves from their marital duties; other devout members of the faithful of both sexes, called *continentes;* and also widows. Deaconesses were appointed from among the widows. For the first four centuries of the Church their function is thought to have been to act as superiors to the wives of men in Holy Orders and to prepare women for baptism and burial. After four centuries their office became extinct. But most especially there were the young women who had espoused themselves to Christ for life. These were the consecrated virgins.

By the second century, consecrated virgins were the "spiritual aristocracy" of every church; they sat in a special place and received Communion before the rest of the congregation. The rite of consecration was a very formal one, conducted by a bishop, during which the young woman received from him her wedding veil, as a bride of Christ, was anointed, and then invested with a crown, ring, and stole. Special rules and customs soon developed for the virgins. As they lived at first with their families, their spiritual director, the bishop, exhorted them constantly against moral pitfalls such as frivolity and pride; they were advised to dress modestly, without jewels, to wear veils, and to avoid appearing at gay or public functions. Certain prayers were to be said privately at home, and together in the church, and other pious duties carried out. A life of retirement, at first only recommended, was later decreed and age limits were set. The virgin's modest garb, consisting of a dark, long-sleeved dress, long veil, and short hair became a kind of "habit," and her life a strict regimen of prayer, fasting, and good works. Both the virgin and the *continente* drew apart from the world into almost complete seclusion. For some, this seclusion took the form of solitary life, on the outskirts of the towns, but for most it led to a common life, lived in a community, under a rule. What may be called the first Catholic *religious* thus appears. Many details of these earliest rules are to be found in the writings of St. Jerome and St. Ambrose, in the fourth century.

By the fourth century another kind of Christian ascetic had also appeared, whose manner of life, like that of the virgin, soon led to the religious community. This was made up of devout men and women who frequented the new basilicas of the East, in order to privately recite the Canonical Hours,[1] and other prayers and devotions, as these had been recited by all the faithful in earlier times. These men and women were called *montazontes* and *parthenae*, respectively.

Although the Faith had spread rapidly in the East, even before its official liberation by Constantine in 313, Christians were now of all types and classes; many were still half pagan and a majority were unable — or unwilling — to devote as much of their time to their religion as the early Christians had done. The single-minded fervor of the first disciples had become diluted; the

---

[1] The recitation of the Canonical Hours (Divine Office) had largely been assumed by clerics. At about this time it was made obligatory for them.

churches were virtually deserted between the times of the Eucharistic Sacrifice, about once a week. Only the *montazontes* and *parthenae* carried on that early fervor. They spent their days and nights in constant vigils within the basilicas.

The good example set by the *montazontes* and *parthenae* soon drew others into their ranks. As a group, they began to recite the Hours together and to practice other corporate devotions. This in turn led to their organizing themselves into associations called *asketera,* under the direction of a priest and presided over by a president, or superior. It was only a step from this closely directed group of ascetics to the religious community under a rule; like the consecrated virgins, they soon were living entirely apart from the world. Evidence that these associations evolved into religious communities is found in the writings of a number of early Doctors of the Church, who highly praise the numerous communities of the fourth century — undoubtedly made up of the consecrated virgins and members of the *asketera.* For monasticism, properly so called, had hardly begun, far away from the centers of civilization and the basilicas, in the deserts of Egypt.

Thus, before Christianity was three hundred years old, this special mode of life — the religious community — evolved. To attain perfect virtue through the Evangelical Counsels of the Gospel it was necessary to turn away from the world's distractions and temptations. This did not mean, however, that the world was forgotten; it was all the better remembered in prayer and good works. Reparation for the world's sins — as well as one's own — and alleviation of its burdens are among the major motives of Christian sacrifice, and are therefore as much motives of the life of the religious as communion with God; for love of Him may not exclude love of neighbor, which is ever "the bond of perfection" for all Christians of whatever spiritual degree.

As a common life centered around the new basilicas was gradually developing, Christianity was elsewhere producing its own brand of that age-old kind of ascetic — the hermit, or eremite, who was to play the most important part of all in organized religious life.

The great Egyptian valley of the Nile, called the Thebaid, has always been particularly suited to hermits; a few exist there even now. By the third century many Christians had fled to the Thebaid from the persecution and corruption of the Roman Empire, until Christian eremites were quite common in all of North Africa's desert regions as well as on the outskirts of towns. The "Pillar Saints" of the fourth century were a common kind of such hermits; they lived atop pillars or towers, in tiny huts, or in cone-shaped cells. The two St. Simeons the Younger and the Elder are the most famous of the Pillar Saints. Fringe-dwelling solitaries continued throughout the Christian era, up until about the seventeenth century.

This partiality for seclusion and austerity in the earliest Eastern Christian was due to many factors other than escape from Roman life and persecution. The temperament of the Eastern people had always contained a strong tendency toward ascetical spirituality; their ancient religions, before the coming of the Romans, were highly moral and spiritual. It is not surprising that the super-imposed mythologies of the Romans were easily enough unseated by Christianity; the people of these regions joined with enthusiasm the uninterrupted current of Judaic tradition, now turned Gentile and opened to them by the teachings of the new Messias. Still another reason for this attraction to the severe and solitary life of the eremite was the influence of the great schools of theology in the East, whose scholars defined and taught the doctrines of the Faith in order to combat the heresies that already assailed the Church. Self-renunciation and complete victory over the flesh was stressed, as a contrast to the licentious paganism of the day, and also as the supreme embodiment of the precepts and counsels of the Gospels. Many found it possible to heed these teachings only in this way.

The first "Desert Father" whose name has come down to us was St. Paul of Thebes, also called St. Paul the Hermit. In 249 he fled to the Thebaid to escape a violent persecution of the Emperor Decius. About thirty years later, a friend of St. Paul named Antony was to join the ranks of desert eremites — to rise

above them as one of the most unique figures in Christendom.
St. Antony of Coma was to become known as "The Father of
Christian Monasticism."

According to St. Athanasius, his first biographer, we find Antony,
a grave young farmer of twenty, attending Mass in his native
church at Coma, in Egypt, in the year 271. He listens intently
to the reading of the words of Christ: "If thou will be perfect, go
and sell all thou hast, and give to the poor, and come follow me."
Deeply impressed, Antony decides to follow this counsel literally;
he will give up his luxurious life and live only for God.

Antony's life had indeed been luxurious; a few years before, he
had inherited a large estate from his parents, and had been left
guardian of his young sister. Arrangements for the disposal of
his property and the care of his sister would take some time. But
Antony's decision was not impulsive; he sold his house and
lands, giving the proceeds to the poor and retaining only enough
to provide for his sister and his own small needs. Leaving his
sister in what St. Athanasius calls a "house of virgins" — one of
the earliest historical references to a convent — he then retired
to the outskirts of his native town to live in seclusion.

Whenever Antony heard of a saintly hermit in the vicinity,
he would seek him out in order to learn how he himself could
advance in wisdom and holiness. An apt pupil in the ways of
mystical contemplation,[2] mortification of the flesh, and self-discipline, he also learned how to make straw mats to barter for
food, that he might do without the last small portion of his
inheritance and live in perfect poverty.

When Antony at last set out alone into the Theban desert, the
devil immediately began to taunt him with the most vicious per-
sistence. All the good that he might accomplish in the world, and
all its wonders, crowded his thoughts. His imagination was induced

[2] Mystical contemplation is the prayer that unites the soul to God by
dispensing with reason and discourse, and obtaining distinct perceptions of God
by a wordless act of love and simple gazing upon Him; also called infused,
or passive, mystical union. It is not to be confused with *asceticism*, which
is the practice of self-discipline, or *austerity*, the practice of bodily mortification and penance.

to reel with temptations: seductive young women paraded before
him, murmuring promises and endearments; derisive noises as-
saulted his ears; and bags of gold and jewels lay glittering in his
path.[3] But Antony's only answer to Satan was longer hours spent
in prayer, and greater patience and humility. He moved even
farther from the world, to a cell which was an ancient, abandoned
tomb carved out of Egypt's rocky hillsides. Antony shut himself
up in it, allowing only a small space for air and the delivery of a
little food, to be brought to him every few days by a friend. Here
he remained for sixteen years, alone except for his satanic tor-
mentors. Although God allowed him to be so severely tried, Antony
had many celestial visions to comfort and sustain him. By such
trials and consolations the saintly eremite became proficient in
virtue of the highest degree.

Antony's great sanctity probably became known and his solitude
threatened, for he left the tomb and sought another abode, this
time in some ruins on wild and rugged Mount Pisper. In exchange
for Antony's mats, a native of the valley below agreed to leave
food by a cistern at the bottom of the mountain. This plan worked
perfectly; at last his beloved solitude seemed insured and complete.
But after twenty years of such peace, Providence deigned otherwise.

One day a small boy was sent to exchange Antony's straw mats
for food. The child was curious; instead of returning to the village
he began to explore the mountain. Coming upon the ruins, the
boy heard a din that sounded like the screaming of a maddened
crowd. He was terrified but, gathering courage, crept on and
peeked inside, where he saw only the holy hermit kneeling alone
in prayer. The dreadful noises were there too, but their agents
were invisible; they were the fiends of hell trying to distract the
saint from his devotions. Fleeing down the mountain, the boy
told the villagers about his experience. Half credulous, they decided to investigate. In a body, they all climbed the mountain
to the hidden ruins where they too heard the screaming noises
and saw the hermit kneeling alone, indifferent to the din.

[3] The "Seven Temptations of St. Antony" are depicted in many famous
paintings.

From that moment Antony's days of solitude were over. People began to flock to his mountain cell, seeking him out and begging his advice. He was besieged with visitors, many of whom stayed on to become his disciples and to follow his example. The caves of Mount Pisper and the ancient ruins were soon quite crowded with hermits! Although Antony could withstand every assault of Satan with equanimity, this kindly invasion of his privacy was more than he could bear. Again he fled, in search of an even more remote spot. But it was too late; followers sprang up by the hundreds wherever he might be.

Each hermit-disciple somehow found a cell of sorts to live in, even though some had to live two or three to a cell. There was also a small garden that the eremite tilled to provide food. The life of the new hermits was a continual round of prayer, contemplation, penance, and mortification of the flesh, with only enough food and sleep to sustain them; only on Sundays did they gather to hear Mass, chant the psalms, and be counseled by "Father Antony." The reawakened virtues of self-renunciation and the quest for spiritual perfection brought the hermit-disciples a mystical joy that reverberated throughout the Empire, and brought even greater fame to Antony. Princes with their entourages, and tourists of every class made long pilgrimages to see him; even the Emperor Constantine and his son, Constans, wrote to him, begging his prayers and blessing. More and more of the pilgrims became hermits themselves; former worldlings — Roman officials, rich merchants, dissolute spendthrifts, nobly born ladies — vied with one another in obedience to St. Antony's unwritten rule of advice and example in its severest terms.

Only twice did St. Antony leave his desert "monastery." The first time was to encourage the Christian martyrs of a particularly severe persecution, in 311, and again, in 338, to preach against the heresy of Arianism that was harassing and dividing the Church.[4]

[4] Arius (256–326) was a priest of Alexandria who taught that the Son was not equal to the Father, but a perfect creature used by God in His works of creation; inferior and of a different substance from the Father. The heresy condemned by the Council of Nicea in 325, was one of the most devastating to ever afflict the Church.

Only when he knew that death was near — at one hundred and five — did he withdraw from the leadership of his huge community. Retiring to a remote cave with two of his disciples, Antony spent the last days of his life in the solitary peace he loved so much. The first great hermit-monk died in 356, after instructing his disciples to bury him secretly, in an unmarked grave. It was not discovered until two hundred years later, in the reign of Justinian. His body was transferred to Alexandria, still later to Constantinople, and finally to Vienne, in France.

Legend tells of many women among St. Antony's followers who organized eremitical communities of their own, but very little is known about them. It was not until thirty years after St. Antony's death that the first famous Eastern "nuns" historically appear — friends of the great St. Jerome. They were four well-born Roman ladies — SS. Melania the Elder, Melania the Younger, and St. Paula and her daughter, St. Eustochium. St. Paula and her daughter founded two communities at Bethlehem; one was for women and one for St. Jerome, who had spent five years in an Antonian community and had then returned to Rome, hoping to establish a community there. Finding this too difficult, owing to worldly interference, he finally returned to the East and remained in the community which St. Paula had founded under his auspices.

Although St. Antony is called the "Father of Christian Monasticism," a younger contemporary from another part of the Thebaid, St. Pachomius, is known as the "Founder of Christian Monasticism." This is because St. Pachomius founded the first so-called order[5] of *cenobites*, or people living together in one establishment under a fixed rule. While the desert was already teeming with Antonian eremites, Pachomius became the first real abbot of a true monastery; the head of a great "order" that suddenly blossomed in the northern Thebaid — only to die again, almost as suddenly.

[5] The term "order," in its true historical and canonical sense, is not used until much later, when constitutions were appended to the rule, for one particular set of confederated houses. Some historians view the Cluny Reform (c. 950) as the beginning of true orders, others the Charter of Charity of Citeaux (1119). See Chapter VI.

Pachomius was a Roman soldier stationed in Egypt when he became a convert to Christianity. Upon his decision to remain in Egypt and to dedicate his life to God, he became, like Antony, a disciple of a wise old hermit. At this time, says the legend, Pachomius had a dream or vision in which an angel appeared to him and dictated a new "rule" for religious ascetics such as he. He beheld a manner of life entirely different from the Antonian kind, and new in every detail. He immediately began to long for the day when he could realize his dream.

When Pachomius left his master he went to live alone in an abandoned temple at Tabennisi, located in the upper valley of the Nile. Joined by a few disciples of his own, and then by more, they soon comprised a fair-sized group. At last there were enough to put the angel's rule into effect; with his disciples, Pachomius set to work creating a kind of religious life so different from the Desert Father's that it might have existed in another age.

Whereas the only communal activities of the Antonians were the chanting of the Hours and assisting at Mass, Pachomius' Rule called for a truly common life in which the monks ate, slept, worked, and prayed together, at fixed hours. The work included systematic maintenance of their establishment through crafts, trade, and agriculture — although the Rule did not compel any member of the community to engage in corporate activities. A monk might live as a solitary in his cell and practice any degree of austerity. The Rule also provided for members of a more temperate character; these were not condemned or expelled for moderateness, but only for direct violation of the Rule. Although no rule, as yet, required vows or was written down — it was learned in conferences with the master of the community — strict obedience to it was required and severe penalties, such as floggings, were imposed for its violation. Altogether, the government of Pachomius' monastery was highly military in character; he was to his monks as a general is to his army, rather than a teacher-counselor as St. Antony had been, or a spiritual father as St. Benedict was to be.

The monastery at Tabennisi, built about 320, was a group of

buildings surrounded by a high wall, each building housing about
forty monks. So amazingly successful was Pachomius' "Order" that
in a few years there were more than seven hundred monks in
the community. The fruits of their labor became a large-scale
business, transported to the ports of trade by the community's
own fleet of ships. Eventually Pachomius founded several more
monasteries for men and one for women, appointing superiors
to each, but remaining their over-all head. He thus became the
first true abbot and superior-general known to Christendom.

After Pachomius' death in 346 his successor was unable to
hold the "Order" together; in a short time it was rent by dissensions which precipitated its speedy decline and extinction. It is
a mystery to historians just how it could have dissolved so quickly;
the only explanations seem to be that Pachomius' genius for
administration was so unique that it could not be emulated, and
that the Eastern temperament preferred the more individualistic
and severer eremitical life of the Desert Fathers. As a united organization, Pachomius' cenobitical "Order" was not again matched
until the Benedictine system emerged five hundred years later.

In the meantime, Antonian monasticism continued to flourish
in other parts of the East, spreading to North Africa and Asia
Minor. Disciples of St. Antony and other outstanding eremites
headed communities composed of thousands of members. In the
Nitrean Desert of northern Egypt alone there were about five
thousand hermit-monks, most of them followers of St. Ammon,
called a "second St. Antony." Eminent churchmen and scholars
would visit the Desert Fathers, live with them for months or
years at a time, and then return to their own lands to establish
the mode of life there. Among these were St. Athanasius, author
of St. Antony's most famous biography; St. Basil the Great, and
St. Hilarion, who is credited with the next important step in
the evolution of the eremite into the cenobite.

Close to the time that St. Antony died, in the middle of the
fourth century, St. Hilarion headed a hermit community of his
own in Palestine. He improved upon the heretofore haphazard
living arrangements of the Antonians by drawing them together

into a kind of "village of cells," called a *laura*,[6] surrounding a chapel and the cell of the master hermit. In this drawing together of the monks into a unit, the first vestiges of truly organized religious life appear in the desert. Following St. Hilarion's example, a majority of the vast number of eremitical communities in the East soon were lauras, some so large that they might well have been called cities, rather than villages, of cells. For about sixty years monasticism flourished in this form, until the growing complexities of an expanding civilization and the problems of monasticism's own growth overtook it. By then, however, the highest ideals of monastic life were already being assumed and carried on by yet another improvement in it.

A number of factors contributed to the decline of the Desert Fathers, which began during the middle of the fifth century. Foremost of these was the breakup of the Roman Empire and the onslaught of the barbarians of the North upon southern Europe. Of the thousands who flocked to the desert communities, some sincerely sought peace and holiness — but others sought only to escape from the barbarians or conscription into the army, to evade debts, or to outwit the law. So numerous did the "hermits" become that they began to encroach upon the towns, causing heresies, schisms — and even riots. Thus did unworthy motive, the primary cause of decline in all religious life at all times, already show its disastrous effects. Also contributing to the eventual failure of desert monasticism was the lack of unity in such huge groups of people. With no organization to speak of, no written rule or binding laws, regularity and discipline were quite impossible. As sincere as some might be in their intentions, uneven standards resulted. Laxity finally became the prevailing fault, with fanatical extremists in the minority and true sons of St. Antony even fewer.

By the middle of the fifth century the tremendous garden of religious asceticism which had bloomed so profusely in the Eastern deserts was overblown and fading. Monasticism did not disappear

---

[6] Literally, *laura* means "alley"; the reason for the derivation is unknown. Any large monastery of the Byzantine Rite is now known as a laura.

from these regions, however. A reform, principally instituted by
four great Eastern saints — Nilus, Sabas, Euthymius, and Theodore — reorganized monasticism and healed many of the heresies
and schisms that had begun to debase the desert communities.
Several great laura monasteries were established and continued
to thrive, the most famous of which was St. Sabas' "Great Laura,"
which still exists and bears his name. But the true Desert Father
was well on his way to oblivion, outstripped by a yet newer and
better form of religious community life.

CHAPTER TWO

THE SHELTERING WALLS

As the links of a chain overlap, so the way to a renewal of monastic life was forged long before the decline of the Desert Fathers. About the middle of the fourth century, almost a hundred years before that decline, a new rule was composed which reorganized monasticism into such a vastly improved pattern that it caused certain characteristics of all Christian religious life to become fixed from that time. This was the rule composed by the Patriarch of the East and Doctor of the Church, St. Basil the Great (329–379).

Basil, son of a devout and aristocratic family, had been considered a prodigy in his boyhood. As a protégé of the Bishop of Caesarea, in Cappadocia, Asia Minor, he rose rapidly in the Church. Honors and admiration were showered upon him in such profusion that he soon began to fear that they would divert him into worldliness and pride. To avert this, Basil turned to the example of his devout sister, St. Macrina, who had organized the first nunnery in that region by converting one of the family's houses into a religious community whose members were composed of her own circle of friends.[1] Inspired by his sister's pursuit of perfection in the Evangelical Counsels, Basil then turned his attention to the Desert Fathers, of whom he had heard so much. He decided to journey to Egypt and study their life.

After visiting many regions where eremitical life had spread, and studying it intently, St. Basil returned to his native diocese of Pontus, in Asia Minor. Here he founded his first monastery, incorporating in its design and in improved form all that he had learned from the Desert Fathers. When he himself later became Bishop of Caesarea, his guidance firmly implanted his Rule in Cappadocia, from whence it gradually spread. Within a hundred years, when desert monasticism had declined and its prestige had faded, the Basilian Rule supplanted the Antonian, to become the established form of religious life for many centuries to come.

The Basilian Rule was the first to be written down as well as the first to require monks to take a vow. Another innovation was the institution of a noviceship, or period of probation, during which the aspirant was trained in self-renunciation and obedience — the monk's greatest means to perfection. The monastery, a laura, was limited to thirty or forty members — in sharp contrast to the thousands that made up the Antonian communities. Certain prayers and the chanting of the Hours, made obligatory, were diversified to avoid monotony; and the necessity of manual labor was stressed — another departure from the Antonian mode, which regarded labor as aside from, and not a part of, monastic life.

[1] St. Macrina is regarded as the founder of religious life for women in the Eastern Church.

Confession of faults to the superior was required, and penalties consisting of a sort of "internal excommunication" were imposed for serious infractions of the Rule. Silence was decreed at meals and work, as was total abstinence from meat and wine; nor could a monk leave the monastery alone or without permission.

As a smaller laura, with the monks' activities well co-ordinated and supervised, the Basilian community was more cenobitical than eremitical, that is, a monastery with communal buildings, enclosed by a wall. As it retained some eremitical features, however — such as the individual cell hut for each monk — Basilian monasticism is called "semieremitical." When "semieremitical" is applied to succeeding religious communities, a Basilian laura is implied. It was not until the sixth century, under St. Benedict's Rule, that this design was altered to any great extent.

For many years the general temper of St. Basil's Rule and its administration was much milder than that of other lesser rules or modes of monastic life in that era. However, the tendency toward rigid austerity in the Eastern temperament soon crept back into Basilian monasticism; eventually it became as severe as the others. This tendency has remained and even today may be noted; Eastern religious life has not developed and changed its form nearly so much as has its Western counterpart, nor has it the elastic qualities that have made Western monasticism so adaptable to different eras and countries. Further cut off from change by the Great Eastern Schism that created the "Orthodox" Churches in the eleventh century, it is without such flexible variations as we see in the many types of orders and religious societies in the Roman Catholic Church. Eastern religious life is not divided into "orders," as we know them, but is entirely Basilian, with some variations. However, those Eastern communities under the Basilian Rule which later made their way to the West are, under Roman Catholicism, as progressive and relatively mild as is all Western religious life.[2]

[2] A number of Basilian orders, of men and women, became established in Rome before the Great Eastern Schism. Still others have become reunited to Rome since, as have other groups of Orthodox Catholics. These latter groups, called Eastern Catholics, have retained their original rites and customs;

It was inevitable that religious community life would spread to the clergy, especially as forms of it had existed among priests since the time of Christ. Although certain saintly clerics had organized groups of priests into monklike communities,[3] these were sporadic until the advent of the true priest-religious, or canon regular, in the latter part of the fourth century.

Monks in those days were laymen; not for centuries would the majority be priests, as they are today. The status of a priest was entirely different from that of a monk, whose only care was his own salvation; the monk was not a functionary of the Church, nor dedicated to its service, as was the priest. On the other hand, a priest was not bound to the practice of the Evangelical Counsels, although he could — and many did — choose "the better way" of voluntary poverty, chastity, and obedience. Celibacy of the clergy was a custom that varied in different regions; although laws regarding it were enacted from the third century onward, they were not as yet uniform.[4] Thus a priest might be married and his material state range from poverty to wealth; low degree in the social scale to high rank. Many had to labor at other work to avoid indigence while others lived in luxury. Such temporal inequalities often made sanctity difficult and interfered with the priest's sacerdotal duties. It is understandable that the stable and ordered life of the monk soon began to attract the clergy.

Religious community life for priests was given its first great impetus by St. Augustine, the great Doctor of the Church whose philosophy is one of the pillars of Western thought. In combining the monastic and the clerical states he strengthened and broadened the scope of both — as each form of religious life was to permanently borrow certain characteristics from the other, to their mutual enrichment.

---

the Basilian orders are of the Roman rite however, under Western customs of religious life.

[3] St. Paulinus of Nola (352–431) was one. He was a Roman statesman who relinquished his place in the world to live a monastic life, although he was a priest. He gathered around his a community of priests who followed his example.

[4] The first definite legislation that we know of on celibacy of the clergy was that of the Council of Elvira, in 306.

As those who are familiar with St. Augustine's famous *Confessions* know, he arrived at his eminent place in the Church by a long and turbulent route. Augustine was born in 354 — two years before St. Antony died — in Tagaste, North Africa, in what is now Tunisia. At sixteen he was already a brilliant scholar, far advanced in his studies as a rhetorician — a promising career of those times. Then, lack of money forced him to suspend his education. This drastic change from diligent study to idleness was Augustine's undoing; he began to sow oats so wild that when he was eventually able to resume his studies he was far gone in profligacy. He entered into irregular but stable relations with a woman who bore him a son. He aspired to become both an actor and playwright, while plunging feverishly into debauchery and vice. His pious mother, St. Monica, pleaded with him, but he resisted her entreaties as "womanish chatter," and made it clear that his only ambition was to become rich and famous.

Augustine finally was overcome with restless self-disgust. In an attempt to achieve some kind of inner stability he embraced a current heresy called Manichaeism, a strange mixture of Zoroastrian dualism, Babylonian folk lore, and Buddhist ethics, with an admixture of some Christian elements. Its somber doctrines concerning the powers of darkness and evil quite suited the present state of Augustine's mind. He was, however, too keen to long remain blind to the paradoxes and discrepancies in his new religion. Augustine then assured himself that these could be perfectly resolved by Faustus, its high priest, but when he met the man he discovered to his horror that the "great" Dr. Faustus was entirely unequal to the challenge. Although this somewhat cooled young Augustine's ardor, he did not give up Manichaeism at once. Still restless and dissatisfied, he continued to pursue his career as a rhetorician.

Despite his dissolute life, Augustine was extremely successful in his chosen profession. He was admired and sought after, and well on the way to becoming as rich and famous as he had hoped to be. But to his surprise, his success failed to give him much satisfaction. There was something lacking. Then, several incidents turned Augustine's mind toward Christianity, among them a chance interview with the holy and learned St. Ambrose, Bishop of Milan. Almost immediately he perceived that here was all the truth and stability that he lacked. This was what he wanted.

It was not without the greatest difficulty that Augustine managed to tear himself away from his dissolute life and the luxury and fame he had considered so important. Accompanied by a few friends, he left Milan and returned to his family home in Tagaste, which he turned into a virtual monastery. He and his friends lived a severely ascetical life; they fasted, prayed, did penance, and discoursed upon the nature of all things. It was at this time that he began to write upon those philosophical and theological subjects that were to contribute so much to his fame, even in his lifetime. After going back to Milan to be baptized by St. Ambrose, he returned to Tagaste, to an entirely new and, at last, happy life. After twenty years, his mother's prayers for his conversion had been answered.

Here in his monastic seclusion at Tagaste, Augustine would have been content to remain, had it not been for another incident that was to change the whole course of his life.

The seat of the diocese in which Augustine lived was in Hippo, not far from Tagaste. The elderly Bishop of Hippo, hearing of this brilliant young philosopher and ascetic, invited him for a visit to the episcopal residence. Augustine accepted the invitation with reluctance. The good Bishop was not only enthralled with the mental and spiritual powers of his guest, but with his talents as a rhetorician and orator as well. Augustine was requested to speak to the congregation.

Augustine's public life might be said to date from this first sermon, as neither the Bishop nor the faithful would hear of his returning to the obscurity of Tagaste. Practically upon the spot, the Bishop ordained him and appointed him his assistant and successor. When Augustine soon became the next head of the diocese, the influence of his great sanctity, inspired preaching, and brilliant writing immediately became extraordinary.

One of the most immediate examples of Bishop Augustine's

influence was its effect upon the clergy of his diocese. The austere life he had led in Tagaste was transferred to his episcopal residence; but instead of the company of his friends, he had the canons of the cathedral, whom he invited to join him in it. He and his priests renounced property and lived under the rule that he wrote for them. Thus they became Canons Regular, a binding together of the clerical and the monastic state that was not entirely monastic, yet not secular either. It was a "quasi-monastic" state, which St. Thomas Aquinas defines thus: "The order of Canons Regular is necessarily constituted by religious clerics, because they are essentially destined to those works which relate to the divine mysteries, whereas it is not so with the monastic orders."[5]

Among the regulations that Bishop Augustine laid down for his Canons Regular were the obligations of preaching, administering the sacraments, and giving counsel and retreats. They were to dress neither poorly nor elegantly, eat simple but sufficient food, and recite the Office in common; in all things they were to observe a golden mean of moderation on the temporal plane, and the highest ideals on the spiritual. This mode of life for priests was not an innovation, as Christ's disciples had lived thus, but it was a renewal of the custom and a much needed revitalizing of clerical standards in a disordered and disorganized time.

Owing to the Bishop of Hippo's influence and inspiration, houses of Canons Regular followed the spread of Christianity throughout the Empire. Wherever churches were built in the expanding frontiers of Catholicism, an adjoining community of Canons Regular usually served them. Secular priests were scarce in the far-flung, semibarbarian outposts of the Faith, and the parish pastor, as we know him, had not yet come into being.

Communities of women also benefited immeasurably by Bishop Augustine's interest in religious life. As chief administrator of the diocese, he was appealed to by the Mother Superior of a nearby nunnery on a matter of discipline; for in those times rules were

---

[5] "Regular" is from the Latin, *regula,* for "rule," meaning priests (canons) living under a rule. Canons secular are secular priests who are functionaries of cathedral or collegiate churches.

vague and the Church's legislation governing religious life was not yet exact; too many far more serious problems and difficulties faced the newly liberated and fast-growing Church. In reply, the Bishop wrote a letter to the nun, outlining a simple and effective set of rules which would correct the controversial matter and serve as a guide for the conduct of the whole community in the future. The extent of the influence of St. Augustine's Rule upon religious communities of both sexes has been tremendous.

By the fifth century, the *continentes* and consecrated virgins, the *parthenae* and *montazontes,* living alone or with their families, disappear, and become cloistered religious. The hermit has become a member of a hermit community, or laura; the huge, scattered laura has become the small enclosed laura monastery. And many secular priests become priest-monks, as Canons Regular, living in a monastic community. Thus do the walls of silence and order rise around these early ascetics in the Church, to protect their pursuit of "the way of perfection" in perfect unity. That those walls would also shelter and preserve Western Culture as well, was as yet undreamed of.

*   *   *

Monasticism was introduced into the West when St. Athanasius — the dauntless foe of Arianism and one of the great "Nicene Fathers" — fled from his Arian persecutors to Rome, in 340, accompanied by two disciples of St. Antony. When his famous biography of St. Antony appeared three years later, the Desert Fathers became the talk of the Christian world; pilgrims, tourists, and disciples flocked to Egypt — but few tried eremitical monasticism in Italy; like St. Jerome, they found that country too densely populated with half-pagan Romans to be suitable for such a purpose. It was not until thirty years after St. Athanasius' visit that monasticism was truly established in Europe, by St. Martin of Tours (317–397), the great patron saint of France.

Martin, son of a Roman military tribune, was a young soldier stationed in Gaul when he became interested in Christianity.

Although the majority of the native Galls were pagans, the Faith had found its way there by way of the Roman soldiers, with whom it had become popular since its liberation by Constantine. It was at this time (c. 350), when Martin was still a catechumen,[6] that the celebrated incident of the cloak occurred. In spite of the loud ridicule by his fellow soldiers, he slashed his cloak in half with his sword to provide covering for a freezing beggar. That night he had a dream in which Christ appeared, dressed in the beggar's half of the cloak, and who said to him, "Martin, yet a catechumen, has clothed Me in this garment." Inspired to great ardor by the incident, the young soldier hastened to be baptized and was about to put himself under the patronage of the holy and learned St. Hilary, Bishop of Poitiers, when his regiment was suddenly transferred to the Rhine border.

Impatient to return to Poitiers, Martin managed to have his tour of duty on the Rhine cut short, whereupon he hastened back to Gaul by way of Italy. After many narrow escapes and much abuse by the Arians on his perilous journey over the Alps, Martin finally got as far as Italy — only to hear that Bishop Hilary had been banished to the East by the Arians, who were then predominating in Gaul. Martin went no farther than an island off the coast of Italy called Gallinaria, where he began the life of a hermit. After Hilary's recall from exile and his reinstatement as Bishop of Poitiers, Martin at last resumed his journey.

Martin was ordained by Bishop Hilary and received permission to continue living as a hermit in a deserted region near Poitiers, later called Ligugé. Here he became known as "Martin the Antonian." Disciples were soon attracted to him who, as they had done with St. Antony, ranged themselves around him until a huge laura grew up. Thus at Ligugé, about 361, was created the first large-scale eremitical community on the continent of Europe.

To a life of prayer and penance Martin and his disciples added the study of Scripture and the Fathers, with which knowledge they armed themselves to evangelize the Galls. For ten years,

[6] A nonbaptized adult receiving instruction in the Faith; a learner.

Martin left his laura only to preach — during the course of which he performed many miracles. He became so celebrated in Gaul that when the Bishop of Tours died the Christian inhabitants of that town were determined that he should be their next bishop. But when Martin refused to leave his community they sent a reputable townsman to the laura at Ligugé to beg Martin to come to Tours and administer the last rites to his dying daughter. Not suspecting that he was being tricked, Martin went. Once inside the walls of the city, he was overwhelmed by popular acclaim and consecrated Bishop of Tours upon the spot!

Although he did not allow his personal preferences to interfere with his duties, the new Bishop of Tours refused to live in the episcopal residence. He chose instead to reside in a small cell two miles from the town — where again a large number of disciples gathered around him, and another laura community was created. This was his second foundation, called Marmoutier, and was to become one of the most renowned abbeys of Europe.

Bishop Martin's inspired preaching and extensive traveling in the interests of the Church made him, for the next thirty years, the greatest religious force in Gaul. In his great charity, no distance or time was too great to spend in pleading for condemned but repentant criminals and heretics, or in wringing concessions for the Church from reluctant officials. The zeal of Martin and his monks did much to win many thousands of Galls to Christianity and Arians to orthodoxy. When he died, in 397, his tomb at Tours immediately became a shrine to which pilgrims came from all over Europe and still come. A succession of shrines was built, each one more beautiful than the one before it. The last two shrines were sacked and looted by anti-Catholic forces, the second during the French Revolution, after which the government built a street through its site to prevent its rising again. All that is left are the basilica's two towers, and a few small relics.

Also contributing to monastic activity in Gaul was the monk John Cassian. In the south of Gaul, in 415, he founded two communities, the abbey of St. Victor for men, and a community for women. For these two foundations he wrote a rule and a number of books on the religious life which were models of their kind for hundreds of years thereafter. Cassian's fame, however, has been dimmed by his controversy with St. Augustine over Pelagianism, a heresy of those times; in it he became so extreme that he was deemed "semi-Pelagian" and his works were officially censored. Nonetheless, he is regarded as an important force in the development of monasticism in Europe.

Cassian is generally credited with establishing the first "double monasteries" on the Continent, a custom that became widespread in Europe for many centuries. These were nunneries and monasteries connected by a chapel used by both the nuns and the monks. One reason for these double establishments was to safeguard the community of women in a rough and pagan land; another was that nuns might use the same chapel — making a duplicate unnecessary — and thus be ministered to by the monastery chaplains, and also that the nuns might be under the close direction of the abbot. As religious life among women has always closely paralleled that of men in its development and growth, rules were usually adapted for women almost as soon as they were written for men, and often new foundations were made simultaneously for both sexes.

In the generation following St. Martin's, men of unsurpassed holiness and intellect emanated from his several foundations in Gaul, who themselves founded great communities. These devout and scholarly monks were in great demand as members of the hierarchy, as missionaries to the North and to the British Isles, and as members of the great schools of theology. In both sanctity and learning, they were the elite of the Church; bulwarks in the struggle against Arianism and all the other disrupting forces at work in that era. Of all the great monasteries that succeeded St. Martin's, perhaps the most noted was Lerins, founded in 423 by St. Honoratus on an island off the coast of Provence. So many great bishops, saints, scholars, and missionaries streamed from this abbey that its influence in molding the intellectual and spiritual life of the whole Middle Ages can hardly be exaggerated. From Lerins came St. Caesarius, Bishop of Arles during the first half of the sixth century. A famous preacher, theologian, and reformer of Church discipline, he wrote a Rule for nuns which is one of the few to survive that antedate St. Benedict's. It is still observed in a number of women's communities today.

All of the monasteries in Gaul after St. Martin were Basilian lauras; that is, separate cells surrounding a chapel and refectory, enclosed by a wall. The highest tradition of Eastern asceticism was maintained among the hazards of a wild, cold country, and its often rough and hostile inhabitants. Yet, to the monk's austere Rule were added scholarship and a great concern for the well-being of the people. Unlike the Eastern monks, they labored unceasingly to share their treasures of faith and learning, and to relieve the ignorance and disorder that threatened to engulf the world as the Dark Ages closed in. Without knowing it, they sheltered within their walls the future of the West.

The Dark Ages began in the fifth century, when the Empire began to crumble in a welter of decadence. Weak, extravagant tyrants wrung exorbitant taxes from the poverty-stricken people, many of whom escaped to the neighboring countries of the pastoral barbarians. In turn, the barbarians infiltrated Roman life and lowered its standards still further. Although the Church had become united with the Empire, interfering rulers caused much trouble, and other tremendous problems seemed to threaten her very existence. Theological controversies raged, Eastern monasticism was soon to lose its prestige; the devastating Arian heresy was rampant, and other dangerous conditions — such as Pricillianism in Spain[7] — were left unresolved by the time of the next great calamity to both the Church and the Empire. This was a fresh invasion of fierce nomad barbarians from the North. Tribe upon tribe of untamed warriors swarmed over Gaul, Italy, Spain, and Britain. Violent disintegration of political and social life ensued;

[7] Almost nothing is known of the Church in Spain during the first three centuries after Christ. One council was held, at Elvira in 300–305, which disclosed a disordered state of Catholicism in that country. Seventy years later Pricillianism was the greatest source of trouble; Pricillian was a wealthy and well-educated nobleman devoted to the ascetical life who became the leader of the *continentes* in Spain; but the authority of the bishops was disregarded and the cult became fanatical, semi-Oriental, and Gnostic. Pricillian was tried and put to death over the protestations of St. Martin, and his remaining

all the arts of peace were forgotten and all the Greco-Roman culture of a once-great civilization was buried. While, in Rome, Leo the Great staved off the barbarians and so ably defended the Church, the monks, as her teachers and missionaries, saved the minds and souls of her children.

The savagery of the barbarians and the decadence of the Romans combined to produce not only boundless cruelty and violence, but abysmal ignorance as well. The churches and monasteries were often the only symbols of law and order that existed in the huge outlying regions of the dying Empire. Out of this wilderness, the monks had to wrest their living. To find their way in it, they had to have a knowledge of astronomy — such as sailors have — and to build monasteries and maintain them they had to have skills as yet unheard of by the invaders. While others lived off the spoils of war, the monks cleared the forests and planted crops, and built foundation after foundation. Only within their walls could the traveler find safety and a bed for the night; and if he were sick or wounded on the way, the monks would take care of him — for there were no inns, almshouses, or hospitals. Sometimes whole families found asylum within the laura's walls.

The monks had to know how to count in order to compute the calendar so that they could determine the times of Christmas and Easter and all the feasts and fasts between. They had to know how to read[8] in order to learn the psalter, to chant the Canonical Hours, and to say Mass. As new members joined the communities and new foundations were made, new copies of Psalters, Missals, Scripture, and other works had to be manufactured in the Scriptorium, where they were painstakingly copied and bound. To these books the monks added works of their own, such as the chronicles to which we owe our knowledge of early medieval history. They also copied ancient manuscripts which had been salvaged and brought with them to new establishments.

---

adherents caused much dissension and factionalism for many years in Spain.

[8] It is thought that for those monks who were illiterate, then, and for many centuries thereafter, the rosary (prayer beads) was used as a substitute "office," consisting of a certain number of Paters and Aves in honor of the

Thus were preserved many Greek and Roman classics that would otherwise have been lost forever.

From these various books in the monastery library the ablest scholars of the community taught the aspirants and the less literate monks. When the number of these increased, it then became necessary to hold classes — the first schools of medieval times. Christian families began to leave their children in monasteries for safety and to partake of the only education available. At first, the parents promised their children to the community as members, but later a decree of the Council of Vaison, in 526, stipulated that these children must be allowed to leave the monastery and marry is they so desired. This decree led to a division of the classes, called "internal" and "external" schools; the former was for members of the religious community only, the latter for children and catechumens. In the "external" school secular subjects such as mathematics, reading, and the sciences were taught, as well as religion. The "external" school led to the great universities of the Schoolmen many centuries later. When the new barbarian lords of Europe found time to stop warring with one another, they found that there was much to learn from the monks besides religion.

Of all the kingdoms of the barbarians, either federated at first with the Empire, or its foes, the Franks in Gaul were the least civilized. When most of southern Europe was Christian, they were still pagans. Yet Gaul was to become the only barbarian kingdom to survive, and the most Christian, for the entire span of the Middle Ages. This was due in great part to the monastic foundations in Gaul which made it such a strong center of Catholicism, and then to the country's Frankish king, Clovis, who was converted to the Faith in 511, soon after marrying a Catholic Burgundian princess. Thousands of his soldiers followed his example, and after them their families.

Except in its remote corners, Gaul thus became the first entirely Catholic kingdom in Europe. The conversion of Gaul was the

---

principal "mysteries" of the Faith. The rosary, a lay devotion and in its final design, was promoted to its present popular status by the Dominicans in the fifteenth century.

first major blow to Arianism and the first piece of good fortune for the Church in a century of disheartening struggles. Upon France was built Catholic Europe, defended and nurtured by Rome, with which Clovis built a bond that became the historic connection between the Frankish Empire and the Papacy.

CHAPTER THREE

THE WHITE MARTYRDOM

Soon after the Roman garrisons deserted Britain in 410, to bolster the Empire's tottering defenses on the Continent, England was set upon by fierce pirate tribes from northern Europe. Marauding bands of Angles, Jutes, and Saxons surged from the mainland, destroying every vestige of colonial life and Christianity. All Christians who could escape fled to Wales in the West and Scotland in the North. The remaining few survivors huddled together in small fugitive groups — priests, nuns, monks, and families — to protect their lives and their faith. In vain the English sent pleas to Rome for help. But communication and trade with Europe was cut off for more than a hundred and fifty years — until the arrival of St. Augustine of Canterbury.

In Wales, the Faith survived well; there the bishops preserved the apostolic succession and were able to build a strong Celtic Church. One cause of its gathering strength was the introduction of semieremitical monasticism by a scholar-priest of Gaul, St. Germanus of Auxerre, who about 430 made two visits to the British Isles in spite of the pirates hammering at their eastern shores. In Gallic-Egyptian monasteries,[1] founded in Wales by St. Germanus, Catholicism's highest traditions of zeal and learning were fostered and carried on. Monasticism's success in Wales was soon to produce that great galaxy of scholars and saints who, with St. Patrick's converts in Ireland, were to create the unique glory that was Celtic monasticism.

In Scotland the Faith survived for a while, through the efforts of its first recorded missionary, St. Ninian. A native Briton educated in Rome and Gaul, Ninian went to Scotland about fifty years after St. Germanus visited Wales, and on the shores of Solway Firth built a monastery called Candida Casa — or "shining house," because of the dazzling whiteness of its stonework. From Candida Casa he kept alive the Christianity that had found its way there earlier and evangelized the native Picts and Scots. Though the Candida Casa flourished, St. Ninian died before the roots of faith had grown very deep; they too eventually died, not to be replanted until the coming of the great St. Columba, about a hundred years later.

In Ireland the druidical religion and the native intelligence and imagination of the people had created a relatively high-level civilization.[2] The Irish Celts were fierce enough, nonetheless; the clans warred with one another ceaselessly and made forays into neighboring lands, whose captured natives were taken back to

[1] It is not known what type of religious community life existed there before this, although it is fairly certain that there was organized religious asceticism of some sort — as there was, by this time, throughout the Church.

[2] Although pagans, the Celts (inhabitants of Britain, Scotland, Wales, and Ireland) were not barbarians.

Ireland as slaves. Roman influence had been barely felt in this distant part of the Isles through the few foreign traders who were hardy enough to get this far north, and the even fewer Roman and Christian captives taken in raids across the Irish Sea. Bishop Palladius, the first Catholic missionary to Ireland, about 425, had met with little success; incurring the displeasure of a native prince, he had been there only a few months before he was summarily banished from the country. Any Christianity that he found there — or left behind him — was even more vestigial than that left by the invading Teutons in England. Completely isolated from the rest of the world, unconquered and unspoiled by any foreign invasions, life in Ireland continued as it had been for many hundreds of years. There was no inkling of the miracle that was to soon change it forever.

In one of their raids on neighboring Scotland, the soldiers of one Irish king called Nial captured a Christian youth of sixteen named Patrick. The boy was then sold to a clan chief, as a slave, and set to herding sheep on the lonely hillsides. For six long years Patrick tended his master's herds, cut off from his homeland, his family, and friends. His religion, in which he had been devoutly brought up, was his only solace. A solitary by force of circumstance, Patrick soon discovered the uses to which solitude could be put; he plunged into the same deep reaches of the spirit as had the great saint-solitaries before him — into mystical contemplation and prayer. It was not long before the young shepherd-slave made up his mind that when, and if, he could escape, he would dedicate his life to God.

In his autobiography, Patrick relates that an angel appeared to him in a dream and told him how to escape. After a perilous flight, he made his way to Gaul, where he spent several years as a monk of Lerins, after which he returned to his own country. But another and constant dream disturbed him so much that he was unable to settle down among his own people. This was a dream of hearing the people of Ireland crying, "We entreat thee, holy youth, that thou come and walk still amongst us!" Convinced that God wished him to return and convert the Irish, Patrick overrode the protests of his family and set out again for Lerins, to prepare himself by further study for his mission.

Patrick at length became a priest — a priest whose burning desire to evangelize the Irish Celts became well known, even to the Pope. When Pope Celestine decided that a missionary bishop should be sent to Ireland, Patrick was considered a candidate for the post. But it was thought that he was unsuited to such an important position; he lacked, it was said, the necessary scholarship and culture. So Palladius was chosen instead.

Patrick's burning wish was not to be denied nonetheless. He received the Pope's permission to assist the new Bishop, and so set sail to join Palladius. Hardly had he started on his journey, however, before he received the news of Bishop Palladius' expulsion from Ireland, and his death shortly thereafter. Again the post was vacant, and again Patrick was considered. This time it was decided to overlook his "rusticity"; he was consecrated Bishop of Ireland by St. Germanus, in Britain, and then continued on his journey, accompanied by about twenty assistants.

It is unfortunate for us that no description of Patrick, the man, was ever recorded. He must have had great charm and extraordinary powers of persuasion, for no sooner had he set foot upon the Emerald Isle, in 432, than he converted a chief, who gave him an old barn for a church. The village of Saul — from *saba,* meaning "barn" — still commemorates the first church he built in Ireland. From here Bishop Patrick and his companions began their mission, which lasted for the next thirty years.

Although the missionaries were continually menaced by the fierce opposition of the Druids, being captured twelve times, no harm came to them. Despite the Druids' hostility, however, the people were awed by Bishop Patrick's eloquent preaching, and a holiness so great that miracle upon miracle was produced by it. Thousands were converted and baptized at a time. So many and so fervent were his new converts that Patrick immediately set about creating sees, founding monasteries, and building churches to which cells were attached for monks or Canons Regular.[3]

[3] It has never been clearly established whether these cells were intended for monks or canons.

The new centers of Christianity that Bishop Patrick established were carved out of the dense wilderness; the churches, monasteries, convents, and other buildings were grouped together into "clerical villages," from which his disciples administered the new sees and the natives were evangelized. Every such center was manned by the ablest men that Patrick could find. Some were native convert priests, three were assistant coadjutor bishops sent by Rome, with a few priests from Wales. Unhampered by barbarian invasions, Roman decadence, heresies, and theological disputes — in the toils of which the Church in Europe struggled so valiantly — this new wellspring of Celtic Catholicism at once assumed a character that was entirely its own. Indeed, it was a character so strong that it was to be felt throughout the Christian world.

The majority of the converts and aspirants to the religious life and priesthood that flocked to Patrick's "clerical villages" were of high social rank. Sons and daughters of chieftains, kings, and princes became priests, monks, and "virgins of Christ." It was one of these "virgins" who was to become, after St. Patrick, the most beloved of all the great figures of Ireland — St. Brigid.[4]

The young noblewoman, Brigid, refused many princely suitors to become a hermitess-nun. Having received the veil from a nephew-disciple of St. Patrick, she took up her abode in the hollow of a great oak tree, where she lived as a solitary. Kneeling alone in prayer throughout the frigid nights was only one of her austerities, to which she added great charity and great charm. Brigid was soon famous throughout the region; so many other women were inspired to join her that the cell in the oak tree became the center of a small laura — and then a bigger one, until a large double monastery stood beside it. Thus, says the legend, was created Kildare — from Cull-Dara, meaning "church of the oak" — one of the most famous foundations and shrines of Ireland, and the only double monastery known to have existed there.

In her monastery Brigid organized schools of art, music, and many kinds of crafts — even a school of metalworking. From the Scriptoria came illumined copies of the Gospels and the Hours

4 Brigid was twelve years old when St. Patrick died, in 461.

that were marvels of beauty; they are said to have exceeded in workmanship and design even the famous Book of Kells, which is today the foremost example of Irish manuscript art.[5] So well respected was Brigid's holiness and ability that she was appointed superior-general of all the nunneries in Ireland, and several monasteries as well. Probably the first woman religious of Great Britain to attain such rank, she was far from the last.[6] Until the Reformation, abbesses ranked on a par with abbots, taking part in all the great synods and councils and, later, even sitting in Parliament.

As high as were the spiritual standards established by St. Patrick in Ireland, they were to rise even higher. About sixty years after his death, a monk from Wales, St. Gildas, and several Irish-trained countrymen crossed over to Ireland to continue St. Patrick's work. As St. Gildas and many other Welsh monks were alumni of the famous monasteries in Gaul, they were not long in introducing into Ireland the semieremitical life of St. Martin and Cassian. The inhabitants of the "clerical villages" were ripe for this innovation; their devotion to perfect order, their austere asceticism, and their intellectual capabilities, combined at once to create a semi-eremitical life that was nothing less than heroic in its intensity. The buildings comprising the "villages" spread farther apart, some to become laura monasteries for both men and women, and practices were instituted that outshone not only the Desert Fathers, but Welsh and Gallic monasticism as well. So incredibly severe was the life in these Irish communities that it became known as the "White Martyrdom" — as distinct from the bloody martyrdom of persecution and death.

The Irish monasteries were rude and simple lauras consisting of small wood or stone huts. There was one or more little oratories, or private chapels, a kitchen and a refectory, all enclosed by a wall. Absolute poverty, chastity, and obedience were publicly vowed for life, and all communication with family or the oppo-

[5] These Kildare manuscripts disappeared during the Reformation and have never been found.
[6] St. Ita (475–570) was another high-ranking nun of the same generation; called the "St. Brigid of Munster."

site sex was totally avoided. Nothing whatsoever could be owned, or meat eaten at any time; and talking during the daylight hours was forbidden. There were two kinds of prayer: the recitation of the Psalter every day, interspersed with readings from Holy Scripture and the Fathers; and penitential prayer, accompanied by many prostrations and genuflections, or with the arms stretched out in the form of a cross — or endured while immersed in icy water. Manual work, crafts, and study rounded out the religious' day; no idleness or illiteracy was tolerated. Severe penalties were imposed for infractions of the rules, which were slightly relaxed only on Sundays and feasts.

Yet charity was not lacking; the sick and infirm members of the community, absolved from its stringent regimen, were cared for with the utmost solicitude. When the communities grew large, the faithful began to share in the monastery life; many families lived within the walls, for protection and to help with the farm work. They also came to share in the liturgical life of the oratories and the learning in the abbey's school. Hospitality was accorded all visitors and pilgrims, who sometimes came with their families and stayed for years!

As the fervor of Irish piety influenced it, Welsh monasticism waxed stronger than ever; as, in turn, the Welsh zeal for scholarship influenced religious life in Ireland. By the sixth century these two forces merged to such an extent — with the Irish brand of stark asceticism predominating — that the British Isles were flooded with its fruits and its influence. Indeed, such prestige did Celtic monasticism shortly attain that the whole structure of ecclesiastical life in Great Britain was to become monastic in cast. All spiritual life began to emanate from, or be channeled through, the many great religious foundations and schools. Abbots were chosen as bishops; but it was more as abbots than as bishops that they ruled their sees; "the see," says Father Hughes, "is lost to view behind the monastery."

Celtic monasticism produced a tremendous galaxy of illustrious saints[7] — famous for their holiness and learning, for the rules

[7] SS. Brendan the Elder, David, Gall, Kentigern, Comgall, Kiernan, Enda, Kevan, Finian, Clonard, Fanchea are only a few.

they composed, the books they wrote, and the great institutions they founded. Not only were these Irish monks great saints, but as personalities they were as colorful as they were devout. Try as they might, official biographers have had little success in fitting them into the gilt and plaster molds that so often rob the saints of their human qualities. Their individuality was largely due to the ardent nature of the Irish temperament, the intense austerity of which that temperament was capable, and the social structure from which they sprang — the fiercely loyal clans. A Church of England clergyman summarizes very well the highly romantic character of the Irish monk: "The hot blood of the chief still stirred in the veins of the cowled monk, and there were often seen strange contrasts in the conduct of the man, whose inherited passions drove him into violent outbursts of anger and indignation while his acquired sanctity made him generally the most patient of Christians."[8]

This description fits many a Celtic saint, and none so well as the two examples that are all that there is space for here: St. Columba, apostle to the Picts in Scotland and superior-general of all the monasteries in Ireland and Scotland; and St. Columbanus, apostle to Italy, France, and Switzerland in the sixth century. Theirs were the two most famous Rules composed in the West before St. Benedict's.

Columba (b. 521) was a nobleman directly descended from one of the Irish kings. Many records and legends tell of his attractive personality, "of an excellent nature, polished in speech, holy in deed." He was handsome and warmhearted, and as sensitive and tempestuous as the rest of his race. Although he became a monk early in life, having studied at the famous Irish abbeys of Moville and Clonard, Columba was also a bard and poet who loved to sing almost as much as he loved God, his clan, and his native land. Yet, at forty-four, he left his beloved clan and country to exile himself forever from them both. How he came to do this is one of the most colorful stories in hagiography.

It is said that Columba, while visiting the Abbey of Clonard,

[8] *Monasticism Ancient and Modern,* F. C. Woodhouse (London, 1896).

stole into the chapel during the night, when all the monks were asleep, to copy out the Abbot Finian's psalter, so that he might take the copy back with him to his own monastery. Columba was discovered in the act by the abbot, who declared that the copy also belonged to him, as it had been made without his permission — which had evidently been refused. Columba denied this, and as neither monk would give in, an impartial court was held by the king to judge the matter. The decision went against Columba; he must return the copy, for it belonged to the abbot "as the calf belongs to a cow." Columba was furious. He thereupon induced his family clan to rise against the king, causing a battle in which three thousand men were lost!

Columba was horrified when he realized what he had done. Distraught, with a heavy conscience, he wandered off alone to seek a manner of somehow making amends. In his wanderings he met a holy old hermit to whom he confessed his plight and asked advice. The hermit counseled the monk to leave Ireland forever, as a penance, and convert as many as were lost in the battle. Columba accepted the penance, and made ready to cross the Irish Sea, to evangelize the Picts in Scotland — St. Ninian's efforts there having quite died out by this time.

With twelve companions, in a wicker boat covered with hides, Columba landed on the small and desolate island of Iona, on Pentecost, 563. Here they began at once to build a crude laura of wattles and planks. It is said that after they had started, Columba discovered that from the point they had chosen he could still see the distant shores of Ireland. But wishing to deny himself even this much consolation, he and his companions removed to the other side of the island, to build their laura there instead.

"Nothing could be more sullen and sad," writes de Montalembert, the great historian of Western monasticism, "than the aspect of this celebrated isle, where not a single tree has been able to either resist the blighting wind or the destroying hand of man. Only three miles in length and two in breadth, flat and low, bordered by grey rocks which scarcely rise above the level of the sea, and overshadowed by the high and sombre peaks of

the great Island of Mull, it has not even the wild beauty which
is conferred upon the neighboring isles and shores." Yet here
was to be the monastic capital of Scotland and the center of
Christian spiritual life in the north of Great Britain.

In his great sorrow and penitence, Columba practiced austerities of the severest sort; and in his intense zeal he achieved great
success in his mission to the Picts and Scots. A legend tells that
when he visited King Brude, in his palace stronghold at Iverness,
the King refused him entrance — having been incited against him
by the Druid priests. Columba made the sign of the cross upon
the palace gates, whereupon they flew open! The King and his
followers, it is said, were baptized forthwith.

When not on missionary journeys or attending councils, Columba
resided at Iona. Similar foundations, under his own Rule and
personal direction, spread over Scotland and Ireland. The severe
plane on which this "Order" existed is quite inconceivable to the
modern mind — but those were the times when the greatest
extremes were commonplace. Columba's first biographer[9] tells of
his extensive fasts and vigils, his great charity and quick sympathy,
and that the "holy joyousness which ever beamed from his coun-
tenance revealed the gladness with which the Holy Spirit filled
his soul." Never for a moment, says the account, did he stop
studying, praying, writing, or preaching. In his lifetime he wrote
or transcribed over three hundred books, two of which — *The Book
of Durrow* and a psalter — are preserved today, as well as the
stone pillow on which he slept at Iona. For over a hundred years
after Columba's death in 597, Iona continued to be the monastic
capital of all North Britain. Celtic monasticism reached its glorious
climax under the Columban Rule, which continued even after the
introduction of the Benedictine system, as we shall see.

The zeal of other Irish monks prompted them to look farther
afield. In spite of the pain of leaving their native land, a steady
stream of Irish missionaries began to flow beyond its borders.
They poured out upon not only other parts of the British Isles,

[9] Adaman (or Eunan), Abbot of Iona, 679. His biography of Columba
is called "the most complete piece of biography that all Europe can boast
of, not only at such an early period, but through the whole Middle Ages."

but upon Gaul, Germany, Switzerland, and Italy. The Catholics of Europe, grown lax through many upheavals were literally frightened into devout living by these amazing monks from a strange northern land. What is even more astonishing, candidates crowded the rapidly multiplying Celtic foundations in Europe; while noblemen and royalty gladly donated lands and money to build monasteries. Europe soon was aware of this entirely different kind of invasion.

Celtic monasticism first came to Europe in the person of St. Columbanus, another of the great Irish missionaries — and a figure quite as colorful as Columba. His rule also created an "Order" which became surprisingly popular and widespread on the Continent — considering the fact that Celtic monasticism was an imported brand of asceticism hardly so well suited to the mixed temperaments and chaotic conditions of Europe as to its originators in Northern Britain.

Columbanus was a well-educated and extremely handsome young man, much pursued by women — and much tempted from the virtue of his upbringing. Seeking the counsel of a pious woman hermit as to what he should do about it, he was told that "there was no safety but in flight." He understood this to mean that he should enter a monastery, which he immediately made up his mind to do. His decision, however, was strongly opposed by his family. His mother flung herself down between him and the door, but he stepped over her prostrate form and proceeded on his way.

Columbanus studied at some of the finest monastery schools in Ireland and eventually became a monk renowned for his learning and piety. Some say he repeatedly heard voices that bade him go to foreign lands as a missionary; others intimate that his high temper made many enemies and that he left for Europe in a huff over something or other. True enough, he often proved bold, harsh, and obstinate, but at the same time he loved God with an intense fervor, and his friends almost as intensely. His letters exhibit the most tender concern for his brothers in Christ — his monks — and his fiery sincerity immediately won over the King of Burgundy, who gave him an old fort for a monastery.

Here he and his monks demonstrated typical Celtic austerity to the awe-struck inhabitants of this remote part of Gaul, where the monasticism of St. Martin and his successors had not yet penetrated.

Soon Columbanus was so overwhelmed with entrants to his monastery that it was necessary for the King to provide other sites for new foundations. Within a short time there were three: Annegray, Luxeuil, and Fontaines. "The new monks," says Father Hughes, "were the most zealous of apostles, the most terrifying of preachers. They knew no other desire than to win souls from sin." The wild mountain country of the Vosges became the center of an amazing spiritual revival; nobles, soldiers, former profligates, plunged from their semibarbarian ways into the uncompromising austerity of Columbanus' Rule.

True to his Irish temperament, Columbanus often came to impassioned grips with those who opposed him or refused to repent. His first encounter was with the French bishops, who at the time had complete control over all the monasteries in Gaul. They resented his independence and growing popularity in general, and, in particular, his insistence on certain Celtic liturgical customs, especially the monks' observance of the Celtic Paschal cycle with its different date for Easter. In reply Columbanus criticized the bishops themselves in no uncertain terms, and ended by offering them some resounding advice. Another encounter was with the royal family of France, whose vices he denounced as fearlessly. For this the Queen Mother had him imprisoned, but he promptly escaped and dashed back to his monastery — only to be chased out of it again by the Queen's soldiers. He and several of his monks then embarked for Ireland, but a storm imperiled the boat and drove it back to the French coast. The captain decided that the monks were bringing him bad luck; they were not, he said, intended by God to go on that journey. So he put them, protesting, ashore.

Columbanus probably decided that the captain was right, for he made no further attempt to leave Europe. He and his monks continued to evangelize in various countries; it is thought that he was the first monk to penetrate as far as Germany, although the inhabitants were as yet too primitive to come under his spell as the already converted Gaels had done. This was to be the privilege of St. Boniface, about a hundred years later. When Columbanus founded his famous abbey of Bobbio, in Italy, his travels finally came to an end. There he stayed until his death in 615.

Although Celtic asceticism was really far too severe for Europeans, Columbanus' Rule provided a spiritual bridge over the last dying phase of semieremitical monasticism in the West, to that time when the perfect Rule for Western monasticism — the Benedictine system — would emerge. Despite the odds against their particular brand of religious life, the dauntless zeal of the Irish monks produced in Europe, for a while at least, monasticism of the highest order. And in Britain the tremendous array of Celtic scholars and saints remains a foundation stone of all Christian civilization.

Chapter Four

THE PERFECT PLAN

Wherever St. Columbanus' monks settled and his new foundations arose, a spiritual renewal took place; Christian morals and
piety were soon revived. Yet in the main, the sixth century was
an appalling morass of illiteracy and immorality. The transition
from paganism to Christianity, from Roman domination to independence, and from barbarism to civilization, took place with
great violence — in spite of the heroic labors of many hundreds
of saints and monks within whose monasteries whole families
sought protection. Many towns, especially in Gaul, originated in

this way. At the end of the century Pope Gregory the Great, "the great landlord" of the Church, held it together against fearful odds.[1]

Outside of the Rule of St. Columbanus, monks fell into sad disrepute. Monasteries housed, all at one time, many would-be rules, and many strange types of men were to be found clothed in a habit — a garb adopted from that of the lowest class, the shepherds and beggars, as a mark of humility. Communities were governed according to the personal will of each superior, and any monks who became dissatisfied with one house could leave it at will and try living in another. When several such malcontents banded together, they might wander about for years, never permanently settling down anywhere. These wandering monks, called *gyrovagi* and *sarabaites*, created widespread scandal and ill-feeling. Between the extremes of Columbanus' Celtic monasticism and the demoralized religious life that existed outside of it, there seemed to be no middle course. Monasticism in Europe appeared to be in the same condition that desert eremitical life had found itself about a hundred years before.

Yet even before Columbanus was born a solution to this seemingly hopeless condition had already germinated in Italy; and as his Celtic monasticism passed across the European scene, that solution was slowly taking permanent root. The year of Columbanus' birth (543) was the year of St. Benedict of Nursia's death; the Benedictine Rule had been in full force at Monte Cassino for ten years. From this island of calm and practical sanctity in a turbulent sea of extremes would come the first truly Western form of religious life — the "Benedictine System."

St. Benedict was born in Nursia, Italy, in 480. At an early age he was sent to Rome to study, but fearing the temptations of the large city, he soon fled from it. Accompanied by his old nurse,

---

[1] The rise of Islam and the consequent loss of the Eastern centers of Christianity was but one peril; the death of Clovis and the division of Gaul among his three brutish sons another. The necessity of defending Rome against the Lombards and placating the exarch in Ravenna was still another of the problems with which Gregory, the "founder of medieval Europe," had to deal.

to serve as his housekeeper, he sought seclusion in a small village where he intended to continue his studies. His great piety and virtue, however, attracted so much notice that when he performed a miracle in behalf of his housekeeper — a large platter which she had borrowed and accidentally shattered was perfectly restored — his fame became quite unbearable; he fled again, this time alone.

The young Benedict — then hardly seventeen years old — took refuge in a cave far down a ravine at a place called Subiaco. A monk from a nearby monastery, happening to meet him on the way, promised to bring him some food every day. The monk kept his promise, often saving a part of his own meal which he lowered down the ravine in a basket — to which a bell was attached in order to signal Benedict of its approach. The youthful hermit lived thus for three years, during which time the devil tormented him continually, just as he had tormented St. Antony. The most famous of these temptations was the vivid memory of a beautiful woman Benedict had seen in Rome when he was a student; so overpowering was it that he forced himself to roll in a patch of nettles until his whole body was burning and bloody, before the memory was obliterated and the temptation overcome.

Shepherds finally discovered Benedict in his cave. Again, as with Antony, this was the end of his solitary peace. People of all degrees, many monks included, came to him for spiritual guidance and counsel. At length he was asked to leave his cave and become superior of a nearby monastery. He consented, knowing of the great need for reformation there. But the monks of the community found his spiritual standards far too high for their liking; they tried to poison him! Only by performing a miracle — he blessed a pitcher of poisoned wine and it shattered instantly — did he manage to save his life and flee.

At this time Benedict founded several monasteries to which he appointed individual superiors, but remaining their superior-general, as had Pachomius and Columba. But again his life was threatened, this time by an envious priest, who also tried to poison him. Again he fled, accompanied by a few loyal disciples, in search of another spot on which to start anew; to establish a community that would be free of the evils that had thus far sprung up on every hand to destroy his efforts. When at last the monks came to a high rocky hill where the ruins of a pagan temple and a Roman fort tumbled dismally together, they saw them as the ideal materials, in an ideal place, for building a new monastery. This became Monte Cassino.

When Benedict's community grew large he saw the practical necessity for a written set of rules and counsels that would impart, with the greatest exactitude, his plan of life for his monks and his views of how they might best advance in spiritual perfection. Rather than making a mere list of laws governing the actions of the monk, he designed his new Rule to be a sort of course or school in the "science of salvation." Not only would it be designed to forestall in every detail the abuses and laxities which existed all around him, but it would set forth as its general premise the purest of monastic ideals, followed by counsels which would embody every virtue and attitude in harmony with that ideal. At the same time, it would not be too severe or too exacting; it would perfectly harmonize with human nature in general, and, in particular, with the character and temperament of Benedict's countrymen. In this St. Benedict's highest point of wisdom and understanding shines forth. He is, above all, the first master of psychology — the doctor of souls and the father of sons-in-Christ. No monastic leader had yet been quite all of these.

Although St. Benedict studied many earlier rules and adapted much from them for his own, he carefully avoided, or modified, all that did not conform to the nature of a European, the climate, or the society in which he lived. He made no attempt to reshape the Western temperament of his monk into an Eastern mold — as previous rules had done or tried to do. The monasticism of Basil, Martin, and Columbanus was derived from the desert;[2] its concepts and traditions were Eastern, on a plane quite unadaptable, on a large scale, to the Romans of St. Benedict's acquaintance.

[2] When a successor of St. Martin of Tours tried to reintroduce some of the severe austerities of the Eastern eremites, it is said that the monks cried, "We are not angels, only Gauls! It is ridiculous and cruel to make us live like angels when we are not!"

Thus this kind of religious life failed permanently to establish itself in Europe. In the reverse order, St. Pachomius' Rule, in the fourth century, had tried to reshape Eastern traditions and the Eastern temperament to fit a concept that was just as unfamiliar and just as unadaptable to the character of his people. The Benedictine Rule was designed *by* a continental man, *for* other continental men. It was in no way contrary to his familiar modes of thought and behavior.

Two principles of the Benedictine Rule were entirely unique. The first was the conception of the community as a *family*, with the abbot as head and father of that family and the monks as true brothers in Christ of one another. The second was the integral part which labor was to play in the life of the community. Columbanus' monasteries were run on military lines; the abbot was the general, vested with complete and autocratic power, and the monks were his soldiers; and nowhere in monastic life did monks have any filial obligation to one another whatever. In the Eastern tradition, manual labor had always been regarded as apart from the devotional life of the monk, to be indulged in only through necessity and not as part of the sphere of prayer and penance. St. Benedict saw labor as within this sphere — a form of religious observance as well as a necessity to mental health and well-being in the natural order. So important did Benedict regard labor that it constitutes one of the two fundamental principles of this Rule; the other is obedience. Each attribute of both these principles is most carefully set forth; the manner in which labor is to be performed, as well as to what kind and for how long; and to all the ways in which a monk owes obedience to his superior is added the spirit in which it is to be offered and to what extent. There is also included directions for the government of the community, the election and appointment of superiors, the regulation of fasts, recreation, and rest. Nothing whatever was left to the chance of error, immoderateness, or relaxation.

First place in the Holy Rule is given to the monk's obligation of chanting the Divine Office; it is his prime duty at all times and no other shall supersede it. To this end St. Benedict made his own arrangement of the Hours, that they should be beautifully and solemnly carried out, as well as fit into the rest of his horarium. This ideal of liturgical worship in Benedictine life is one that has never faltered; it has always remained one of its main characteristics.

Next place of importance in the Holy Rule is given to the obligation of study — that is, reading — in order that the monk, in learning and understanding of God, might ever advance to a higher point of perfection in his union with Him. Scholarship was not made an end in itself, for Benedict's monks were simple laymen at that time, not priests, intellectuals, or teachers. Thus we may well see in these two most important ideals — that is, the liturgy and study — how prayer and knowledge are ranked above self-mortification or penance. In the Eastern conception of religious asceticism the ideal was, so to speak, the other way around; severe austerity ranked first, as conducive to union with God and high spiritual virtue. The liturgy was secondary, and labor had no place in the ideal at all.

In St. Benedict's time, the vow of obedience was the only specific one made; poverty and chastity were implied under it. To this vow he added two others: conversion of life, and stability. The former means the vowing to live in all ways, and only in ways, which do honor to God; the latter is the vow that binds the monk to the community he has entered. In view of the conditions of religious life to be found elsewhere at this time, this was a wise innovation. Guided by this manual of the perfect religious state and the perfect community, these new patterns became a monastic code to be known as the Benedictine System. With it Western religious life found its proper media. And under it, yet unimagined heights would be attained.

The Benedictine Rule included religious life for women as well, for St. Benedict's sister, St. Scholastica, had founded a nunnery close to Monte Cassino and had adapted her brother's Rule for it. It is said that brother and sister were accustomed to meet once a year, at a house between the two monasteries, to confer with one another on spiritual matters. At their last meeting Scholastica, having foreknowledge of her imminent death, begged Benedict to stay and talk with her throughout the night. He refused, telling her that he and the monks that accompanied him could not so breach their Rule, and chided her for suggesting it. In tears, Scholastica prayed that her brother would change his mind, at which a violent storm arose, making it impossible for the monks to leave until the morning. Three days later, Father Benedict had a vision of his sister's soul entering Paradise.

The exact circumstances under which St. Benedict wrote the Holy Rule, ten years before his death, are unknown. Some historians believe that he wrote it at the express order of Pope Silverius, in order to reform all religious life, but this is an unproved point. More general opinion holds that St. Benedict had no intention other than to draw up a rule for his own monastery — and any others wishing to adopt it; but so suitable was it to the Western temperament, so successful at cutting away, all at one blow, both the untenable severity of Celtic monasticism and the evils of relaxation, that it took natural root of its own accord. St. Benedict was not a missionary; he did no traveling or evangelizing as Columbanus did; for this reason his Rule was virtually unknown outside Italy in his lifetime. It was not until fifty years after his death, when his system acquired its first champion in Pope Gregory the Great, that it began to be known.

Gregory, while still abbot of his own monastery in Rome, had occasion to observe closely a few Benedictine communities that had been driven to the city by the wars then going on. The perfection of the Benedictine mode of life so impressed Gregory that he immediately became an enthusiastic advocate of it. After becoming the first monk-pope, he wrote extensively in favor of the Holy Rule and finally decreed that it should be adopted in all new foundations. Within the next hundred years — by the eighth century — the Benedictine System was universal except for a few monasteries in Spain and Ireland. By historical standards, this is an exceptional rate of speed for so widespread and so enduring a development, especially in a time that seemed wholly unripe for such exactitude and harmony. Yet without this miracle of the steady growth of the Benedictine System, the whole advancement of the Western world would have been retarded by many hundreds of years. Together with the cathedral schools, the great Benedictine abbey schools of the Middle Ages were the fonts from which all Europe drew knowledge and sustenance for its cultural growth.

One of the first triumphs of Benedictine monasticism — as well as of Gregory the Great — was its introduction into Britain, in 597, by St. Augustine of Canterbury, a Roman and one of Gregory's own monks. As the Anglo-Saxons in England had invaded southern Britain in the previous century and either massacred the Celts or driven them into the West and North, England was, at this late date, largely pagan. The Celtic monks, for all their missionary zeal, abhorred the new race in the south as their enemies, not worthy of the Faith, nor were they familiar with the Anglo-Saxon language; only the northern tip of England had they tried to evangelize. Thus Celtic monasticism was almost unknown in England; it was virgin ground in which to implant the new Benedictine Rule.

Although he instituted it immediately, and was cordially treated by the King, Bishop Augustine's headway was nonetheless fraught with so many obstacles that at one moment the whole mission came close to being doomed and, at others, difficulties arose that seemed all but insurmountable. The greatest of these difficulties was the rewelding together of the Roman and the Celtic Churches — so long cut off from communication with one another. Bishop Augustine called a council to meet with the Celtic bishops in Wales, but very few of them came; they were aggrieved that the Anglo-Saxons should receive so much attention from the Holy See, and resentful of the rumor that Augustine meant to change their old-style calendar to the one now used by Rome, their monastic rule, and some of their liturgical rites. This was true enough; the new Roman calendar brought the date of Easter at a different time, and the Roman baptismal and marriage rites differed in some of their forms, although not in content.

The Celtic monk's tonsure, also, was of a different fashion; it was customary to have the head shaved in back, leaving the hair long in front, with charcoal smeared around the eyes. The Roman tonsure was a shaved head, with a ring of hair all around – and no charcoal. As trivial as seem some of these causes of the Celtic-Roman controversy, to the northern monks they were matters of grave concern, signifying an authority and discipline other than their own – to which they had become wholly unaccustomed. They adamantly made the most of every point, especially the matter of the date of Easter, and refused to co-operate with Augustine.

Because of this refusal by the Celts to co-operate with the new Bishop of Canterbury the reconversion of England and the Christian consolidation of the Isles was made much more difficult, and took far longer than it would have otherwise. The evangelization of eastern Britain *should* have come from the West; that it did not, spoiled Augustine's plans and almost the whole venture. It was saved only at the last moment, after his death, by the conversion of one of the petty kings called Edwin, who married the daughter of one of Augustine's first converts, King Ethelbert of Kent, and his French-Catholic queen. Edwin spread the Faith in his conquests in the Midlands, so that by the time he himself was defeated and slain in battle, Roman Catholicism was well entrenched.

The estrangement of the Celtic bishops and the Roman mission continued to cause so much trouble that it was decided to settle the matter once and for all. A great council, or synod, was called to be held at St. Hilda's[3] Abbey of Whitby in 664, to rule on which authority was right and authentic, the Roman or Celtic. After all the arguments had been heard, King Oswy – one of the two presiding rulers – decided that the Romans should prevail: the Pope and the Holy See were the true font of Catholic practice as well as doctrine. Only one Celtic priest, Tuda, submitted to the ruling, and he was consecrated a bishop at once – and the entering wedge was made. It was already the beginning of the end of a near-schism.

[3] The first Anglo-Saxon nuns were trained in Gaul. The first native (Northumbrian) nun is said to have been one Heia; the first two to become outstanding abbesses were St. Hilda of Whitby and St. Ebba of Coldingham (c. 650).

In protest, many of the Celtic abbots removed themselves, their monks, and their precious relics farther north; but it did no good. All the backward and schismatic parts of Christianized England fell into line, with most of Wales, Scotland, and Ireland gradually following. Under Augustine's successor, Theodore of Tarsus, England was fully organized into dioceses and bishoprics; monasteries, nunneries, schools, and cathedrals were founded, and all the culture and traditions of Rome and the East were introduced. Manuscripts, paintings, relics, vestments — even masons, glaziers, and singers — were imported from Rome by St. Wilfred, Abbot of Ripon,[4] and St. Benedict Biscop. Britain was at last reunited to the culture of the Continent through its reunion with Rome.

Entrenched in a few places in the North, Celtic monasticism, and all the controversial points to which it held so obdurately, lasted for two hundred years more. But it was a dead issue; Benedictine religious life, gloriously flourishing in England, eventually overcame it completely. All that Augustine had hoped to do — and felt that he had failed in doing — was accomplished.

For over a hundred years, until the Danish invasions in the ninth century, Britain was unaffected by those elements of the Dark Ages that were rife on the Continent. Through this first triumph of the Roman Catholic Church, and St. Benedict's Rule, England rose to a height of early medieval splendor not approximated in Europe for centuries to come. There the success of the Benedictine System was further off; tremendous difficulties had to be overcome. For if the sixth and seventh centuries were bad, the eighth was worse.

In Gaul, where all the forces of Western culture converged, the last of the "do-nothing" Merovingian kings had created "a regime of despotism tempered by assassination." When the Merovingian rulers were deposed and the Carolingian line took over France (as it may now be called) conditions grew worse; Charles

---

[4] Wilfred (634–709) was the great figure of the Whitby Council; St. Benedict Biscop, an Anglo-Saxon monk of Lerins, founded the abbeys of Wearmouth and Jarrow and is said to be responsible for introducing into England the art of making glass windows.

Martel, the first "strong man" of the new dynasty, was as ruthless and bloodthirsty as any barbarian chieftain had ever been.

Columban monasteries, though quite numerous, were often saddled with abbots who were laymen, appointed by nobles for political reasons. Even at best, Celtic monasteries never received any continuous support from the ruling class however. Although the Bishop of Mans had invited St. Benedict to send some of his monks to Gaul, he had died before they arrived and the new bishop had refused to receive them. However, one of the Frankish governors had offered the Benedictine monks an estate on the banks of the Loire. Here St. Maur, Benedict's disciple, and four companions had built a monastery — the first, and for a long time the only, Benedictine monastery in Gaul. Pope Gregory's later decree that all new communities should adopt the Benedictine Rule helped little, as Celtic monasticism prevailed and very few new foundations were made that had even heard of the Holy Rule. Thus was religious life in France very much in the same condition in which St. Benedict had found it in Italy, except in the few extremely severe Columban monasteries remaining.

In Germany, which was cut up into small barbarian kingdoms, the people who had been once converted by the doughty Irish missionaries had reverted to paganism and heresy. The priests, monks, and Christians that remained were without any organization; even the high standards of Columbanus' rule were for the most part debased by invalid and unorthodox practices. Christians — monks and priests included — were wont to participate in pagan rites and festivals as well as their own, often combining the two in a heterogeneous mixture. Resurgent paganism had all but dislodged Christianity's first foothold in Germany; it was well on the way to disappearing altogether.

The turning point came in the middle of the eighth century, brought about by the two greatest figures of that chaotic age — Pepin the Short, son of Charles Martel, and the first king of the new French dynasty; and St. Boniface, the Anglo-Saxon monk who was the apostle and savior of Germany. Between them, the Dark Ages, although not over, began at least to show some signs of light.

St. Boniface, born Winfrid in Devonshire, England, about 670, was educated by the Benedictine monks of Exeter, and later became one of them, in spite of the protests of his aristocratic father. He was a brilliant man and the most talented and holiest of monks — a poet, musician, Latin scholar, and eloquent preacher — and the head of his abbey school at Nutsshall. The Benedictines in England expected much of him, awaiting only the day when he should become one of the great abbots of his country. But such considerations were the furthest from Winfrid's mind; he thought only of going to northern Europe, to the country of his forebears, the old Saxons, as a missionary. Other missionary monks had told him of the sad conditions of Christianity in one of the northern Frankish provinces called Frisia; only one missionary bishop — the aging St. Willibrord — had managed to have any success there. With difficulty Winfrid prevailed upon his superiors to let him join Willibrord. With a few companions he set out, but at that moment the King of Frisia turned against his Frankish overlords and the Church; the little band was beaten back and had to return to England. A few years later, as he was about to be elected abbot of his monastery, Winfrid persuaded the monks to elect another in his place and returned once more to Europe, first going to Rome to receive the sanction of his plans by Pope Gregory II. At his meeting with the Pope he received the name Boniface, in honor of an early martyr whose feast had occurred the previous day, and to signify his intimate union with the Holy See.

Boniface then returned to Frisia, the rebellious King having died, and for three years assisted the aged Willibrord, who was so delighted with Boniface's talents that he wished to make him coadjutor bishop. Boniface, however, desired a freer hand and a wider scope for his labors than this position would have given him, so he left Frisia and proceeded to central Germany. In these wild lands, harried by disorganized, semipagan Christianity and fierce heathen tribes, his success was so unusual that the Pope recalled him to Rome to consecrate him a bishop and strengthen his hand by further plans, a brief, and letters of safe conduct. Boniface traveled about on horseback with tireless zeal, living in tents and peasant huts, and converting thousands at a time. He confounded the pagans by destroying their shrines and the unworthy monks by wooing away their followers with his preaching, miracles, and saintly personality.

The next pope, Gregory III, made Boniface archbishop of all the territory that now comprises Germany. For ten years he labored to build a native clergy, and to found monasteries, nunneries, and churches. His friends in England responded nobly to his appeal for aid; holy men and women flocked to join him, bringing with them books, manuscripts, vestments, and other fruits of their British culture. A hundred thousand converts were made in Hesse and Thuringia alone as Boniface continued to reorganize and reform, adding still more countries and thousands more converts to his triumphs. Then, as he reached the age when his lifework should be nearing completion, yet another project called for his great talents and his powers as the Papal Legate, which he had now become. This was the reform of the Frankish Church.

When Pepin the Short — a good man, wholly unlike his father — became king of the Franks in the middle of the eighth century, he was crowned and anointed by the Papal Legate, Boniface, at Soissions in 751, and three years later by the Pope himself. Thus was born the ideal of the *Christian State* and the theory of the "divine right of kings."

Pepin and his brother Carloman[5] immediately interested Boniface in ecclesiastical reforms for the whole Empire, brutalized as it had become under their father, Martel. The task was gigantic, but armed with the help of the Holy See, Pepin and Boniface did their best. The first general council in France for almost a century was called, with others following, at which the most

---

[5] The Frankish Empire was at first divided between Pepin and Carloman, but Carloman later entered a monastery (said to be Monte Cassino) in Italy, and Pepin became sole ruler.

stringent reforms were legislated. One of the laws was that the Benedictine Rule should govern all monasteries henceforth.

While helping Pepin reform the Frankish Church, Boniface never forgot the field of his missionary labors. He returned to Germany and began the work of carrying out one of his most cherished plans: the foundation of a monastery which was to be the monastic center of Germany. In it he would train priests and missionaries and cultivate the arts, to make it a perfect example of Benedictine life. This was the great Abbey of Fulda, completed in 744. Before the death of Fulda's first abbot the abbey numbered four hundred monks, and in succeeding centuries it trained many great ecclesiastical scholars. Whenever he could rest from his labors, Boniface would retire to Fulda to refresh his soul and hold conferences on the Holy Rule.

In spite of advancing age and illness, Boniface still burned with missionary zeal — especially for Frisia, which had reverted to paganism upon the death of Willibrord. Seeking one last victory for God, he returned there. As usual, thousands were converted and baptized, heathen shrines were demolished, and chapels were built in their stead.

Seeing their false gods crumble to dust, the disgraced pagans were furious; they skulked in the mountains, secretly plotting revenge, while St. Boniface planned the mass confirmation of several thousand converts, on a June morning in 754. As he prayed in his tent before dawn, and a few converts began to gather, the pagans struck; Boniface and fifty-two of his converts were murdered. The others, when they arrived, carried his body to Fulda, where it was interred in the chancel of the abbey church.

"St. Boniface had a deeper influence on the history of Europe than any Englishman who has ever lived," says Christopher Dawson.[6] "Unlike his Celtic predecessors he was not an individual missionary, but a statesman and organizer . . . a servant of the Roman order. . . . It was through the work of St. Boniface that Germany first became a living member of the European society."

[6] *The Making of Europe,* pp. 210–211.

After two hundred and fifty years of chaos, Europe at last was molded into a Christian world, with its own culture. Thenceforth would her rulers assume the principles and traditions taught them by the great Benedict, Gregory, Augustine, and Boniface. From this point onward the struggle is wholly a Christian one, divorced forever from the paganism and primitiveness of the past.

CHAPTER FIVE

THE CASTLE AND THE ABBEY

When Charlemagne, the grandson of the terrible Charles Martel, succeeded to the throne of the Carolingian Empire in 768, some semblance of order was to begin. The great Charlemagne's "Holy Roman Empire" was built on "the new conception of Christendom as the ultimate social unity." All that Gregory the Great and St. Boniface had hoped for would be attained through Charles; he was the true successor of them both, for their work might not have survived or matured without him. Though neither a scholar nor a saint, Charles built an empire on his deep respect for a culture and a faith in which he himself was little schooled. For thirty years, he practically *was* the Church.

Charlemagne's favorite book, which he had read to him when he dined, was St. Augustine's *De Civitate Dei* (*Of the City of God*). He set out to create "the city of God" on earth. To this end was every law enacted,[1] every detail of life considered, every battle fought. If his exalted ideal fell short of complete realization, it was because no mortal man, dealing with other mortal men and with so few material aids or resources, could have done better. Culturally, his first and greatest aid and resource was, of course, the monks and the clergy who became the imparters of all the learning which they alone possessed, as well as the shepherds of souls and the upholders of the King's laws — based as they were upon the laws of God and of the Church. Worthy bishops and scholarly clerics were appointed to newly created sees and schools; churches, monasteries, roads, bridges, and a multitude of other public works rose under Charles's forceful hand. From faraway Ireland and England, as well as Rome and Germany, he gathered in the best minds of his age to help him carry out his objectives. The "Carolingian Renaissance" was fully matured by 800, when his achievements were, quite literally, crowned by Pope Gregory III on Christmas Day in Rome — the climax of Charlemagne's triumph, its reward and confirmation.

So high was Charlemagne's regard for education that several different kinds of schools were set up — all conducted by religious and clerics. First, there were the village schools, in charge of parish priests, for the elementary education of all children; then came the monastic and cathedral schools, in which the Seven Liberal Arts — grammar, rhetoric, logic, arithmetic, geometry, astronomy, and music, in addition to theology — were taught. Schools of singing and church music, for which two authorities were imported from Rome, were conducted for clerics. All of these schools were open and free to all; the sons of serfs were as welcome as

[1] Civil law and Church law were equally valid before the State, and infractions thereof punishable by the State, as well as by the bishops. This led to an overlapping of authority which was often a disadvantage to both Church and State.

those of freemen. A palace school, at Aachen, for the education of the children of the nobility, was established, and to an Academy of Arts and Sciences, held at the imperial court, were invited the most distinguished scholars of the time, to lecture and hold "conversation classes." In consequence of all this intellectual activity, monasteries and cathedrals became active institutions of learning, as priests and monks had first to attain the high standards set by the Emperor before they could pass them on to others. "The abbeys of Charlemagne's time were no longer merely convents of monks, whose lives were given over to prayer and mortification," says Father Hughes. "They were the great centers of national life, functioning in the social organism as the cities had functioned in the Roman Empire."[2]

Charles expressly desired that "all clergy should be monks and canons living in common." With characteristic directness, he sent to Monte Cassino for an authentic Rule of St. Benedict, and urged it upon all the monasteries. Although one of his blind spots was the inability to grasp and appreciate contemplative asceticism, Charles well realized the benefits of monasticism in the furtherance of his aims. Not only his patronage, but that of the many nobles who donated lands and money for the foundation of abbeys (often entering them as well) made monasticism flourish. Many of the abbey schools thus created became great seats of learning throughout the Middle Ages.[3]

That clerics might be encouraged to live a common life, Charles called upon a scholar-priest whom he had summoned from Germany, St. Chrodegang, Bishop of Metz, who helped draft plans that would regulate priests' educational requirements, property, conduct, work, and support. St. Chrodegang also composed a rule for all canons (priests of a cathedral church), modeled on St. Benedict's, which served to reorganize and systemize the now large households of clerics and student-clerics which surrounded the bishops and the large churches. St. Chrodegang also instituted

[2] *A History of the Church*, Vol. II, Chap. IV, p. 151.
[3] Mabillon cites 27 abbey and cathedral schools in France alone. Several were to become great universities during the High Middle Ages (Paris, Lyons, Tours).

a number of liturgical reforms by introducing the Roman Rite and Gregorian Chant, making, with the Emperor's sanction, every effort to encourage the bishops to adopt all of these new laws and policies.

Though only the extraordinary Charles could keep his vast empire together, the momentum he created continued for about thirty years after his death in 817 before it began to slacken. Under his heir, Louis the Pious, Carolingian culture continued to advance, taking deeper root in the second generation than it had in the first — on whom it had been more or less imposed by Charles's forthright methods. Intellectual life, no longer enforced, but bred of the genius of Alcuin, the great English scholar-monk, and the extensive education offered all citizens, produced abundant results as Louis continued his father's policies to the best of his ability. On one point, at least, Louis superseded his father; he understood the true nature of monasticism. He saw the religious state as a life of prayer, in monasteries which were sanctuaries where the perfect following of Christ through the evangelical counsels might be realized. This principle had been endangered in his father's time by arrogant and ambitious men who began to see profit in dictating to the abbeys and cathedrals which their munificence had helped to found. These men often appointed their own candidates to Church offices, or sometimes even entered the ranks of the Church themselves, to gain their objectives. This practice had prevented Charlemagne from fully realizing his educational policies and was also detrimental to the spiritual life of the people. Moreover, it threatened the discipline of the Benedictine System, as religious life continued to expand — especially as each monastery was an autonomous unit without outside supervision, except that exercised by the bishop. Temporal and intellectual progress was often at the expense of piety as the insidious custom of appointing "commendatory abbots"[4] took hold. But

---

[4] A commendatory abbot was a prelate or layman who held an abbey *in commendam;* that is, who was appointed abbot through rank or influence, and who was usually not a member of the community, or living in it. He also was granted the revenue accruing to the community for his own use, a monk usually being appointed to act in his stead, as superior of the house.

relaxation was forestalled by Louis, to whom these dangers were evident, by an historic advance in the structure of religious life; the first milestone in the history of monasticism after the adoption of the Benedictine Rule. This was the advent of monastic constitutions, or *capitula.*

In order to find means of safeguarding the monastic ideal, Louis conferred with one of his ecclesiastical advisers, Benedict of Aniane. Benedict, one of the many soldier-nobles who had entered the cloister during the reign of Charlemagne, was a man of austere piety and great executive ability. He immediately called for the assembling of a great conference of abbots and bishops to formulate corrective measures; and to this end a synod was held at Aix-la-Chapelle, now Aachen, in 817.

First of all, the adoption of the Benedictine Rule was made mandatory by imperial decree as well as Church law, for although Charles had advocated and encouraged its use, it had not been obligatory. Benedict of Aniane then proposed a set of qualifying bylaws or *capitula,* to be appended to the Holy Rule. Uniformity, especially in regard to the discipline and government of monasteries, was his aim, in order to combat the relaxation of piety and interference from outside the cloister. Although the pronouncements and opinions of Benedict which resulted in his new "constitutions" were somewhat rigid and severe, his austere and energetic guidance was a needed tonic; everything he proposed was agreed upon and adopted by the conference at Aachen.

The word "constitutions" is one which becomes identified with the history of religious life from here on. Up to the drafting of a general constitution for religious life, monasteries were completely independent of one another, and ruled by no other law than the Rule itself and the authority of the abbot. There was therefore quite a lot of variation in the interpretation of the Rule, and many consequent offenses against its letter, either by omission

---

There were many other Church offices and benefices (property and income) that were often thus appropriated. Lay investiture and benefices held *in commendam* were very harmful practices which took many centuries to erase.

or commission. Nor was the interpretation of the Rule by one monastery of any interest or concern to another.

St. Benedict of Aniane's set of eighty *capitula* put an end to such latitude and created a uniform monastic system for the first time in continental religious life. His own monastery, Corneli-münster, which was built for him by Louis near Aachen, set the standard for the new discipline which other great foundations — such as Corvey, in Westphalia, and Fulda — followed. To offset the emphasis now placed upon scholarship, the necessity of manual labor was restressed and ascetical practices were multiplied in order to keep piety in the forefront of the monk's daily life. Carried on by several successors after his death in 821, the reforms of St. Benedict of Aniane — although seemingly short-lived in the disorders that were soon to follow — established traditions and set standards that exercised a permanent influence on all subsequent religious life; so permanent, in fact, that he is called the "Second Founder of Monasticism in the West."

In the same year that the Council of Aix-la-Chapelle was held, new constitutions for canons and non-Benedictine nuns — called canonesses — were also issued, for, since the previous century, both canons and canonesses had become divided into types that needed clearer definition and more specific regulation. Like the Benedictine Rule, St. Augustine's and St. Chrodegang's Rules needed "tightening" by added constitutions, as the complexities of a growing culture created more and more variations in religious life.

Since the time when St. Chrodegang had composed his Rule for canons, about 750, many of them had abandoned the common life, to live in separate, personal quarters. These had become known as secular canons, while those that continued to live in community were known as regular canons. Thus arose the term "canons regular" at this time; one not specifically used before and therefore causing many historians to place the origin of canons regular at about the time of St. Chrodegang. However, since canons living in common under a rule began with St. Augustine and even before, it would seem that merely the term, rather than the mode of life, originated in this era. The additional constitutions of 817 further molded the life of religious priests into the form that we know today.

For nuns who were not Benedictine, St. Augustine's Rule had sufficed since the time he wrote it. These nuns, known as canonesses, recited the Divine Office, made altar linens and vestments, and specialized in the education of girls. Some communities of canonesses strictly adhered to St. Augustine's Rule, as well as constitutions modeled on those of St. Benedict of Aniane, but the majority had never carried any of these out to their fullest extent. Only two vows — chastity and obedience — were taken, which could be abrogated at any time. These communities of canonesses were largely made up of noblewomen and soon, therefore, acquired valuable property and much wealth. Their abbesses often held princely rank and were vested with feudal authority. This combination of rank and wealth led to a laxity which set them apart from the less aristocratic — and more austere — canonesses. New constitutions were now decreed for the canonesses by the Holy See to induce a more regular observance. Those that were successfully reformed, to become strictly cloistered with a resumption of the three perpetual vows, became known thenceforth as Regular Canonesses; those that continued in their customary way of life became known as Secular Canonesses. In later ages, when active, uncloistered, congregations emerged in history, Secular Canonesses were to become a valuable branch of the Third Orders Regular, but in these early times their spiritual prestige was not great.

The extensive missionary activities carried on by the Church under Charlemagne were continued by Louis. Of the many hundreds of missionaries who worked to Christianize the North, the most celebrated is probably St. Ansgar, a Benedictine monk. He completed the conversion of Denmark and north Germany in about the year 850 — begun by Louis' foster brother, Ebbo, Archbishop of Rheims — by spending seventy years in those regions, accomplishing what St. Boniface had done in central Germany and the Irish monks had done in the south. Also, like St. Boniface,

Ansgar created a second Fulda in Hamburg, which included a cathedral, monastery, school, and library.

After the death of Louis the Pious in 840, the Carolingian dynasty began to crumble rapidly. Under Charles's weak grandsons the Empire was divided and subdivided until no strong central authority remained to stem a fresh onslaught of barbarians from both the North and the South. In lesser hands than Charles's, the alliance between the State and the Church proved all but disastrous; the Papacy was turned into a tool of princes, to be debauched to such a scandalous degree that no merely mortal institution could have survived. As the struggle of the Papacy to extricate itself from this "legal secularization" went on, bishops protested in vain; monasteries and churches were sacked, towns were burned; clerics, laymen, families, and noblemen were slain as the barbarian foe made systematic advances. Great Britain, aloof before from the ravages of the Dark Ages in Europe, was now engulfed in it too; nothing that Britain had experienced before could compare to the annihilating ferocity of the Danish invasions of England that coincided with the new onslaughts on the Continent. A darker age than ever swept over the West. When the great army of Northmen penetrated the very heart of the Carolingian Empire, Christendom seemed to be making a last desperate stand.

But the seedbed of Catholic unity and culture so briefly cultivated by Charles the Great withstood this final assault. When the climax of the storm had passed, Europe was still Christian and still Catholic. Only the branches had been stripped; the roots were there to stay — "a terrible test which burnt away anything that was weak and superfluous and left only the hardest and most resistant elements which were inured to insecurity and violence."[5] Into this time of insecurity and violence, born of the will to survive, to preserve Latin power and Christian values, there emerged the "feudal system."

No time in history so catches our imagination as the feudal

[5] C. Dawson, *Religion and the Rise of Western Culture*, p. 101.

era. Gaily retold in song and story, it seems only a time of high romance — of brave knights, beautiful ladies, and towering fortress castles. Actually, it was a time of great extremes, its darkness of tyranny and bloodshed shot through with bright flashes of beauty and valor. Evil existed — but as a sin to be expiated and a wrong to be righted. If Christian values were debased or exploited through bad motives, the values themselves were not altered thereby; they waited only to be reaffirmed by a society that was convinced of their changelessness.

Historians disagree as to the worth of feudal society; it is regarded by some as a thoroughly depraved era, while others hold that such depths have been exaggerated and that it held much that was good. Its effects were, it is true, bad enough, but as a manner of life it seemed the only possible mode of self-defense and self-preservation at the time — the price of saving European civilization and Christianity. An expedient that successfully did both could not have been so terrible as some have pictured it. And that it did not become much worse and thereby, perhaps, lose in the struggle, is entirely due to the close relation of the castle and the abbey, the prince and abbot, the serf and the monk — in the little kingdom that was the great landed estate and its fiefs.

With southern and eastern Europe besieged by the Northmen and divided up into small kingdoms, princes who had been granted large landholdings, or put in command of remote territories, became laws unto themselves — although they were nominal vassals of the Emperor and owed him taxes which were paid in soldiers who were fed, housed, and trained on their great estates, which were the personal kingdoms of each prince, to hold at his own peril. The castle was the little kingdom's fortress and ruling court. Lesser nobles, relatives, or friends were granted land in exchange for their military support, which land they ceded back to the estate as fiefs, themselves becoming vassals of the lord. Nothing ruled the lord of the castle but his conscience, the court confessor, and possibly the proximity of the abbey — and his Catholic heritage.

These feudal overlords were generous in support of the Church;

they willingly gave part of their lands for the building of monasteries and endowed them handsomely. Once established, the
monastery was ceded back as a fief, to become a part of the
feudal community. The abbot helped to rule the estate with his
advice and to serve its spiritual needs, while the lord protected
and provided for the abbey. It was to the lord's interest to see
that a worthy and competent abbot was appointed to the monastery
that was his fief — an appointment that only he might confer.
When, however, the abbey later became a powerful and wealthy
part of the feudal community it was too often to the interest of
the feudal lord to appoint abbots for other reasons; a favored
relative or supporter might covet such an honor and the material
benefit attached to it. Sometimes the lord even invested himself
as abbot! The custom of lay investiture then began to spread to
a nefarious degree; even lesser Church offices began to be sought
after, schemed for, and conferred or bought, as political and
material prizes. When bishoprics and abbeys themselves became
great estates — as they sometimes did — they were often ruled
in commendam by absentee, or titular, recipients of these rich
benefices, which revenues were drained off to be enjoyed elsewhere. All offices requiring any degree of literacy had to be filled
by clerics, as they alone knew how to read and write; thus poorly
paid parish priests and ambitious clerics filled or fought over every
post that called for such requirements — too often to the detriment
of their spiritual welfare. So enmeshed was the Holy See in the
larger disorders of the time — the beginning of the "Iron Age"[6] —
that protesting bishops and abbots were unheeded by Rome; or,
if heeded, little could be done about their complaints. Quite in
vain did several popes and members of the hierarchy attempt to
put down these growing evils. The feudal barons with their
overweening pride and great privileges — whether churchmen[7] or

[6] "The Iron Age of the Popes" is an historical parallel with the last of the
four great ages in mythology, supposed to be characterized by abounding op-
pression, vice, and misery.

[7] Abbots and bishops, if landowners in their own right, were also vassals
of the Emperor, and owed him taxes in money and men, just as did the
other vassal lords.

princes — were, it seemed, a "necessary evil." They were the power that held the West together.

It is easy to imagine what such practices did to the morale and discipline of the clergy and religious. All feudal society, however, was not so degraded; there were good feudal lords as well as bad — or ignorant, or headstrong — and there were prelates, priests, and religious whose holiness, scholarship, and integrity well outrode the dark times. Such great abbeys as St. Gall in Switzerland; Fulda in Germany; Fleury, Corbie, Reichenau in France, stood their ground with distinction; their great libraries and schools produced immortal writers, poets, and philosophers. Although many monasteries were destroyed, or religious life in them made impossible by the monks having to defend their countryside against the infidels, as happened at Lerins, others continued to be built and endowed by feudal princes. Ascetical life suffered much, but it was far from destroyed. Although many a Christian principle was ruthlessly violated in feudal society, Christianity lost no ground in the West; men like St. Ansgar and SS. Cyril and Methodius converted the Scandinavians and Slavs; and the Viking conquerors of Great Britain and France — to whom Christianity had not been unknown — became Christian almost immediately upon settling in these countries. As the ninth century turned into the tenth, embattled Catholicism was braced for a storm that was to grow even worse before it was over.

By the beginning of the tenth century, Charlemagne's ideals and their partial realization seemed completely dissolved in confusion and decay; the bright promise of his Holy Roman Empire had come to nothing. The picture was black, indeed, as the feudal "system" now used the religion it had so well protected to further the most debased ambitions of power and wealth. From this cause the Church began to weaken perilously from within, and from without the onslaughts of the Northmen, Saracens, and Magyars beat down its institutions and brutalized its followers. The prelates of the Province of Rheims drew up a document that read, in part:

"The Cities are depopulated, the monasteries ruined and burned, the land is reduced to solitude. . . . The powerful oppress the weak, the land is full of violence against the poor and the plunder of the goods of the Church. . . . In the case of the monasteries some have been destroyed by the heathen, others have been deprived of their property and reduced to nothing. In those that remain there is no longer any observance of the rule. They no longer have legitimate superiors, owing to the abuse of submitting to secular domination. We see in the monasteries lay abbots with their wives and their children, their soldiers and their dogs. . . . God's flock perishes through our charge. It has come about by our negligence, our ignorance and that of our brethren. . . ."

But in the very fact of such an admission was the seed of regeneration. Even as the bishops drafted their declaration, forces were gathering that would end the so-called "Iron Age of the Popes" and clear the way to a new and glorious era.

The regenerating force came, as it must, from within the Church; not in the edicts of kings or councils, but in the souls of her children and ministers — beginning with the monks and nuns. Within the monastic life of the Church, there began, in the tenth century, a revolutionary movement which was to expand and include far more than the religious. The whole Western world was to share in it.

That a movement which began only as a monastic reform could so quickly spread beyond the abbey's walls to society in general was due to the fact that, unlike religious life in previous times, monasticism was now bound up with all Carolingian tradition and culture. As missionaries, teachers, judges, and mediators in feudal society, monks were highly conscious of their social responsibilities. Nor had apostolic zeal died out. In the north, especially the Low Countries, Scandinavia, and Germany, successors of SS. Ansgar and Boniface continued to build monastic foundations, establish sees, and gather the last of Europe's pagans into the Christian fold. As exploited and secularized as were so many of the monasteries, the Benedictine Rule was still the consecrated norm of ascetical life; the Holy Rule — even as the Gospel of Christ and His Church — had not been destroyed, but temporarily distorted and abused by men. That the spiritual energy of grace

may always transform man and lift from him the burden of his
sins, was still the legacy of St. Augustine's philosophy to a
Christian world.

Nothing could better prove St. Augustine's premise than the
history of the next three hundred years, when the Church would
rise to its Golden Age in the renaissance of the twelfth century.
And that great era begins with the Abbey of Cluny, in France.

The Abbey of Cluny was one of the many new monasteries
founded by the nobility. In 910, William the Pious, Duke of
Aquitaine, donated his entire domain for its foundation, with
the stipulation that it should be free of all lay interference whatsoever and subject only to the Holy See. William chose for its
first abbot the holiest and most learned man he could find —
Berno, then abbot of another monastery. Abbot Berno immediately
instituted a very austere form of Benedictine life. To the *capitula*
of St. Benedict of Aniane he added others which introduced many
extra devotional exercises and votive offices — such as the Office
of the Dead, of Our Lady, and All Saints — as well as the fullest
possible exercise of the Benedictine laws of fasting, abstinence,
night offices, strict obedience, and rigorous discipline. The Cluniac
constitutions also made all sister foundations subject to the authority of the Abbot of Cluny, thus creating a "chain" of houses, all
closely related to one another. This was a most important point
of the reform and one that would have far-reaching consequences
in the history of religious life.

There was a tremendous response to these high standards set
by Berno in spite of the immorality of the times. Almost at once
a full-fledged community came into being, to be led by a succession
of some of the greatest abbot saints known to the Church. One
of these was the second abbot of Cluny, St. Odo (927–942). A
prolific and scholarly writer of the utmost vigor, Odo boldly
attacked the social injustices of the times, the evils within the
Church and without, and wielded the philosophy and theology
of St. Augustine as a weapon against them all. The Cluniac
reform movement spread as far as the Low Countries and England,
and to the south of Italy; other new foundations followed, led by

equally zealous men,[8] and many existing houses asked to be incorporated with Cluny as a part of the new system. Independent of the bishops, according to William's original charter, Cluny was able to extend its influence into feudal society by becoming, itself, a kind of chain of feudal estates serving as an exemplary model for the other great landowners.

In 1080, after the guidance of five saintly abbots had raised Cluny to the height of temporal success and spiritual prestige, an abbey was built on the same site to match the greatness of the community. Five hundred and fifty-five feet in length, the abbey church was the largest in Christendom until the building of St. Peter's in Rome. Together with its conventual buildings, the entire monastery covered an area of twenty-five acres, exclusive of its land. It was the wonder of the early Middle Ages, to become, for the next two hundred years, the "school of popes" and the home of some of the greatest saints and scholars in the history of the Church.[9] Its library was a collection of fabulous treasures — which were stolen and lost when the abbey was sacked and destroyed by the Huguenots many centuries later.[10]

Up to this point in our story of religious life, it has been with reservations that the word "order" has been used, as not being within the full meaning of the modern term. The true religious order here emerges in the now accepted sense: a congregation of aggregate houses, centrally governed, with its own "mode" or interpretation of the rule set forth in its own constitutions, or bylaws. Thus Cluny may be called the first modern order. The conception of an order would develop still further, with the advent of the Cistercians, and later still when orders must conform to canon law, and be formally approved by the pope. But with Cluny the word begins to mean what we now understand it to mean: one particular society of religious, as distinguished from another,

[8] SS. Gerard of Brogne; Peter and Bavo of Ghent; and Omer, Bertin, and Chislain in Metz and the Low Countries; St. Abbo of Fleury; St. Poppo of Stavelot; and St. William of Volpiano.

[9] Four popes; also SS. Berno, Odo, Odilo, Mayeul, Hugh, Peter the Venerable, and others.

[10] Only a small fraction was ever found, to be preserved by the French government.

spread out into many foundations. From this main trunk of the Benedictine tree sprang all the branches that were to follow.

In Great Britain the new spirit was one of revival rather than reform, for England's glorious beginning, so relatively free of the devastation caused in Europe by the breakup of the Carolingian Empire, had been cut short by the second invasion of the Northmen in the ninth century. England was virtually in ruins; monasteries, cathedrals, and churches were sacked; priests, monks, nuns, and laymen were massacred by the thousands. In some abbey convents nuns cut off their noses and lips to save themselves from being attacked by the Danes. The cruel fury of the pirates, whose only intention was to rob and destroy, made up for their lack of numbers. They did tremendous damage before they were finally repulsed, or absorbed into English civilization, when Alfred the Great rebuilt England.

During the lull that followed the Danish invasions, the Church began a slow recovery under one of England's first great churchmen and statesmen, St. Dunstan (909–988), Abbot of Glastonbury and Archbishop of Canterbury. Dunstan set to work on the task with the utmost vigor. He rebuilt churches and restored the liturgical life within them, reorganized monasticism under the Benedictine Rule, and set in motion large-scale reforms of the clergy and laity. When he was appointed Bishop of Wells, Dunstan traveled all the way to Rome to receive the pallium, dispensing such lavish charity on the way that one day his attendants protested that nothing would be left for the remainder of the journey. But Dunstan was undeterred; he urged them to "trust in Christ." By evening a monastery came in view whose abbot offered Dunstan and his company a hospitality so equally lavish that they were well provided with enough for their journey.

On his return from Rome Dunstan became virtual ruler of England. For the next twenty-eight years, he pushed forward all-embracing reforms in which he himself took active part — as a teacher, abbot, priest, scholar, and statesman. So gentle and patient a teacher in the cathedral schools was he that it is said that for many years after his death boys were accustomed to pray for his protection against harsh masters, and that their prayers were well answered. As a scholar he corrected manuscripts in monastery libraries, and as a craftsman made bells and organs; as a judge he protected widows and orphans, and became the patron of foreign students and scholars. Celibacy of the clergy was strictly enforced; either canons under rule or monks replaced secular priests in the cathedrals, and observance of the Holy Rule was patterned after Cluny.

Much of this achievement was halted when the Danish wars were resumed, and some of Dunstan's work was nullified. When peace came again after many violent and bloody years, the Danish King of England, Canute, repented of his cruelty and became a devout Catholic; he even made a pilgrimage to Rome in 1026 and sent British missionaries to Denmark. What Dunstan had begun continued anew, to join the awakening spirit of reform in Europe.

On the Continent this spirit enlisted several of the chief rulers of Europe and resulted in a line of popes through whom the papacy regained its dignity and prestige. The first great strides were made in Germany, where Otto the Great (936–973) briefly revived the Carolingian line. Otto sincerely desired to put an end to the humiliating subjection of the Papacy to political machinations and to establish a Holy Roman Empire such as Charlemagne had envisioned. His efforts were at least well rewarded in his own country through his brother, Bruno of Cologne, a youth of only seventeen when the Emperor appointed him abbot of the two large monasteries of Corvy and Lorch. Soon after he became archchancellor. Bruno re-established a strict observance of the Benedictine Rule in both houses and also proved to be as brilliant a statesman as he was a priest and monk. As Archbishop of Cologne, he improved relations between France and Germany, arbitrated royal and episcopal quarrels, and induced, through his love of scholarship, a renaissance of learning in the cathedral and monastic schools. Through his brother's efforts, Otto's policy of perfect union of Church and State was realized. Without him it is doubtful that Otto would now be called "The

Great." But Bruno was, first of all, a zealous priest; the wide influence of his holiness was, in Germany, the cornerstone of monastic and clerical reform there.

All of these first glimmerings of the "Golden Age" to come were, it must be remembered, achieved under the greatest possible difficulties. The breakdown of the feudal system into small kingdoms of feudal states resulted in continual warfare among them and with the Church. Moreover, the deeply intrenched evils of lay investiture and the vices of simony and clerical incontinence were so common that the average man barely remembered any other customs. Nowhere in history is the remarkable vitality of the Catholic Church more evident than in her ability to rise out of such conditions to yet unimagined heights. And though the heights were barely in sight as yet, they already influenced the cause of all the trouble — feudal society. It began to change and improve. Slowly the iron darkness turned into the light of the Golden Age.

CHAPTER SIX

FROM IRON TO GOLD

It was not until now, in the year 1000, that the feudal knight
fully realized the chief victory of his conquest. It was his heritage
of faith. Pressed on him by the renewed Church, Christian values
began to replace brutal expediency as the knight gradually turned
from an uncouth, ruthless soldier into a courtier and a Christian
hero — vowed to uphold virtue as well as his lord. Chivalry,
knight errantry, and the *chanson de geste*[1] were born. The besieged castle and its estates turned into the palace of a duchy,

[1] An epic poem narrating heroic exploits.

adorned with gay courtiers and fine ladies; fierce loyalty and jealous might were replaced by the ideal of honor, for the knight who fought in an honorable cause was a martyr as well as a hero. Had he not defended the Church against the Saracens and Magyars and Moors? Feudalism was a high price to pay for the saving of Christianity and Western culture, but it was worth it.

The great revival and reform of monasticism that took place in the eleventh century naturally revived Christian culture in all its other aspects as well. As the movement of revival matured, many scholarly abbots became its leaders who, in turn, exercised a tremendous influence on Europe's rulers. Consequently, the relations between the Papacy and the Empire began to improve; despite defections and much factionalism,[2] harmony existed between a number of truly good rulers and equally good popes. When Leo IX became pope in 1048, he imported many leaders of the reform from central Europe to Rome, thus wresting much power from the Roman nobles in the papal court and infusing vigorous new blood into the Vatican. The centuries-old conflict over lay investiture came to a crisis when the first truly great reforming Pope ascended the throne of Peter in the middle of the tenth century. As Papal Treasurer and saintly Benedictine, Hildebrand had been the power behind the papal throne for twenty years, and his fearless integrity was well known. As Gregory VII he now — in reluctant and prayerful trepidation — armed himself for a spiritual battle with the last dangerous forces of entrenched reaction.

Gregory attacked the evils of this era of transition with an experienced and masterly hand. The most stringent decrees against the prevailing decadence of the clergy were formulated, and the right of lay investiture was definitely canceled by new canons far more drastic than any heretofore. He deposed simonical prelates and put in their places only those who would carry out his reforms, and valiantly fought to instill regularity in all monasteries still

[2] Much of this was due to the still-accepted Carolingian tradition of the divine right of kings. The reforming parties looked first to royal power, rather than the ecclesiastical or papal power, for their support; the duty of the prince to intervene in the Church's affairs was taken for granted.

outside the influence of Cluny. There were, of course, storms of protest — from the clergy, from the feudal princes, and even from the Emperor himself. In the course of the struggle, civil war broke out in Germany, and Rome was sacked by the Normans — who came to defend the Pope but whose ferocity got out of hand. The deposition of Gregory and the election of an antipope, by the Emperor, made a bloody ending to this last stand of the State's entrenchment in the Church. Gregory died in seeming defeat — at Salerno in 1085, where he had fled. Nevertheless, his reforms had taken such a firm hold that in 1122 the Concordat of Worms brought the long controversy over lay investiture to an end; freedom of election to ecclesiastical offices was guaranteed. Lay investiture was limited to a ceremony by which the layman-lord bestowed upon the Church-elected prelate or abbot all temporal possessions attached to his office.

In the meantime, the destiny of England had been fused with that of Europe more completely than ever by the Norman Conquest. Leaders of the reform in Normandy — which had raised that country to one of the cultural centers of the Continent — were imported to Canterbury by William the Conqueror. From one of Normandy's great new foundations, the Abbey of Bec, came its renowned teacher and prior, Lanfranc, as Archbishop of Canterbury, to be chief counselor of the King and vice-regent when William was absent. After Lanfranc, came one of his most brilliant disciples at Bec and a fellow Benedictine — St. Anselm (1033–1109). As Archbishop of Canterbury under William's disagreeable son, Rufus, St. Anselm staved off any damage that the violent Rufus might have done, for Anselm's sanctity was so respected that even Rufus dared not go too far in opposing him.

In England, as on the Continent, the chief problem was lay investiture; the King refused to bow to the new canons against it or unseat the improperly invested prelates and abbots whom Anselm had found occupying many offices on his arrival. Before the matter was settled, Rufus died a violent death, but his successor, Henry, carried on the quarrel. Although the aging St. Anselm was, above all, a scholar and contemplative — not by

nature an administrator like his predecessor, Lanfranc — he was
forced to journey back and forth between Rome and England in
a long drawn-out series of negotiations between the King and the
Pope, constantly interrupted and complicated by outside partisans
of both sides. But Anselm finally won out and was allowed to
end his days in peace.[3] Renowned as a champion of the rights
of the Church at this crucial time, he is even more famous as a
writer and thinker; as one of the great Doctors of the Church,
his influence on Catholic theology and philosophy has been deep
and far-reaching. It was as a teacher-philosopher and devout
monk that he broke down the resentment of some of the English
monasteries and the clergy — who regarded him at first as an
usurper from abroad — and won over the English people. By
his example and his solicitude for the religious life — a life which
he had, to his sorrow, been denied by his responsibilities —
monasticism in England began to flourish once more, interrupted
as it had been by the Danish wars, the Norman Conquest, and
the laxities of feudalism. By 1077 there were several Cluniac
houses in England and many more were to follow.

As the eleventh century was the turning point in the history of
the Church, so it was the gateway to the renaissance of the
twelfth and thirteenth. When every violent and evil force, every
false motive and sapping weakness of the Middle Ages and the
fallen nature of man had seemed bent upon the ruin and annihila-
tion of the Church, she yet managed to throw off the husk of
these dangers. And the major counterforce which threw them off
was born in the cloister. It is by this token we may ever after
look to the ascetical life in the Church as a key to its condition.
Not an adjunct, or a self-contained "department," religious life
is the wellspring of the Church's spirituality. The Cluniac Reform
was but the first large-scale evidence of this fact.

The almost fabulous glory of the Cluniac "system" lasted for

---

[3] Many historians consider that neither side won, owing to the concessions
of both, but considering the fact that this agreement was made in 1106,
fourteen years before the real settlement of the matter at the Diet of Worms,
it surely constitutes a victory for St. Anselm that is hard to match elsewhere
at this time.

over two hundred years. As the seat of an order consisting of more than three hundred houses,[4] with ten thousand members spread over Europe and Great Britain, the great Abbey of Cluny was next to Rome as the center of the spiritual life of the Church. The gradual change in the character and status of the monk as a member of society — from a layman recluse to a public figure with public functions and responsibilities — was completed with Cluny, not to recede for five hundred years. Monasticism was one of the pivots of Western culture.

Both spiritual and temporal factors peculiar to Cluny helped to set the stage for monasticism's influential role throughout the remainder of the Middle Ages. One factor was the Rule's horarium of greatly increased offices and other devotions; hardly an hour went by that did not require the presence of the monk in the abbey church — not for private or contemplative prayer — but for liturgical or public prayer. For this a high degree of literacy was required, and the abandonment of manual labor was necessary. This emphasis on the liturgy led to the desire of the religious to enter into it more fully through Holy Orders, for which the now well-educated monk was well equipped. In becoming priests the monks could not only live fuller lives, as religious, but could serve the needs of the community and those of the laity, for whom the abbey was the epitome of Catholic spirituality — and the antithesis of the ills that affected much of the secular clergy. Thus the monk, while still remaining an ascetic and contemplative, was also a teacher, scholar, and cleric; an aristocrat, indeed, on the spiritual and intellectual plane.

The temporal factor which combined with this spiritual one to raise still further the prestige of monasticism, through Cluny, was the growing wealth of the Order, heaped with endowments by public enthusiasm and the ownership of feudal property. In order to carry out the liturgy with fitting solemnity, a renaissance of ritual music and art sprang up; the abbey churches began to be richly decorated, the priests wore exquisite vestments, and the offices were chanted with great precision and beauty. The liturgy

[4] Rising to eight hundred houses by the fifteenth century.

took on an unprecedented splendor. And it was natural enough that such pomp should soon spill over into the rest of the house, to principally rest about the position of Abbot General — a virtual monastic pope by reason of the autocratic power invested in him by the Cluniac constitution. He was regarded as a prince of the Church and a personage of great spiritual and social importance. During his visitations of the sister houses and on other missions, he traveled with such a great train of attendants that a separate residence was required to house them all at various points.[5] Monasteries were feudal estates in their own right, requiring the services of hundreds of villagers and villeins. As the castle of the feudal prince turned from a rough fortress into a glittering court, so the abbey became similarly conscious of adornment and dignity; the monastery and the castle were part of the same world, awakening to an artistic awareness that was hitherto unknown.

Like every human institution, Cluny's uniform magnificence could not be sustained indefinitely. About the year 1100, it began to slacken. In some of the houses mitigation of the Holy Rule, allowable by St. Benedict, led to relaxation; and among the thousands of members of the Order there were those unworthy of a religious vocation. Moreover, abbots began to be appointed according to rank rather than worth or fitness for the post. It was not the end of Cluny's glory, however; under Peter the Venerable (c. 1150) the Order was reformed and had a resurgence that many historians regard as its true zenith, but this first spiritual lag led to a recoil which resulted in another order of even greater and more enduring significance than Cluny — the Cistercians of Citeaux. When the final decline of Cluny did take place, it was to the Cistercians that the ideal of Benedictine life passed. With it we emerge into familiar territory at last, for the Cistercians of the Strict Observance, or Trappists, are sons of the same order, in unbroken line.

Robert, abbot of the Cluniac Abbey of Molesme (c. 1090), strove in vain to bring his monks back to the community's first austerity. After years of fruitless effort, he asked permission of

[5] What is now the Cluny Museum in Paris was the town house of the abbot.

the Holy See to found another house on entirely different lines; one that would return to the primitive Rule of St. Benedict, without the additions of the Cluniac *capitula*. With permission granted, Robert set out with twenty of his monks to find a suitable spot for their venture. They chose a desolate wasteland in Burgundy called Citeaux — from the rushes or "cistels" that grew there. Its feudal owner gladly ceded it to the monks, as it was otherwise useless. Here, on March 21, 1098, they began to build their new community — a collection of small cells and cabins.

Robert put into effect a very simple but austere form of Benedictine life. The new community was devised as an association of penitents, deprived of everything but that which was necessary to their bare existence; neither property nor food nor intellectual pursuits (a candidate need not know how to read) was to distract them from this central idea. Fasting and total abstinence was continuous, silence complete and without a break; every vestige of the pomp and privilege of Cluny was swept away at one blow. This contrast with Cluny marks a cleavage in the character of monasticism at this point; it is henceforth to be of two types — active-contemplative, and purely contemplative, or penitential. Both were (and are) necessary in encompassing the needs which the ascetical life of the Church both fills and serves.

The monks of Molesme, stung by the scandal created by the departure of Robert and twenty other monks, brought pressure to bear on the Holy See to have Robert return. This he was ordered to do; after only a year he was forced to leave his beloved project and go back to Molesme, where the monks now readily submitted to his stricter rule. The Citeaux community he left in the hands of his twenty disciples, several of whom at different times became its abbots. Of these one was an Englishman named Stephen Harding, who, in 1119, drew up a new constitution aimed at correcting the faults of the Cluniac *capitula*. It definitely legislated against all those luxuries and additions that had, by Citeaux's custom, already been done away with. A now-famous document in the history of religious orders, the new constitution was called "The Charter of Charity."

In this fresh interpretation of the Holy Rule, every detail was covered that could possibly be a loophole for mitigation; only Celtic monasticism could compare with it in austerity. The charter also set forth a new system of government, one far more flexible and democratic than that of Cluny. A yearly general chapter, or meeting, of the whole order was called for, with the election of several officers in whose joint hands the administration of the Order would rest, but shared with the general chapter as well. The abbot of each sister house in the federation was elected by his own monks — not appointed by the Abbot General at Citeaux — and each house was autonomous, bound to Citeaux only by the "laws of charity," the visitations of the administrators, and the general chapter. This was a far-reaching pattern and ideal, the tradition still in effect in the Benedictine Order.

In the new charter, the offices were shortened and many of the extra devotions — which had become a burden at Cluny — were omitted entirely. Great stress was laid on manual labor (five to seven hours a day) with only a few hours of scriptural study allowed. The habit was changed to approximate that which St. Benedict's own monks wore five hundred years earlier. This was white, in contrast to the black habit of the Cluniacs. From another of the contemplative orders founded during the twelfth-century renaissance (the Vallombrosans, mentioned later), the Cistercians borrowed the custom of having lay Brothers, those members of the community who were freed from the time-consuming liturgical duties of the choir monks in order to engage in the heavier labor and material affairs of the house. These lay Brothers were called *conversi* and shared completely in the life of the community, with no distinctions being made "during life or after death."

Although the community at Citeaux became a separate and duly approved new order by "The Charter of Charity," and its members relaxed not a moment in their devout austerity, their number seemed to be at a standstill; not a single entrant was able to get through the severity of the novitiate for the first fourteen years. Then, to add to this discouragement, the region around Citeaux was attacked by a virulent plague; the monks were struck down and began to die at the rate of several a day — to the malicious glee, it is sad to report, of their Cluniac "cousins," who declared it to be a result of their condition, so weakened by austerities. It was, the Cluniacs said, a judgment of God upon the Citeaux community for their presumption.

Stephen Harding, then abbot, was desolate as he saw his ranks thinning to a bare few. In his anguish he began to fear that perhaps the Cluniacs were right; his Order was about to be extinguished. Prayer seemed to bring no relief or light as to what should be done. Finally, as a last resort, he could think of only one way to storm the gates of heaven for an answer. It was a novel and daring course.

Approaching the monk who was undoubtedly going to be the next to die, St. Stephen instructed him, under obedience, to return and "inform us, according to His will, what we are to believe concerning our state and the life we are leading." The expiring Brother duly promised and then died as expected. A few days passed. At last he appeared to St. Stephen with the glad news that he enjoyed "that happiness and peace incomprehensible, which surpasseth all the thoughts of men to conceive," and that their way of life was pleasing to God, who would shortly send a great number of entrants, many "noble, wise, and mighty," to fill the house and overflow it into all parts of the world.

In renewed faith and fervor the Cistercians waited. Not many days had passed before there was a knock at the monastery door and there, crowded on the threshold were thirty young men, all clamoring for admittance. It was St. Bernard, five of his brothers, and a company of his friends and relations whom he had persuaded to join him in dedicating their lives to God. Citeaux was saved, and its brightest star, St. Bernard of Clairvaux, began to shine from that moment. The radiance that emanated from this nervous, intense young aristocrat, to be known as the "Perfect Monk," was to illumine all Europe. The "sweet-souled and eloquent" Bernard was to stamp his personality on the age and influence the whole history of Christendom. With the possible exception of St. Francis of Assisi, no man has been any more loved and esteemed than

St. Bernard; we will meet him at many points of monastic history
in the forty years that succeeded that fateful day when he knocked
upon the door at Citeaux.

This sudden influx of recruits was the turning point in Citeaux's
fortunes; the community grew with astounding speed, and soon
included a Second Order of nuns, founded under St. Stephen's
direction in 1125. By the time St. Stephen died, in 1134, there
were 70 houses; 350 existed at the death of St. Bernard nineteen
years later, and 530 by the end of the century. Some of these
were not new foundations; other Benedictine communities of
both sexes and colleges of Canons Regular joined the ranks of
the Cistercians in wholesale numbers. Thus the reforming forces
of the tenth century turned into a full-scale spiritual renaissance
in the eleventh.

Nor were the Cistercians the only form of this resurgence of the
contemplative, penitential spirit. St. Peter Damian (1009–1072)
also added great luster to this plane of monastic life. A famous
teacher at Parma and Ravenna, he retired to a hermitage, where
he eventually became superior of the hermit community of Fonte-
Avellana. Peter Damian instituted the use of the "discipline"
(small whip) in self-mortification, and also the siesta, or afternoon rest, to overcome the fatigue caused by the long night offices.
He later became a cardinal and did much in reforming the secular
clergy. Adding yet more impetus to the new fervor was the influx
of some Eastern monks into Italy, when they fled the wars in Egypt.
Interest in their eremitical life produced several very severe, semieremitical orders,[6] one of which was the Carthusian. Of all the
orders in the Western Church today, this one may be called the
most unusual, for the Carthusians have remained semieremitical,
unmitigated in their austerity, and undefiled by decadence at any
point in their history. Completely steadfast to the ideals of its

[6] Two of these semieremitical orders which still exist are the Camaldolese,
founded in 1012 by St. Romuald, and the Vallombrosans, founded in 1030
by St. John Gualbert; both are Benedictine. The former have two hermitages
and one cenobitical congregation; the latter became entirely cenobitical. Both
are confined to Italy.

founder, St. Bruno, the Order carries them on to this day exactly as he established them.

St. Bruno, founder of the Carthusians, was born in Cologne of wealthy and aristocratic parents, who sent him to the episcopal school of Rheims to study for the priesthood. A fine scholar, he became a member of the faculty at an early age and a brilliant career as an ecclesiastic opened before him. His reason for suddenly abandoning it is a colorful legend, made popular throughout Europe by a series of famous paintings by Lesueur, centering around the burial of Bruno's most revered teacher, the Canon Raymond, at the school in Rheims.

When the apparently sainted Raymond died, and the funeral was well under way, the corpse is said to have suddenly risen from its bier and cried in an anguished voice, "By the justice of God, I am accused!" Whereupon it fell back into the coffin. The funeral was postponed, but proceeded again the next day. At the same point in the rites Raymond again rose up and cried, "By the justice of God, I am judged!" and again fell rigid into his bier, as on the previous day. The obsequies were halted in great consternation; no one wanted to continue. But continue they did, the next day, in "fear and trembling." In horror the attendants and priests saw Raymond rise a third time and in a terrible voice cry, "By the justice of God, I am condemned!" In the last of the series of paintings by Lesueur young Bruno is shown in deep meditation before a crucifix while, in the background, the body of Canon Raymond is being hastily thrown into an unhallowed grave.

Not long after this incident is supposed to have occurred, Bruno persuaded six of his companions to leave the world with him. They first proceeded to Citeaux, where St. Robert was establishing the Cistercians, but they found that their vocation did not lie there. Several miles from Grenoble they came upon a desolate place known as *Le Grande Chartreuse,* a high and rocky spot covered with snow almost all of the year. Here they built a chapel surrounded by cells; a laura much in the manner of the Camaldolese. They had brought with them two lay Brothers to

take care of their material affairs and of the manual labor of
the house, so that the monks could give themselves over to a life
of complete contemplation — prayer and study — in absolute poverty and seclusion.

In the thirteenth century the Carthusians built some of the
most beautiful churches of that artistically fertile period, and
their fame as scholars and copyists spread. Yet they never departed
from their austere Rule. In combining the gentle steadfastness
and humanity of the Benedictine Rule with the determined
avoidance of all worldly intercourse embodied in the eremitical
ideals of St. Antony, St. Basil, and St. Martin, the Carthusians
stay within bounds that are never breached — avoiding rigidity
or inhumanity on the one hand, and mitigation or materialism on
the other.

The design of a charterhouse — as a Carthusian community is
called — is semieremitical; each cell is a small stone house, built
around a cloister and a chapel. In this cell hut the Carthusian
monk eats, sleeps, studies, prays, and works; he has a storeroom,
workroom, cell, and study. Outside he has a small garden, the
tilling of which is a part of his manual labor. There is another,
lesser, cloister for the lay Brothers surrounded by the Brothers'
cenobitical living quarters made up of cells, workshop, refectory,
and chapter house. A large part of a Carthusian monk's day, and
three hours during the night, is devoted to three offices: the Great
Office for the day, the Office of Our Lady, and the Office of the
Dead; the rest of the day is given to mental prayer, study, and
manual labor. His only recreation is on Sundays and feasts, when
he takes a walk with his fellow monks and is allowed to talk.
Except during the conventual Mass (preceded by litanies and
adoration), two Offices, and supper in the refectory, he spends his
life in his hut, alone.

St. Bruno lived only six years at the charterhouse at Le Grande
Chartreuse, before leaving to establish another at Calabria. This
was of a slightly different design, almost exactly like that of the
Camaldolese, but it did not long survive. It was later absorbed
into the Cistercian Order while the original charterhouse flourished,

and in spite of various setbacks and persecutions continues to the present time. The proceeds of the Order's famous business of liquor and cheesemaking — when not used in the building and maintenance of the charterhouses — are entirely devoted to charity. One foundation has very lately been established in the United States.

The Premonstratensians, or Norbertines, made a duly approved order in 1126, were as much of a milestone in the story of Canons Regular as were the Cistercians in the history of purely monastic life. They not only infused the same austere spirit into the life of regular canons, but instituted revolutionary methods of educating priests, organized new kinds of devotions for laymen, and set the design of modern contemplative-active orders of Canons Regular.

St. Norbert of Gennep, a courtier as well as a subdeacon of the collegiate church in Xanten, Germany, lived the thoroughly worldly life of many a cleric in those days. Not until he was thirty did a near-fatal riding accident cause him to change his course; he withdrew from the world to live in "silence and retirement, wore a hair shirt next to his skin, and spent his time in tears, holy prayer, and meditation." After being ordained, Norbert preached penitence, healed feuds, and reconverted whole parishes that had become demoralized. Selling his estates and giving away the proceeds to charity, he petitioned the Pope for permission to continue his itinerant preaching, and at the same time organize an order of Canons Regular that was monastic and contemplative in character — as well as apostolic in action. The Pope was doubtful of such an innovation, but the Bishop of Laon, in France, had such faith in it that he became Norbert's patron, giving him the choice of several sites for a foundation. A lonely valley near Laon, called Prémontré, was chosen, where — much like the monks of Citeaux — Norbert and thirteen of his disciples erected their first community. The future order soon grew to forty members, while St. Norbert and his disciples, according to their plan, went about the country preaching and reorganizing other houses of canons.

Unlike the Cistercians, the Norbertines had a strict requirement of knowledge and study, as it was necessary to the apostolic part of the life, while monastic austerity was just as necessary to the community life. Definite courses of study, such as Latin and grammar, were prescribed, and progress in knowledge was made a condition of ordination. In every other respect, the canons of Prémontré lived very much the same as their monk brothers, the Cistercians; perpetual silence reigned in the house, severe fasts, and total abstinence from meat and wine were observed all year, and the predominating character of their daily round was severely penitential. After St. Norbert's death, his successor, Hugh of Fosse, drew up a rule. By this time the itinerant nature of the canons preaching had been largely replaced by the serving of parishes which they themselves founded. The Norbertines are credited with organizing the first sodalities and establishing popular devotion to the Holy Eucharist. Their abbeys became so famous as schools for the priesthood that they may be said to have been the first seminaries for the parochial clergy — as, up to this time, the clergy had been trained in the houses of the canons attached to churches or cathedrals; special establishments for their education was not yet a custom.

A Norbertine rule for women was also composed by Hugh, to govern the communities of nuns the founder had established in a parallel movement. The Premonstratensians — called the "White Canons" — spread to every country in Europe and to Great Britain; St. Ninian's "Candida Casa" in Scotland became one of their abbeys. By the thirteenth century there were over a thousand abbeys and about half that number of convents. Although the Order declined after the first two hundred years, owing to a series of commendatory abbots, it was successfully reformed and is now one of the flourishing orders of Canons Regular in the world.

From the eleventh century onward, orders begin to spring up in great numbers. It will be possible to mention only those that are most significant in the development of religious life. Like buds, some of them bloomed long and well, some briefly,[7] but

[7] A few of these were: the Canons of the Lateran (1063), under whose jurisdiction Canonesses Regular were placed; Congregation of St. Rufus (1039), Congregation of St. Victor (1113), Congregation of St. Genevieve (1060), Monte Virgine (1119), Grandmonte (1120). Cluniacs and all other

all added richness and luster to the High Middle Ages, when life in the West finally outgrew its feudal primitiveness.

Particularly numerous were congregations of regular canons, mostly in the towns. With no central authority or common observance to call upon, they suffered from the same debilitating evils and laxities that infected the secular clergy throughout the Middle Ages. The efforts at reform of St. Peter Damian and two popes (Nicholas II and Innocent III) helped, but were not by any means universally accepted; it was therefore up to individual zealots to reorganize and reform various chapters. These reformed chapters gave rise, in turn, to movements which resulted in "orders," or congregations, with limited approbation. It was not until the middle of the thirteenth century that many of these congregations of canons amalgamated and, under the Rule of St. Augustine, became definitely known as the "Canons of St. Augustine."

Out of the surplus of feudal landownership rose the medieval city — an economic unit of free men bent on a common interest in work, trade, property, and peace. Religious confraternities and tradesmen's guilds, educational and charitable institutions, and the *commune,* pledged to peace and obedience to law — all fostered by the Church — now took form. Historians speak of this "highest point of the medieval spirit" as the foundation and beginning of modern civilization; it may well have been the peak of modern civilization also. There was, of course, a reverse side of the picture — class conflict and much internecine strife — but never again has the whole Western world been so united in its culture, ideals, and faith. Out of that culture came the great Schoolmen and the universities; out of those ideals came the Crusades; and out of the faith came saints and scholars whose unmatched stature of soul and intellect has towered above all time.

Benedictines, not Cistercian, were called Black Monks; the Cistercians were known as the White Monks, the Norbertines as the White Canons, and the Augustinians as the Black Canons.

Chapter Seven

KNIGHTS AND SCHOLARS

From the time of Constantine the Great, the Holy Land had been the goal of the Christian pilgrim; his most devout dream was to make the long and perilous journey there. At first, only a lucky — and wealthy — few were able to realize this dream. Later, the little bands that had set out, attended by much ceremony and celebration, enlarged to thousands. However, when the Turks took over Palestine, in 1070, Christian shrines began to be desecrated, and pilgrims insulted and persecuted. In Europe, resentment and indignation mounted until saving the Holy Land from the infidels

94

and restoring it to Christianity became an all-pervading ideal. The
new conception of knighthood as a sacred consecration to lofty
motives needed only such a spark to set that ideal in motion;
when Pope Urban II urged every knight to become a soldier-
pilgrim, and promised him every protection and privilege of the
Church, the Crusades began — to be one of the dominating forces
of history for the next two hundred years.

Since knights and monks were the dominant figures of the age,
it was natural that they would fuse in the pursuit of a cause that
so perfectly combined the enthusiasm of both. The "Military
Order" was this perfect combination. Many a monk wore armor
over his habit, and many a knight became a monk of a monastery-
hospital-fort in the besieged land to care for sick and destitute
pilgrims, to ransom captives, and to fight when necessary. The
military orders were usually composed of knights — who had renounced their worldly interests to succor pilgrims and crusaders
— and priests and lay Brothers, all of whom took the three vows
of poverty, chastity, and obedience. They not only became a
permanent force in the East, but as their "chapters" multiplied
in Europe, they formed an important link between the East and
the West. As active orders of mercy, they were forerunners of
the mendicant friars, whose functions and activities were so similar
in many respects.

The first of the military orders was the Knights of St. John,
also known as the Hospitallers, which originated with the building
of the Hospital of St. John, in Jerusalem in 1092. In a huge fortress monastery lay Brothers nursed the sick — who were attended
by several doctors and surgeons — and cared for the indigent.
The knights defended the stronghold or provided military escort
for the arriving and departing pilgrims — a dangerous duty which
required a large force; many died in carrying it out. The knights
were of two classes — externs, who served only for a time, and
professed knights, who were permanently bound to the order by
vow and were counted as religious as well as soldiers. After the
last defeat of the Christians, the Hospitallers retired to Rhodes,
which they defended for the next two hundred years. After the

capture of Rhodes, the Emperor Charles V bestowed the island of
Malta on the order — the origin of the Maltese cross. They then
became known as the Knights of Malta. Endowed by alms from
all over Europe, and by the wealth of noblemen recruits, the
Knights of Malta became very rich. Their houses, many of which
were on the Continent as well as in the East, were known as
"commanderies," and the office of commander or "grand prior"
of a community became a much-sought-after prize. Thus wealth
and power, as well as the latter-day military character of the
order, led to its decline as a religious society. With the confiscation
of much of the knights' European property during the Reformation,
and then the treacherous surrender of Malta itself to Napoleon,
in 1798, the Order was reduced to a mere remnant. It now retains
only a small nucleus of members, in Europe. The members are
called the Knights of Justice. They take vows and devote themselves to works of charity. Other degrees of knighthood are conferred on laymen.

The Templars, or Knights of the Temple — whose first headquarters was a temple in the Holy Land — were founded by
nine French noblemen who vowed themselves to the protection and defense of Christian pilgrims. When they sought approval of their Order at the Council of Troyes in 1128, St. Bernard,
who was present at the council, was so impressed that he wrote a
rule for them, persuaded them to adopt a white habit similar to the
Cistercians but with a red cross, and did much to promote the
growth of the Order of Templars through a treatise on it, which
he called "In Praise of the New Knighthood." Favors of every
kind were heaped upon the Templars, and entrants flocked into
the Order in spite of its strict regimen. The Templars had commanderies in every country in Europe but were most numerous
in Germany and France.

The Templar, unlike the Hospitaller, was a soldier *and* a monk;
there were no unhabited knights, externs, or temporary members.
Unswerving obedience to both religious and military rule made
him the most formidable of soldiers and probably the bravest of
all Crusaders. The Mohammedans were awed by his cool deter-

mination in the face of certain death and the perfect discipline he exemplified. As the rule forbade offering ransom for release, he would stand his ground against the severest tortures, refusing to deny Christ or his own cause, but preferring to die as a martyr instead. The price of such fidelity was great. It is computed that in the less than two hundred years that the Order flourished, almost 20,000 Templars perished; owing to these losses, recruits eventually were permitted to waive the probationary period required by the rule; thus the first high standards were not maintained.

As with the Hospitallers, the great wealth and many privileges enjoyed by the Templars excited ambition within the Order and jealous envy outside of it. It is said that Philip the Fair of France, coveting the many commanderies and estates in France and the East, persuaded the Pope to let him investigate the Order through a royal commission. The secular clergy, already antagonistic toward its power, were all too ready to testify to alleged crimes and heresies. Especially had the secrecy of the Templar's initiation rites caused the most extravagant speculation and suspicions — probably unfounded, since the nature of these secret rites — as grave a mistake as was the secrecy — has never been ascertained. Philip then persuaded the Pope to suppress the Order[1] and saw to it that the decree was accompanied by punishments of the utmost cruelty and violence. Much of the Templars' property was ceded over to the Hospitallers — a crushing defeat for the Templars, as the two societies were bitter rivals. In the ensuing welter of charges, counter-charges, admissions, and recantations, it is impossible to tell how much was truth, and how much was rumor, fabrication, or admission induced by fear. At any rate, the Order was dissolved in ignominy and its Grand Master and several officers were burned at the stake in front of Notre Dame Cathedral. None of the charges of heresy or even deviation from orthodoxy could be proved, though the Order had indeed been over arrogant and certainly too wealthy.

[1] The Pope instituted his own commission to investigate the charges, but too late to recover any semblance of truth concerning them.

The Teutonic Knights originated in Acre, in 1189, when some German knights set up a tent hospital. Made up of knights, priests, and Brothers, the Order transferred its commanderies to Europe, undertaking to convert the pagan Prussians with a violence that later earned the Knights much unpopularity. This caused their decline in about 1400, and in 1805 they became a secular society. The Order was reorganized in 1834, in Austria, and is now in two branches: one of professed knights, priests, and Sisters who serve the sick — called the Order of Justice — and an order of honor, for laymen.

The only Crusade order that has survived as an international religious society is the Trinitarian, founded by St. John de Matha and an aged hermit, St. Felix of Valois, in 1198. It was one of several orders that originated for the purpose of ransoming the Christian captives[2] of the infidels and was made up entirely of religious, who either begged alms for ransom money or allowed themselves to be held as hostages until it could be paid. The Trinitarians became very popular with kings and popes; St. Louis of France installed them in the palace of Fontainebleau as advisers and chaplains, and by the end of the twelfth century they had over two hundred and fifty houses in Europe. Their rule was strict and their poverty severe — as two thirds of their revenues and all of the alms they collected were used for ransom. They had many colorful and persuasive ways of soliciting alms; preaching, tableaux, and parades were carried out with such dramatic force as to be extremely successful. The dangerous and prolonged procedure of ransoming captives they carried on with the greatest intrepidity, redeeming many thousands of Christians. They also engaged in many hospital and parochial charities, further draining their resources and keeping their struggle with poverty acute — but their motives purely spiritual. In time, the Trinitarians separated into three congregations of strict and mitigated observances. Rivalries and disputes arose as to which branch was entitled to the revenues from various localities, which disputes were finally settled in the

[2] The Order of Our Lady of Mercy, established at Barcelona in 1223, by St. Peter Nolasco and St. Raymond of Penafort, was another.

nineteenth century, when the Order was united again, to be known thenceforth as the Mendicant Canons Regular of the Holy Trinity. Trinitarian Sisters did not originate until the seventeenth century, although it is probable that there were nuns serving in the Order's hospitals before that time.

The only religious order not related to the Crusades which rose to prominence in the East during this time of close commerce between the East and the West was the Carmelite. Whether it originated in the twelfth century, together with the military orders, or many centuries before, is a point that has never been entirely settled. Some have the conviction, shared by members of the Order, that the "Sons of the Prophet" (disciples of Elisius and Elias in the Old Testament) were a community of hermits living on Mount Carmel, who had been followers of St. John the Baptist. Discovered by the Crusaders, the hermits were joined by Berthold, a European monk of Calabria, who organized them into a community on Western lines, erected a chapel to our Lady, and became the community's first abbot. The community, it is said, was thenceforth known as the Hermits of Our Lady of Mount Carmel and its numbers swelled with the inrush of Christians to the East. Another view is that, on the advice of Berthold, who was merely one of the community's Western members, Albert, the patriarch of Jerusalem, was asked to draw up a rule. This he did on Augustinian lines but semieremitical and far more austere, prescribing a red and white habit similar to the mantle the prophet Elias was supposed to have worn. Thus St. John the Baptist is considered by some to have founded the community (or Elias and Elisius); others call Berthold its founder, in 1155, and still others maintain that it was Albert.

Communities of Carmelites, whose life was very similar to that of the Carthusians, spread well beyond the vicinity of Mount Carmel into other parts of the Eastern deserts until the Saracens overran the country, when their hermitages were destroyed and they began to be persecuted. Mount Carmel was temporarily lost, and most of the monks fled to Europe. Under regulation by the Pope, their Rule of St. Albert was mitigated to allow cenobitical communities, and their habit changed to brown, with a white mantle. The Order soon became well established in France, Italy, and England. The third General of the Order, in 1247, an English-man named Simon Stock,[3] introduced the Carmelites into many prominent seats of learning so that his monks might become better educated, and also to reap vocations to it from the ranks of university students. In this he was very successful, in spite of Carmel's austere Rule — which did not permit its houses to be erected near cities — and the Order's extreme poverty. The Carmelites were especially popular in England, where they took an active part in evangelical and scholastic life, and made many important contributions to mystical theology.

There was a great deal of antagonism toward Carmel in the thirteenth century, however; the other orders judged them to be existing in defiance of the Fourth Lateran Council — which had forbidden the erection of any new religious orders after 1215. They, on the other hand, insisted that theirs was the oldest order in the Church. Simon Stock had resourcefully obtained an interim approbation which did not gain full and final approval until 1275, when the Carmelites were permanently approved as a mendicant order — an expedient that prevented suppression, permitted them to retain their active scholastic life, yet allowed them to keep their contemplative character at the same time. The storm raised by their opponents did not abate, however; it shifted to their claims to antiquity, hotly contested by the other orders and as hotly defended by the Carmelites. This led to much of Carmel's literary talent being dissipated in the dispute. In consequence, Carmelite participation in scholasticism was less extensive than that of the Benedictines and the other mendicants. The controversy over their alleged antiquity provoked a "literary war of over thirty years' duration and almost unequaled violence" until 1698, when the Holy See imposed silence in the matter on all parties. The once burning question is now reduced to one of merely academic interest.

[3] St. Simon Stock was never officially canonized. The story of the Brown Scapular, given by our Lady to St. Simon, is a legend only.

In spite of the diverse activities that mark Carmel's history in medieval times, the Order has always adhered to its devotion to the contemplative life. Penitential in its austere rule — which is mitigated in some branches — with attention centered on the liturgy of the Divine Office, and mystical in its theology, its character has always been far more monastic than mendicant. Also it has always held more constantly to the ideal of absolute poverty. Even at the height of the Order's prominence, when Carmelites were the royal confessors, and held other important offices at the English court and at Oxford, they subsisted on such meager means that it was necessary to sell the monasteries' trees and benches in order to maintain themselves. Nuns of the Order did not originate until the fifteenth century, when several communities of semireligious women, called Beguines,[4] asked to be incorporated into it. The same rule and constitutions were given to them, together with other special regulations. The female branch spread rapidly to France, Belgium, Italy, and Spain, producing two blesseds (Frances d'Ambois and Jane Scopelli, in this era). But their original austerity was of comparatively short duration. Although there were large communities, especially in Spain, and abbesses ranked high and possessed a great deal of power, the life became much relaxed — to be renewed to its former vigor by St. Teresa of Ávila in the sixteenth century.

The influence of the Crusades on all monasticism in Europe was very great; knights left their domains in the hands of the monasteries, to be inherited by the orders if they should fail to return — and of course many did not. Knights also made large donations to the monks as votive offerings for their safe return from the Holy Land, or for the success of their missions — these donations became even larger when they returned safely when their missions succeeded. But the prestige of the monasteries was far from inherent in property and wealth only; there were other causes of greater importance. One was the spiritual revival that began with Hildebrand and found its most vivid embodiment in the Benedictine abbeys — of both Black Monks and White — the

[4] Beguines: see p. 106.

new congregations of regular canons such as those of St. Norbert, and the austere "hermit" orders such as the Camaldolese. The other cause was the learning and literary production, originating in the abbey, which produced the great universities and the Schoolmen.

As feudalism waned and the Crusades grew more and more hopeless in the accomplishment of their objectives, morale was lowered and chivalry declined. Europe began to turn its attention toward education and the intellectual life. Education was sought for the purpose of career-building, in arts, science, and law; and intellectual attainment was sought for the purpose of perfecting the relationship of philosophy, reason, and theology. With the rediscovery of Greek logic and Roman law, coupled with the necessity for personal success built on individual merit — rather than hereditary caste — the independent man of the medieval city demanded knowledge and skill hitherto either denied him, or unneeded. To this end he sought masters and crowded into classes — as the impecunious university student so familiar to succeeding generations.

The diocesan monastic schools began, in the middle of the eleventh century, to attract students in all parts of Europe, drawn by the fame of the scholar monks. Similarly, the cathedral schools, especially those whose patrons were often kings and high-ranking nobles, drew both clerical and lay students who eagerly learned from masters who specialized in one subject or another, or one viewpoint as opposed to another. This led to the growth of large followings of the different masters or certain "schools" of thought, or of certain subjects. Thus there were many schools — each approximate to our colleges — which later united into universities. In Italy the foremost early center of scholastic culture was Monte Cassino, and in France it was Bec, under Lanfranc and St. Anselm. Later the Paris and Bologna cathedral and episcopal schools grew into the largest of the great medieval universities, crowded with students who chose their masters from among clerics, both monks and seculars, brilliant in the arts of disputation, in philosophy, science, law, metaphysics, medicine, art, and a hundred other learned subjects. With the increased application of the Greek theories of logic, disputation turned into the science of thought, demanding precise expression and a deep and well-disciplined scholarship. Philosophy and theology were coupled, and to them was applied the test of this new science of logic, in order to define and systematize every spiritual and doctrinal subject. This naturally led to diverse pronouncements and controversies by the masters and their followers, with the Church keeping a wary eye on their course. Much latitude was taken and given; only when particularly dangerous premises became overpopular and threatened to become widespread cults was any action taken by the Church. St. Bernard, for example — who dominated the twelfth century in a hundred ways — wrote many letters to the bishops of France complaining of the dangerous line being taken by the most famous master of the Cathedral School of Paris, Peter Abelard — "that incomparable seducer of minds and hearts." The action finally resulting from St. Bernard's protests is a short act upon the medieval stage that epitomizes this large-scale tournament of wits in which the Schoolmen were protagonists and stars, watched and hailed as avidly as were the jousting knights of the previous century.

The eloquent and handsome Abelard was the "idol of Paris." Literally thousands of students from all over Europe sat at his feet. His great brilliance as a rhetorician and philosopher made a lasting contribution to Western thought; and he was, moreover, a sincerely devout Catholic whose loyalty to the Church was never in doubt. Time and time again his overweening pride and ambition — by his own admission — had got him into serious moral and theological difficulties. The seduction of Heloise was but one of them. But after each time that Abelard had submitted to chastisement and sought peace as a Benedictine monk (first at St. Denis, then St. Gildas de Rhuyes, and finally at Cluny) he would soon find himself in fresh difficulties. His hypercritical tongue and presumptuous zeal would whet his ambition once more; and again he would become the center of a huge and loyal set of disciples and students. His skill in the art of dialectic led him far afield on a number of points which, in general terms, might be summarized as a system of theology and philosophy based entirely on Aristotelian logic, without giving place to mystical devotion or purely revealed religion. St. Bernard, one of the greatest mystical theologians of all time, seriously objected to such a premise and the errors to which it had already led Abelard. But Abelard was so sure of himself that he was unawed by the reputation of his revered critic; his reply was to suggest a debate between Bernard and himself. It was agreed that the debate should be held at Sens (1140) before a jury of theologians and bishops.

The proposed debate caused intense interest and excitement. Royal families, whole courts of nobles, clerics, officials — and anyone else who could get in — flocked to Sens. Bernard, though the most revered churchman and famous preacher of the time, shrank from the spectacle and was only persuaded by the pleadings of his friends. The experienced tongue, clever wit, and romantic appeal of his protagonist nonplused even him. Armed with excerpts from Abelard's writings to prove his points, Bernard reluctantly stood ready for the attack. He, the huge audience, and the judges waited for Abelard to begin what would undoubtedly be one of the most brilliant displays of the great master's pyrotechnical talents. But they were completely dumfounded at what happened. Abelard either would not, or could not, open his mouth; by not a single sentence did he defend himself!

The cause of Abelard's strange and so entirely uncharacteristic behavior on this occasion has been ascribed to various reasons, miraculous or practical. His excuse that he had, at the last minute, decided to submit the questions at issue to the Holy See without deigning to put them to the test at hand, seems inadequate under the circumstances, especially as the damaging material collected by St. Bernard was immediately submitted to the Pope, who, recognizing the errors, sentenced Abelard to silence in the cloister. Just as strangely acquiescent, Abelard retired to Cluny, where he was kindly received by Peter the Venerable. Through Abbot Peter, Abelard was even reconciled to Bernard. This marked the complete surrender of Abelard's turbulent soul: after twenty-five stormy years he finally found peace as a monk of Cluny, where he eventually died, it is said, quite "in the odor of sanctity."

The foregoing incident is only a fragment of the career of the great St. Bernard. The foundation of Bernard's power was his supernatural asceticism; his discipline of the senses was so complete that, under all circumstances, his communion with God was undisturbed, his humility intact — yet he was fired with the passion of a poet and the insight of a genius. He "moved among men like a being from another world," always carrying with him the detachment of Citeaux and inexhaustible spiritual resources. While the Cistercians went into their "golden age," with its center at St. Bernard's own monastery of Clairvaux, the saint was forced out of the cloister where he would so much rather have been — to mediate between prince and pope, counsel bishops and clergy, and preach to thousands. It is said that in the churches where he was preaching the crowds were so thick around him that the sick had to be forced in through windows and over roof tops. In his great charity, none was turned away and a prodigious number of miracles were wrought through him. Bernard organized the Second Crusade, intervened in wars, and settled theological disputes. His theology, based on St. Augustine, he formulated into a synthesis in the highest tradition of Scholasticism, to become the founder and author of medieval mysticism.[5] His prayers, hymns, sermons, and other devotional works became a rich source of spiritual sustenance for all subsequent generations of Christians; he was the brightest star in a galaxy of unequaled brilliance — in that time, or any other.

Religious life played, as we have seen, such a predominant part in the age that it literally spilled over into secular life; variations occurred that combined the two states. It was not enough that religious became very active in secular life; laymen, too, became active in religious life — as semireligious *conversi* and

[5] The two basic schools of thought in medieval Scholasticism may be said to be St. Bernard's theory of mystical devotion, as opposed to the theories derived from reason alone, typified by Abelard.

confraters. Conversi were lay Brothers, as has been pointed out, and *confraters* were, in the Benedictine Orders, the lay members of a monastery (not of the whole Order but attached to one house) who shared in its spiritual privileges — often living and working within — without taking vows or wearing a habit. These lay members were later to be called Oblates by the Benedictines, and Tertiaries, or members of Third Orders Secular, by the mendicants and others.

Semireligious communities of women also grew up — of which the secular canoness was one type — wherein women lived half in the world and half out of it, so to speak; a development which was to encompass men to an even greater extent in the next century. The chief form of this combination of world-and-cloister was to be seen in huge communities of semireligious called Beguines. They were laywomen under temporary vows of chastity and obedience, who maintained themselves by their own incomes and were free to leave at any time. The origin of the Beguines is not clear; the best accepted opinion is that their communities were an outgrowth of the Crusade era, when the many widows and other relicts of crusaders joined the female solitaries who had lived on the outskirts of towns from the time of the Holy Roman Empire. As many were well to do, often nobly born, the community was usually made up of many little houses, surrounded by a wall, each house inhabited by one or two ladies, with their own household furnishings and servants. If not of independent means, the Beguine maintained herself by teaching girls or doing craftwork; at the same time engaging in various works of mercy. The Beguines were especially numerous in the Netherlands and Belgium; beguinages, as the communities were called, came to be made up of thousands of members and had a great deal of influence in the revival of piety and mysticism in that region during the fourteenth century. However, they eventually became very class-conscious; some beguinages admitted only nobly born ladies, while others were for women of humbler stock. Thus some communities were all too sumptuous while others degenerated into indigence — causing decadence in each case. A few that were not eventually suppressed by the Church, for later heresies and irregularities, or that joined the ranks of regular orders, survive in Belgium today.

The Beguines and lay canonesses may be said to represent an experiment that has been tried countless times throughout history; that is, a combination of two life states in a quasi-religious society, built on well-intentioned motives and often having many beneficial effects. But those good motives and effects have ever been temporary, at best; a proof that the inner and outer discipline, and the graces accruing thereto, imposed by the three vows and the rule of the true religious is absolutely necessary to those who would successfully embrace the evangelical counsels.

During the High Middle Ages there were almost as many communities of women as there were of men. Nor was it only through such half-lay, half-religious societies as the Beguines and the secular canonesses that women religious entered into the main stream of medieval life. In the twelfth century, the nun was not strictly cloistered; she was allowed to leave the cloister with permission on any legitimate errand, and to travel if necessary. Only at the famous Benedictine Abbey of Fontevrault in France — a double monastery whose superior was the abbess — was very strict cloister observed. Women religious were scholars, teachers, artists, and craftsmen; and abbesses ranked on a par with abbots, their only nominal superiors the bishop of the diocese — except for the Cistercian nuns, who were under the Abbot of Citeaux. Thus the nun was almost as active a member of society as the monk. This was to change later, when scandal ensued and reforms were instituted, but in the twelfth century the nun was very much a part of the colorful pageantry of the times, contributing a goodly share to it.

The growth of religious life during this era was truly amazing; it is estimated that there were ten thousand religious in England alone, out of a population of three million. The Benedictines (Black Monks and Cistercians) acquired vast estates and built beautiful churches and abbeys whose Gothic stonework, frescoes, and stained glass mark the apex of artistic creativeness — of this, or any other time in Western history. St. Norbert's Premonstratensians and William of Champeaux's Canons of St. Victor labored valiantly to achieve the standards set by Pope Gregory, assisted by a hierarchy much purified by the Gregorian reforms and the Concordat of Worms. The unswerving austerity of the orders of regular canons, and their ministrations to the people of the towns, brought them a spiritual prestige that temporarily overshadowed even the Benedictines, especially in England. Benedictine monasteries, having shifted their attention to scholarship and liturgical grandeur, became cultural and economic centers of medieval society. Abbeys were often elegant retreats where nobles and scholars pursued higher learning or the arts; or they were busy colleges of one of the great universities, housing hundreds of students equally dedicated to scholarship. Nonetheless, by sheer force of numbers and grandeur, brilliant intellectual attainments, and beautiful architecture — and permeated with the spiritual influence of such great figures as the Cistercian Bernard, the Carthusian Hugh of Victor, the Cluniac Peter the Venerable, and the Benedictine mystic, St. Hildegarde of Bingen — monasticism crowds every corner of the medieval scene.

CHAPTER EIGHT

THE BEGGARS AND THE HOUNDS

As the cultural life of the twelfth century moved to its climax,
so did the power of the Papacy. While rulers fought and schemed
for all the crowns of Europe, the Pope was looked to as the one
mediator, arbiter, and judge. The Crusades, the Pope's victory in
the investiture struggle, and the intellectual attainments of the
great Schoolmen made respect for the Faith and the Church
universal. The organized devotional practices of the guilds and
communes and the preaching in the vernacular by the Canons
Regular in the beautiful Gothic churches made Catholicism very

much a part of the content of ordinary men's lives as well. It was, indeed, the "Age of Faith."

Such brilliance also cast its shadows, however. By the thirteenth century many new problems had arisen. For one thing, the dominance of the Papacy was far from an easily held victory. Despite the Concordat of Worms (1122), states continually interfered in ecclesiastical matters, encroached upon the Holy See's feudal jurisdictions, and appropriated revenues needed by the Church for its maintenance — financially depleted as it was by the Crusades and the Hundred Years' War with the Hohenstaufens. (A system of taxation for support of the Holy See, known to us as Peter's Pence, had not yet been established.) Ceaseless conflict was also fomented through the attempts of Innocent III to maintain spiritual as well as political order among the rulers of Europe. Moreover, the monastic orders were becoming too numerous and wealthy, often at the expense of unworldliness. Materialism and the struggle for place and power began to overrun a great part of society — the religious orders included.

Innocent III (1198–1216), one of the greatest popes of the medieval era, tried to deal with all of these problems by holding the Fourth Lateran Council in 1215. Attended by over a thousand bishops, abbots and priors, and representatives of all the European states, it was the most important synod of the Middle Ages. Seventy disciplinary decrees were promulgated, many having to do with religious orders, as well as with the secular clergy. The founding of any new orders was forbidden; no abbot was to rule more than one monastery, to encroach upon certain episcopal rights, or to be exempt from tithes. Most important of all, a common chapter, or meeting, of abbots or priors, was to be held every three years, presided over by four Cistercians. The object of the chapter was to review the state of monastic life, enact needed reforms, appoint abbot visitors to all monasteries and nunneries, and to define the duties of bishops toward the orders. Such legislation went far in clarifying the confusion that resulted from the tremendous number of religious communities, and in disentangling the overlapping prerogatives of clergy and religious.

Much was accomplished by the Fourth Lateran Council, but not by laws alone could deeply entrenched customs, evils, and complexities be wiped out, or faulty motives be transformed into good ones. Nor were materialism and ambition any longer the province of one class; as feudalism waned, all the free men of the free cities must now live competitively, by their wits, as it were. The necessity of creating and trading in all manner of goods and services devolved upon the usually illiterate individual. In the crowded medieval town, pestilence, poverty, and vice abounded, and petty wars were waged constantly between towns, families, and political factions.

A reaction to all these elements began to show itself in the formation of pious societies of laymen not sponsored by the Church. At first these societies were perfectly orthodox; they were but a reaffirmation of the gospel's counsels of unworldliness, humility, and high moral standards — in opposition to frequent clerical arrogance, immorality, and wealth. Their leaders were mostly good men, many of whom were monks, whose only quarrel was with the unworthy clergy, the lay control that nominated them, and the system that permitted them to exist. These lay movements, at first, aimed only at a return to primitive Christianity; but these aims were soon vitiated by an extremism that verged into spiritual anarchy.

The most celebrated of these anticlerical movements was the one organized by Peter Waldo, a wealthy banker of Lyons, in 1176. Taking Christ's admonition to "sell all thou hast, and give to the poor . . . ," as his sole ideal, he and his disciples set out to preach that poverty was the only possible way to perfection.

This, of course, incurred the displeasure of many bishops, and Waldo appealed to Rome. The Pope blessed the Waldensians' manner of life and gave them encouragement, but he upheld the ban on preaching without diocesan approval. This first minor break in the Waldensians' relations with the Church was followed by more serious breaches caused by disobedience to the ban; the "Poor Men of Lyons," often ignorant and poorly informed in doctrine, began to take many unorthodox lines in their preaching.

They ended by condemning the Mass, the priesthood, purgatory, indulgences, veneration of the saints, and other doctrines. This led to censorship and finally excommunication. Nevertheless, they continued to do much harm to the traditional faith in France, Bohemia, and Poland. Later, the Reformation absorbed what was left of them as a Protestant sect.[1]

A far more disrupting influence than these penitential brotherhoods that floundered in heresy, however, were the antisocial, anti-Christian movements revived by the introduction of Eastern culture via the Crusades. These (Paulicians, Bogomiles, Catharists) combined under the heading of Albigenses — a cult that grew out of Manichaeism, the heresy that had ensnared St. Augustine. The Albigenses — as had the Manichaeans — taught that there were two gods, one good and one evil; all created matter was evil, ruled by the devil-god, and the soul was only redeemed to good after many reincarnations. Marriage was condemned, having children abhorred as a crime, all animal food — even eggs, cheese, and milk — was forbidden, and suicide was a great virtue. Only the "Perfect" — a higher class of believer — lived in rigid austerity, a state from which the majority shrank in horror. Most of the believers preferred to follow the cult's morbid doctrines at a safer distance. The heresy was violently anti-Catholic and anticlerical, of course, and attracted many followers only for these reasons. Churches and monasteries were pillaged, priests insulted, and Christians massacred. It seems strange that in an era of such intellectual enlightenment so unpalatable a set of doctrines could gain so much ground; but every coin has its reverse side. To the superstitious and brutish, Albigensianism was an easy explanation of evil and a license to indulge in it.

All of these and a number of other heresies were severely condemned and repressive measures were set up, of which the Inquisition was one. But these measures, too often carried to extremes by imperious prelates and orthodox rulers, only made matters worse. Violence and hate mounted on both sides, and

[1] Among other such groups were the Joachimites, followers of a Cistercian mystic, and the Humiliati, who became so anticlerical that they allowed laymen to say Mass — provided they wore sandals.

neither was any the better for it. But as these dangers to the Age of Faith began to mount ominously, an entirely new spiritual force suddenly emerged to save it. This was the mendicant order — a brand that burned away all the evils of the moment, and set fresh fires of faith that would spread around the world. And the first great light of that consuming fire was the "little poor man of Assisi" — St. Francis. Here, at last, was the "little people's" own saint. He was the first great manifestation of the power of the ordinary citizen of the free cities; a remanifestation of the Church's power to be ever born again from within.

St. Francis' brotherhood of beggars was not so different, at first, from the "Poor Men of Lyons" and the other antimaterialistic groups. But by calling on the resources and the protection of Mother Church and exemplifying them so freshly — rather than cutting himself off by lapsing into hate and heresy — he transformed his brotherhood into a new-yet-old conception of Christian life, which was entirely Catholic and entirely obedient to the changeless core of doctrine guarded by Rome.

No early portents or special graces marked Francis Giovanni Bernardone for his amazing role. The lighthearted and spendthrift son of a wealthy merchant, he joined the "smartest" clique of young nobles in the town. With seriocomic abandon they engaged in all the petty wars that waged unceasingly and, between times, concentrated on frivolous pleasures. In one neighborhood battle Francis was captured and held prisoner for a year. For the first time in his life he had time to think, lying ill and alone in an enemy dungeon. He resolved to settle down to a serious military career, and to try to remember that he had a soul to save; but that was all. After his release Francis joined an expedition against Naples but before long he fell ill and had to return to Assisi. He again took up with his old friends, but his heart was not with them and they teased him unmercifully for his distrait air.

In this arid state of mind Francis one day stepped into the half-ruined old church of St. Damian. As he prayed he heard a voice say, "Go, Francis, repair My house which you see is falling into ruin." Taking this literally, he dashed off to his father's house and impulsively gathering up a load of merchandise, sold it for enough to repair the old church. When the astounded pastor refused the donation Francis threw the money on the ground. When his angry father appeared upon the scene, the son took to his heels.

After a month of hiding, Francis returned to the town. Ragged, filthy, unshaven, and gaunt with hunger, he created an immediate sensation. Embarrassed and angrier still, his father dragged his son home and locked him in his room as a lunatic.

With his mother's help, Francis escaped and sought refuge at St. Damian's, where the priest gave him sanctuary. This time Bernardone Senior sent the police, with orders for Francis to appear before the town consuls to forever forswear himself as his father's heir. This his son was all too willing to do. "Henceforth I desire to say only, 'Our Father Who art in Heaven.'" he cried, and proceeded to strip himself of his clothes! Borrowing a beggar's cloak, he rushed off.

Francis wandered about for some time with the staff and cloak of a pilgrim, doing various good works. He collected stones for the repair of St. Damian's and other ruined churches, worked as a scullion in a monastery, and nursed lepers. The numerous lepers were, incidentally, the most despised and shunned of creatures in medieval society — victims of a cruel heartlessness unimaginable by us today. They repelled Francis too, but as a supreme act of humility and love he kissed the most miserable one that he could find.

The Gospel tells how our Lord's disciples are to possess neither gold nor silver, nor scrip for their journey, nor two coats, nor shoes, nor a staff, and that they are to exhort sinners to repentance and announce the Kingdom of God. Here, Francis thought, lay his true vocation! He threw away his staff, shoes, and cloak, and clothed himself in a garb of the lowest of Umbrian peasants, with a knotted rope around his waist. He began tramping about, preaching penance, brotherly love, and peace to the people of the countryside.

The people ceased suddenly to scoff. As first they were awed, then they were impressed. They were quite literally astounded when a wealthy merchant of the town renounced his position and property to join the "Poverello" as his first recruit. Then the next recruit, a popular canon of the cathedral, joined them. The Friars Minor were a reality. As others joined the first three, Francis wrote out a short and simple Rule. It was just enough to formally present to the Pope for his approval — although such approval was not necessary, however, as the "little brothers" were not monks, but merely religious beggars (mendicant friars) without any foundation or fixed abode. Dressed like Francis, the Penitents trooped to Rome in a body to see the Pope.

The Bishop of Rome was not impressed at all by this ragged band of pilgrims and they were somewhat curtly dismissed. It is said, however, that the Pope had a dream that night of young Francis bolstering a tottering Lateran Palace on his shoulders. The Penitents were then summoned back. Approval was given — a shock to the disapproving cardinals, who held that such a plan of life was impractical and unsafe. The name Friars Minor became official — "minor" after *minores,* or humblest class. They then returned to Assisi, preaching along the way.

When the number of Friars Minor increased, they were given a tiny chapel, called St. Mary of the Angels, by the Benedictines of Subasio, around which they built huts of wattles and mud to serve as cells. But they had no cloister; their cloister was the world. They slept anywhere, worked at any job, begged if necessary, and preached penitence, not with sternness and gloom, but with compassion and joy. Men of all classes became "minstrels of God," singing His praises and bidding all to enjoy the riches of poverty and brotherly love; by the thousands they threw away their tools and purses and followed Francis like a people bewitched.

This, in essence, was the revolution in religious life which the Friars effected. Heretofore, true religious life had been contemplative and liturgical, within the solitude of the cloister, its center. The monastery was the monk's world; he was pledged to stay in it, nor was he happy outside of it. But the friar's monastery was the world at large; his vocation was a dedication to action, not to study or contemplation. The apostolate of prayer and the apostolate of action here become two branches of the same life, the same purpose — which is the glorification of God and the sanctification of self. For the first time, the familiar terms "active order" and "contemplative order" become a reality in the history of religious life.[2]

Francis had no intention of confining his Rule of poverty and love to his brotherhood of friars alone; *all* people needed those graces, should be a part of that brotherhood, should reflect the Divine Image! He planned for this to be accomplished by way of a Third Order, for laymen, in addition to a First Order, for men, and a Second for nuns. No one would be excluded.

Some historians contend that *only* a Third Order was Francis' first conception of his brotherhood; that his dream was of whole families — men, women, and children — being Minors no less than the friars themselves. Others hold that the lay society was a somewhat later development, springing from the dilemma of so many married men and women desiring to join the First and Second Orders. At any rate, as thousands joined the First Order, as many thousands joined the Third Order. These wore the Franciscan habit also, but shortened to knee length. These also were bound by the same simple Rule — but not under pain of sin — and were to do, as far as possible, the same work in the same spirit of charity and poverty.

The Second Order[3] was organized under Francis' direction by St. Clare, the lovely daughter of a wealthy Roman with an estate at Assisi. After hearing Francis preach a course of Lenten sermons at the Church of San Georgio, she sought him out and begged him to show her how she might "live according to the Gospels." Together they made plans, for Francis recognized in her the means of bringing his order to virgin women who aspired to a contemplative life of poverty. In her he sublimated his own desire for

[2] The majority of monastic orders today are contemplative *and* active, although the pivot of monastic life is the liturgy rather than the apostolate. Action is regarded as one of the fruits of contemplation.

[3] "Second Order" will henceforth refer to all female branches of equal status as the same order of men.

the wholly contemplative life; for he was, in spite of his activity and his generosity of spirit, a mystic of the highest order.

At night, accompanied by her sister and an aunt, Clare secretly left her father's castle and went to the friar's little chapel, Porziuncula, where Francis and his brothers met them with lighted candles and led them into the chapel. Here Clare laid aside her fine clothes and donned the rough tunic and knotted rope; and Francis cut off her hair and placed a coarse black veil over her head.

Clare was pursued by her father for a while, but he finally relented after the friars built her a chapel and huts on some property given them by the Benedictines. Here began the Order of the "Poor Ladies of Assisi," or the Poor Clares. Francis and Clare remained devoted friends, depending much on one another's advice and consolation — for Francis was often troubled in his desire for a contemplative life, and felt unequal to the complexities of his rapidly expanding Order.

The Second Order, in spite of its great austerity and poverty, soon spread over Europe, just as did the friars. As the Poor Clares were far more secluded in their life than the friars, they were able to maintain a greater degree of uniformity in the observance of the Rule. Since they depended on the alms gathered by the Brothers — they were not able to beg or preach themselves — many ecclesiastical authorities tried to persuade Clare to own certain property and moneys against necessity; but she stood firm in her vow of complete poverty. After Francis' death, Clare twice delivered Assisi from disaster by her prayers; together with numerous other miracles, this made her almost as far-famed as the Poverello himself.

The Order of Poor Clares has retained to this day the same character designed for it by its founder. Its first Cardinal-Protector (Ugolino) gave to it the Rule of St. Benedict, and decreed that the growing Order hold certain property under a curator. But Clare was dissatisfied with such a compromise of Francis' principles; before her death she drew up a Rule more nearly approximate to the Franciscan, which she successfully had approved by

the Holy See. Those Poor Clares who remained under the Rule
and constitutions of Ugolino — who was made Pope Urban IV —
became known as Urbanists. The Urbanists outnumbered the
original Poor Clares until St. Colette, in the early fifteenth century, received permission to reform the Order and restore St.
Clare's Rule. Although St. Colette's reforms were extremely
successful, the Order has remained split into two branches, one
Urbanist, the other Colettine.

The Poor Clare's life is divided between contemplative prayer
and work; total abstinence is observed, the full Office is recited,
and silence — except during certain brief intervals — is imposed.
The Order has produced many saints and blesseds; it is one of
the few entirely contemplative orders in the United States.

St. Francis burned with many holy ambitions — to convert the
Mohammedans, to go apart and unite himself in mystical union
with God, and at the same time to bring all men into his brotherhood. In pursuit of these aims, he left Europe to evangelize the
Saracens, and also went to Spain, to be gone for two years,
secluding himself in the mountains for intervals of contemplative
prayer between missions. It was during one such interval that he
received the stigmata. When he returned at length to Assisi,
Francis found the Friars Minor in a confused and somewhat
chaotic state, owing to its all-too-rapid growth. In order to help
restore regularity, Francis was prevailed upon to write a more
detailed rule and to outline constitutions for the Order's government. A General Chapter was then called, at which five thousand
friars were present. The Order was formally organized into
provinces, with superiors for each province, and the friars' activities were regulated and restricted to controvert the irregularities
and laxities that had begun to cause scandal. Thus renewed and
fortified, with amazing speed the new Order spread into England
and as far as the East, gathering momentum as it grew.

The friars all but remade society; they cared for the sick,
preached holy poverty and love, and brought out of servitude
to war, vice, and greed a whole generation of men. Materialism
abated because Francis preached — and lived — holy poverty;

cruelty turned to kindness because Francis taught — and showed — charity. The whole world of nature, taken for granted before, was held up as a mirror of God's goodness and beauty. And no law but sincere example effected this tremendous change.

On one of his visits to Rome, St. Francis met an aristocratic Spanish canon named Dominic Guzman. The Spaniard was also there to petition the Pope for approval of another new kind of order. Just as Francis had been, Dominic was turned down this time. Nonetheless, he was already raising the banners of the next great army of mendicants. No two men and no two religious societies could present a greater contrast to one another and still be members of the same family of orders and of the same religion. The Dominicans and the Franciscans so well complemented one another that almost between them they possessed the soul of Europe.

Much less is known of St. Dominic's life than that of his contemporary, St. Francis. Before Dominic was born, in 1170, his mother was much alarmed by the repeated dream of a black and white dog, holding a lighted torch in his mouth. A saintly old confessor told her that the dream presaged wonderful things for her unborn child. At Dominic's birth his grandmother is said to have seen a bright star hovering over his head; and his earliest childhood was marked by an extraordinary piety, extreme even by the standards of such a devout family as the Guzmans.

While he was studying at the University of Palencia, the austere and charitable character of Dominic's piety was so obvious that he was asked to become a priest-canon of the cathedral chapter. He accepted and effected that chapter's reform, as well as some others, and was then appointed superior to the chapter of canons at the Cathedral of Osma. For the next nine years he hardly went beyond the chapter's gates except to preach. Once he sold all his books to relieve the starving poor of Palencia, and twice he offered to sell himself as a slave in order to raise money for liberating Christians held by the Moors.

When Bishop Diego of Osma was commissioned by the Spanish king to travel to the north in the matter of arranging a royal marriage, Dominic was chosen to accompany him. This was the turning point in Dominic's life. On the journey he and the Bishop were appalled at the prevalence of heresy in the south of France; whole towns and provinces had turned Albigensian, and Catholics were cruelly persecuted. The two journeyed to Rome to petition the Pope for relief from their posts in Osma and to ask permission to stay in France. Although the Pope consented, he dismissed their suggestion of a new order, founded expressly for the purpose of combating heresy. He gave Dominic and his companion permission only to join the Cistercians, who had been commissioned to reconvert the Albigenses.

When Diego and Dominic arrived in Languedoc to join the Cistercians, they were dismayed to see the monks conducting their campaign with such pomp that it only added to the controversy. The two Spaniards persuaded the Cistercians to alter their methods — at which a marked change for the better ensued and many were reconverted. At the same time they planned an entirely different line of attack. Dressed plainly and armed only with a few books, the Spaniards set out to do battle with the Albigenses in their own way.

Dominic's university training and brilliant scholarship was an ideal weapon against the heretics. Those who were not converted by his arguments found no better defense than to threaten him with violence. At two points in the verbal battle, it is said, he and the enemy disputed by "ordeal of fire"; that is, they both threw one of their books on a pyre. The story goes that the Albigensian's book was immediately consumed, but Dominic's leaped three times out of the fire and remained unharmed.

It was at this time that Dominic saw the necessity for an institution to protect Catholic women from the influence of the heresy and from the resentment of their Albigensian families; also for the children of Catholic nobles to be given the opportunity to study in other than Albigensian institutions. To this end, in 1206, he established a convent in Prouille, his headquarters, to which he gave a rule and special constitutions. Thus it might be said that he founded his Second Order first, for he was not to realize his dream of a men's order until six years later.

Two years later, in 1208, that overzealous crusader-knight, Simon de Montfort, angered by the murder of a Cistercian legate, took up arms against the heretics. The bloody battles that ensued have been laid at the door of the Church ever since, and Dominic himself has been continually besmirched by the many legends concerning his part in it. In view of Dominic's famed tenderness and charity toward the suffering, the shadow is quite unmerited; but more than that, it has been dispelled by far more valid accounts, from more authentic sources than the highly colored prejudices of the two succeeding centuries, when opinion was too often presented in the guise of fact.[4]

The fame of Dominic's sanctity and talent became so great that three efforts were made to raise him to the episcopate, but he threatened to flee if the offices were pressed upon him. In the meantime, a small band of disciples had gathered around him. Again he thought of an order devoted to combating heresy, a plan which he put before his superior, the Bishop of Toulouse. The Bishop not only approved of it but gave Dominic a chaplaincy, that he and his fourteen followers might have a source of revenue. The group soon was joined by a wealthy citizen who donated his own large house for their community, and here, in April, 1215, the first convent of the Order of Preachers was canonically erected.

Dominic was happy to have accomplished this much, but he was far from satisfied with a merely diocesan congregation. What he wanted above all was a world-wide organization to combat heresy everywhere in all its forms and to propagate Catholic

---

[4] That Dominic was the first ecclesiastical judge (and an extremely harsh one) of the Inquisition is another popular charge against him. This is refutable on two counts: he was still a student at Palencia when the Inquisition began, six years before he was appointed to it. But he was never a judge; he was given the role of examiner, for orthodoxy, of the depositions of the accused. That he often tried to mitigate the sentences of the civil court of the Inquisition is a matter of record.

truth. He again went to Rome, accompanying his Bishop to the
Fourth Lateran Council, then in progress. When he heard the
aims to which the council was dedicated — "the improvement of
morals, the extinction of heresy, and the strengthening of the
faith" — Dominic was overjoyed. The aims of his Order were
exactly the same; he was sure that he now would receive the
approbation he sought. But the council also legislated against the
formation on any new orders. The conservative Curia looked with
scant approval on such a project by a stranger from heresy-ridden
France. Dominic returned to Toulouse empty-handed.

Despite this setback, Dominic and his followers immediately
began to plan on how the "no-new-orders" stumbling block might
be circumvented. It was decided that their new rule would be
scrapped and in its place would be substituted the Rule of St.
Augustine — which was not only ancient but was general enough to
be adapted to whatever form a religious community might take.
Dominic also decided to alter the character of his congregation
from one of canons regular to a "brotherhood of priests," or
priest-friars — neither monks nor canons. Armed with this revised
pattern, he once more made the journey to Rome for the long-
sought approbation. The Pope at last sanctioned the new Order;
and he not only gave the Dominicans a church in Rome, but wrote
a bull for all bishops, abbots, priors, and priests, that they were
to favor the Order and give it their protection. Whereupon the
sixteen friars preachers dispersed, and two by two, spread over as
much ground as they could cover — dressed in much the same
black and white habit we are familiar with today. Dominic's
mother's dream symbols were exactly realized; Dominic, the "hound
of God" (*Domini-canus*) went out to combat the darkness of
heresy with the flaming torch of truth.

So tirelessly did St. Dominic travel and preach — often several
times a day — while practicing austerities that would have broken
most men, that he became known as an "athlete of Christ." The
Dominicans' root principle was study, but not scholarship for its
own sake. Intellectual prowess that is concentrated, exact, and all
to one single purpose is the aim of the friars preachers. A contrast,

indeed, to the ideal of St. Francis, who abjured scholarship in any form!

Established in a monastery in Rome with the post of "Master of the Sacred Palace,"[5] Dominic set about forming a definitive rule and constitutions for his Order, at the same time undertaking the reform of many convents there. At the first Dominican General Chapter, in 1220, the Order was officially reshaped into a mendicant — rather than canon regular — type; the houses were to be known as convents or friaries, not abbeys, and a strict rule of poverty was put in force. Also the Rule which Dominic had given to his nuns at Prouille and his constitutions were considerably altered. These were rearranged again, twenty-five years later, by a famous canonist and third general of the Order, St. Raymond of Penafort, and remain the same, with a few minor modifications, to this day. A Third Order grew up, more or less spontaneously, in imitation of the Minors — rather than as a result of an original plan or intention of its founder. The seventh master of the Order wrote a rule for a Third Order Regular, and there is still a Third Order Secular, for laymen.

The Dominican preaching mission soon naturally evolved into a teaching one also. Every class of men, lay and clerical, heretic and faithful, was preached to, reformed, taught. What the Franciscans did not encompass and make over, the Dominicans did. Their instruction was based upon such a thoroughly well-organized system of knowledge that Dominic has been called the "first minister of public instruction in modern Europe." The Order's schools, in Oxford, Cologne, Montpellier, Bologna, Naples, Florence, Barcelona, and elsewhere, taught the liberal arts as well as the "sacred sciences." At many of the great universities the chairs of theology were occupied by Dominicans and their prolific literary output extended into all spheres of learning. Princes and bishops called on their services and royal courts, especially in France, heaped favors upon them. So thoroughly have the Dominicans always acquired the intention and spirit of their founder that the Order

[5] The office of head theologian of the Vatican, a post held by a Dominican since that time.

may be characterized by the same term — "athletic." All activities are to be carried out "briskly." Even the liturgy of the Dominicans is somewhat different, cut to fit this pattern. Modern Catholics may have noticed that the Dominican Mass is shorter.

Although the two great mendicant Orders, the Franciscans and Dominicans, seemed to exist to complement each other, they also learned much from one another. The Franciscans grew so numerous that they needed the example of the Dominicans' great organizational talent in order to prevent a breakdown into irregularity. For in spite of Francis' repugnance for "book learning," the quality of the Friars Minor — at least that of the First Order — had to be safeguarded against heresy, schism, and excesses of asceticism. On the other side, the Dominicans, as mendicants, shed more and more of their canonical character. They were strictly forbidden to accept episcopal office, except under obedience to the Pope, and their rule of poverty forbade them to own property. The First Order of Friars Minor began to produce more priests, instead of lay members or those in minor orders (St. Francis was a deacon only); and the Dominicans' Third Order Regular, or Brothers of Penance, increased its ranks. Yet neither Order lost its own distinctive qualities.

The mendicants were the first great battalion of the Church Militant: born that the contemplative life might be reborn and bred to combat hate with love and ignorance with knowledge. Through the friars, every quarter of the world would be flooded with a new spiritual energy. Because of them, compassion began to temper the harsh extremes of the time and an unprecedented awareness of religion quickened the spiritual life of the people.

Thus did the songs of God's Beggars and the baying of the Hounds of Heaven find response in the minds and souls of men.

CHAPTER NINE

MENDICANTS AND MYSTICS

The great tapestry of the Middle Ages becomes a virtual riot of crowded color by the middle of the thirteenth century — with the predominant figures in religious habits. Mingled with the brown-clad Beggars and the black-and-white Hounds of Heaven are imitators and emulators by the thousands; diocesan communities, with no uniform rules, habits, or observances, fairly overrun Europe. The "no-new-orders" decree of 1215 did little to stem the tide, after all, for congregations — not orders, in the canonical sense — needed only a bishop's sanction. As rivalries, duplication of effort, and underorganization grew among these communities, it became increasingly evident that additional and different measures would be needed before enthusiasm toppled into heterodoxy and disorder.

The Second Council of Lyons, in 1274, sought to remedy such conditions by suppressing many of these communities — as having been founded after the prohibitions of the Lateran Council of 1215 — and by bringing those deemed worthy of survival[1] under the superior-general of the Hermits of St. Augustine, one of the new monastic societies founded in 1256. The Rule of St. Augustine, the same habit, and little variation of observance was made mandatory. Many of these congregations incorporated into the Hermits of St. Augustine were of a semieremitical character; but when, some years later, the Order was put into the ranks of the mendicants, the "Hermits" soon lost much of its seclusive character (except for the Brittinians), to become prominently active in the same way as the Minors and Dominicans. Of the noted mathematicians, astronomers, musicians, scientists, teachers, that have graced the Order, perhaps the most familiar is Abbot Johann Mendel, who discovered the Mendelian Law of heredity. Missionary activities have always been a particular province of the Hermits; their wide-scale activities in this field, beginning in the Philippines, have branched out into China, Japan, Australia, and South America. Austerity of observance varies with different provinces, but all have retained, to some degree, respect for the "hermit" tradition; the Discalced (shoeless) branch of the Order observe strict fasts and silence, and every province has a "house of recollection," or hermitage, where members may retire to practice penance and contemplation.

Another monastic society to survive the reorganization was the Sylvestrines, a Benedictine community founded by St. Sylvester Guzzolini in 1231 on Monte Fano. The interpretation of the Holy Rule by the Sylvestrines was primitive and very austere, laying

[1] The Williamites, Hermits of the Holy Trinity, Bonites, Brittinians, Brothers of Penance of Christ, and others.

special stress on the observance of strictest poverty. Eleven members of the original community were subsequently beatified, and by 1326 the Order had grown to one thousand monks in thirty monasteries.

The great flux of friars in the thirteenth century caused other complications which the Second Council of Lyons sought to untangle. The clergy complained that their rightful functions were usurped and taken over by the mendicants, and bishops protested the friar's privileges. On the other hand, in some dioceses the friars were treated as laymen and refused any of the rights and privileges which they were supposed to have. The Council decreed drastic measures against abuses by both sides, but, at the same time, strengthened the Dominicans and Minors by praising and protecting them anew.

Besides the Hermits of St. Augustine and, as we have already seen, the Carmelites, the only other mendicants to emerge in the thirteenth century were the Servites, or Servants of Mary. This Order was founded by seven young aristocrats of Florence, who came together for the purpose of venerating Our Lady of the Seven Dolors. On the feast of the Assumption the Virgin appeared to them, advising them to withdraw from the world and devote themselves to eternal matters. The young men chose Mt. Senario, a secluded mountain near their native city where again our Lady appeared with instructions to wear a black habit and to adopt the Rule of St. Augustine. They then elected a superior, took the three vows, and began to admit new members.

The Servites flourished, at first under the approbation of the papal legate; but later were in danger of losing their identity as a separate order when the decree of Lyons was promulgated. With aggressive tenacity St. Philip Benizi, their superior and one of the founders, pursued the matter in Rome until approval was granted in 1304, soon after his death. The Servites spread with remarkable rapidity. By the fourteenth century the Order had expanded to all the countries of Europe — except Scandinavia and Great Britain — and to India and Crete. A Second Order of cloistered nuns originated from the women converts of St. Philip;

a Third Order, called "Mantellates,"[2] was founded by St. Juliana
Falconieri, niece of St. Alexis Falconieri, one of the seven founders; and also a lay Confraternity of the Seven Dolors — all of
which flourish at the present time and are to be found in all
parts of the world. Ten members of the Order have been canonized and several have been made blesseds. Many distinguished
scholars of Scripture, theology, Canon Law, philosophy, and
mathematics may also be counted among the members of the
Order.

One of the Servites' most interesting saints is St. Peregrine
Lazosi, who, as an aristocratic young Florentine of the Ghibelline
faction, heartily detested the Church. When he met St. Philip,
who was on a preaching mission of peace, Peregrine rudely struck
and insulted him. Abashed by the Saint's mild reception of the
assault, Peregrine not only begged Philip's forgiveness but asked
to join the Order. So great was Peregrine's humility and holy
patience that it was only with great difficulty that he was persuaded to become a priest. Admiration of Peregrine's virtue — he
was often called "a second Job" — did much to further the fame
of the Servites. He founded a monastery in Florence and never
ceased working for peace in that time of continual strife. Peregrine
died in 1345 and was canonized in 1726. His body remains incorrupt to this day.

Coming as they did toward the end of the Middle Ages and
during the first phase of the Renaissance, the mendicant orders
provided the Church with a tremendous array of saints, artists,
writers, mystics, and scientific scholars. Among these may be
mentioned St. Anthony of Padua, famous preacher and miracle-
worker, who was appointed by St. Francis to teach theology to
his friars; Roger Bacon, Franciscan teacher, philosopher, and
scientist, whose remarkably advanced encyclopedia comprises
eighty volumes; Duns Scotus, Franciscan philosopher-theologian,
whose theories, based on Aristotle and St. Augustine, are an

[2] *Mantellate* was a common name for Third Order Sisters in Italy, derived
from the distinguishing dress which they wore (short sleeves and veil), in
order to facilitate their work among the needy. Now, only the Servite Mantellates bear the name.

integral part of the history of philosophy; and Albertus Magnus, lecturer and writer of the Dominican school at Cologne who was teacher of the greatest star of them all — the prince and master of Scholastic theology and philosophy, St. Thomas Aquinas (1225–1274). No man since Aristotle has exercised such a powerful influence on the intellectual world as Aquinas, the "Angelic Doctor."

With St. Thomas Aquinas and his friend, St. Albertus Magnus, Scholasticism reached its peak. Dominated by the mendicants, the universities perfected a "classic" system of theology and philosophy, based on Aristotle, which combined all learning into one harmonious synthesis; and in the towns, the churches of the four great mendicant orders were large preaching halls where a huge "militia" of tertiaries — members of Third Orders Secular — thronged. Sodalities and penitential brotherhoods honoring the Eucharist, the Sacred Heart, and the Virgin flourished. An excess of ardor so swelled the ranks of a brotherhood known as the Flagellants that they marched through the streets scourging themselves. St. Vincent Ferrer even encouraged this practice, but it was prohibited later and the Flagellants were suppressed. Devotional works, translated into the vernacular and issued by the mendicants, poured out to create new forms of piety and an understanding of the Faith heretofore unrealized by the average layman. Books of St. Bernard's sermons, St. Gregory's lives of the saints, meditations on our Lord's life by St. Bonaventure, were widely read and gave new life and direction to medieval Catholicism.

As the greatest of the mendicant preachers and writers were mystical theologians, their influence created an exuberant wave of mystical piety among both laymen and religious throughout Europe. The North, especially, seemed a particularly fertile soil for this tendency; in Germany, whole convents of Benedictine and Dominican nuns were noted as mystics. In the Netherlands, Switzerland, and Belgium as well, followers of the growing movement sought perfection of the interior life through mysticism devoid of scientific theology, and through simple asceticism and charity. In this it was a revolt against Scholasticism — which had become, after St. Thomas, more and more complex and controversial — and against the growing materialism of the later Middle Ages. Known to historians as the New Devotion (also *La Vie Devote* and the *Via Moderna*) it was the last great force of the mendicant's impact on society, but it was one which had — indeed still has — a tremendous effect on Christian thought and practice.

Paradoxically enough, the first great leaders of the New Devotion were among the most learned Schoolmen. Johann Eckhart (1213–1329) was a Dominican professor at Paris and Cologne. A master of German prose and a preacher of great simplicity and depth, his originality of method and thought caused as much controversy as acclaim, but his stature as a mystic has remained unshaken; called, even in his lifetime, "The Master," he is considered the founder of Northern mysticism. Two of Eckhart's disciples, Blessed Henry Suso and John Tauler, were the next great leaders of the movement. Suso's widest influence was on convents of women and on individuals rather than on the masses; his erudition had much effect on German letters, while his austerity inspired religious, and his charm those in the world. Tauler, another Dominican, is considered one of the greatest of the preacher-mystics of the Middle Ages, having developed still further than Eckhart the doctrine of blessed contemplation, or knowledge of the Divine Nature, based on the theology of Aquinas. Eckhart, Suso, and Tauler have been claimed by Protestants as "reformers before the Reformation," but, in reality, they were all perfectly orthodox; Eckhart, in the year before he died, withdrew a number of his propositions — which inclined toward Pantheism — and made full submission to the Holy See; nor did any one of the three, while stressing contemplative spirituality, deny or fail to uphold all the other doctrines of the Catholic Faith. To draw all men closer to it, by a contemplative method, was their only wish.

Preached and written exposition, by such men as these, of the soul's communion with God in the contemplative, interior life, opened a spiritual frontier heretofore thought to be reserved for religious and saints alone. Inspired by this new theory that the mystical life was possible and open to all, rather than to a gifted few only, thousands of laymen and hundreds of clerics formed themselves into associations for the practice of this idea, of which the achievement of personal virtue through apostolic charity and ascetical living was a part.

One of these associations, the Friends of God, might be said to have been the cradle of the New Devotion. Under the direction of Tauler and Suso, the association effected such a revival of fervor and a reform of religious observance that a fresh school of mystics — both religious and lay — resulted. This, in turn, led to the establishment or growth of other such societies. A male counterpart of the Beguines was one of these, called the Beghards, whose ranks swelled with men of the lower levels of society, usually craftsmen of the guilds. The Beghards, like the Beguines, lived in communities, with a common purse and board but with no vows or rule, and through the guilds they were able to have wide influence and do much good. Houses of both Beguines and Beghards were very numerous in Belgium and the Netherlands throughout the remainder of the Middle Ages. However, owing to the Beghards' loose organization and the liberal nature of their piety, they went astray in many ways soon after they had reached their height. With the waning of the craft guilds they lost much of their prestige, and decadence brought them lower still. Unlike the Beguines, whose decadence caused them to either be suppressed or incorporated into regular orders, the Beghards continued for two hundred years more, then finally dissolved during the disturbances of the fifteenth and sixteenth centuries. Eventually, the Friends of God suffered the same fate. As long as they were under the direction of such men as Tauler and Suso, their fervor was channeled into paths of the best influence; later, however, they were led by men who had become tainted with the latitude of the Beghards and the overmystical deviations of the Franciscan Spirituals, one of the controversial factions of the Friars Minor, later suppressed. By the end of the fifteenth century the Friends of God was also defunct. But the New Devotion had not been extinguished; it was to be carried to far greater perfection by a new association called the Brethren of the Common Life.

The Brethren of the Common Life was founded by a Dutch deacon, Gerard Groote, in the middle of the fourteenth century. A scholar of several universities and a wealthy canon, Groote was influenced by several mystical writers of the day to resign his church offices, give his personal fortune to the Carthusians, and go into seclusion as a mystic and hermit. After seven years of retreat he emerged to preach penitence and love of God, and to denounce materialism and the evils which still continued to affect much of the clergy. The result of his preaching was a fresh upsurge of ardor; he was surrounded by disciples, both clerical and lay, who joined him in his apostolic labors and formed the nucleus of a community much on the order of the Beghards. As the movement soon included women, it became known as the Brothers and Sisters of the Common Life, whose well-organized, closely knit community life was based, like the Friends of God, on cultivating the interior life, on work, and charity. Their difference was their attitude toward learning: other such societies, in their anti-Scholasticism, regarded learning as a sin of pride. Groote was a scholar who wished to controvert the excessive classicism and formalism of the universities by simplicity — not by illiteracy, which was almost total in the Netherlands at this time. Thus the work of the Brothers and Sisters consisted of teaching religion and letters as a part of their apostolic labors, and copying manuscripts, while the clerics of the community studied and preached.

Sanctioned by the Holy See, Groote's society was just beginning to flourish when its founder died, in 1384. Leadership of the Brethren was then taken over by Florent Radwyns, whom Groote had, upon his deathbed, appointed his successor. In his last consultation with Radwyns, Groote advised him to try to form a canonical congregation out of the association, as the members of it were not true religious — either regular canons, monks, nuns, or friars — and had therefore been subject to some hostility on the part of the orders. This Radwyns immediately set out to do by establishing a new foundation at Windesheim, in Holland, as an abbey, under the Rule of St. Augustine, with six of the Brethren as its first members. Within the next eighty years the Canons

Regular of Windesheim had eighty-two houses. The Brethren that did not pass over into this more canonical type of religious life became famous as teachers and copyists. Throughout the fifteenth century they offered the most advanced secondary education to be had in northern Europe, making use of the new invention of printing and the best aspects of the new "classical," or Renaissance, standards of learning. Both the Windesheim Congregation and the original Brethren of the Common Life preserved intact the influence of Groote, to which was added that of Groote's pupil, Blessed John Ruysbroeck, another of the many mystical writers of the time and founder of another congregation of Canons Regular in the North. Thus did both forms of Groote's society hold back the tide of extremism and laxity fostered by the Renaissance.

Although the New Devotion would be chiefly immortalized by one of the Windesheim congregation in his *Imitation of Christ,* this work of Thomas à Kempis was only one of the hundreds of books, tracts, and pamphlets put out by Windesheim and the Brethren, to inspire and spread this new kind of piety. Not only in their literature, but in their teaching and example did the Brethren and the Canons help controvert the growing cynicism and savagery of the secular writers of the time; and they had, as well, a most salutary effect on both clergy and religious — who sorely needed such bulwarks in the disasters through which the Church was soon to pass.

Besides such leaders of the New Devotion as Eckhart, Suso, Tauler, and its societies and their founders, there were great saint-mystics who both caused and consummated the movement; men and women who had immense influence, not only on religious thought and practice, but on the political and ecclesiastical life of the time. Their advice and prophecies were sought and respected by princes, prelates, and statesmen; and their writings — often composed while in ecstasy — were extremely popular. Nor were these saints solitary contemplatives, who must be sought out in hidden retreats; active work in the world was as much a part of their lives as contemplation. With the exception of that of Bernard of Clairvaux, no other age has produced such a dazzling combination of intellect, sanctity, and humanity as the period of the saint-mystics of the thirteenth and fourteenth centuries.

St. Bonaventure (1221–1274), the General of the Franciscans, was one of this brilliant company, as was his friend, St. Thomas Aquinas. Bonaventure, called the "Prince of Mystics" by Leo XIII, was a preacher to kings and popes and a writer of utmost originality whose works comprise a treasury of knowledge in Scholastic philosophy, theology, and scientific thought — second only to Aquinas. He arbitrated between the warring factions of his order with a bold hand, defended it, and reorganized it. He was also a friar whose humility was startlingly simple; when, much against his will, he was made a cardinal, the papal envoys found him washing dishes outside a convent on the outskirts of Florence. He cut short the ceremony by telling them to please hang the red hat on a nearby tree until he had finished!

In the North, St. Gertrude the Great (1256–c. 1302) was the star of the "Mystics of Helfta." Helfta was a Benedictine convent in Saxony famed as a center of Northern mysticism. Although Gertrude was hidden in the cloister from a very early age, her mystical treatises, *Legatus* and *Revelations,* exercised a widespread influence in her own time as well as on posterity; she was one of the earliest writers to promote devotion to the Sacred Heart, and her work was particularly favored by the theologians and saints of the sixteenth century. St. Bridget of Sweden (c. 1303–1373) was still another member of this company of saints — another writer-mystic of influence and the founder of what has been called the only important religious order to come out of the fourteenth century. The widow of a nobleman and the mother of eight children, Bridget worked ceaselessly to raise the spiritual standards of the court of Sweden, and in Rome — where she went in 1349 — she worked for the return of the popes from Avignon. Her Order of St. Saviour, or Brigittines, she founded at Vadstena as a double monastery in 1346. The nuns were strictly cloistered and the monks were preachers and missionaries whose example and zeal did much to extend the fervor of the New Devotion into a fast-declining era.[3] When, to her bitter disappointment, Urban IV returned to Avignon after two years in Rome, Bridget prophesied his imminent death, which occurred a few months thereafter. It was not to be she, but the Dominican tertiary, Catherine of Siena, who was to be responsible for the end of the "Babylonian Captivity." The last of this great company of saint-mystics, Catherine is the most dazzling of them all.

Catherine of Siena (1347–1380), called "a great statesman as well as a great saint," is one of the most remarkable women of history. No phase or plane of life escaped her concern, and her burning charity poured out upon high and low alike. Her intrepid adventures and trials as an immensely influential diplomatist rival those of the hardiest ambassador or general. No mortal circumstance or creature could deter her; for every action seems to have been directed and dominated by the Divine Will — not by human reason or instinct at all.

When Catherine was only a child she experienced visions and practiced austerities unheard of in one so young. At the age of sixteen she became a Dominican tertiary, wearing the habit of the Order and living in a cell in her father's house. Her family heaped all manner of abuse on her for her way of life, mainly because she was beautiful and was therefore expected to make a highly advantageous marriage. Oblivious to all this, however, her soul transcended all mortal obstacles to ascend into the loftiest reaches of union with God. During this time she had three years of practically uninterrupted celestial visitations of various kinds, after which she went out among the poor and sick — upon divine command — doing the most difficult and menial work. At the same time she endured the calumnies of her neighbors, family, and even envious members of her own Order with charming patience.

[3] The Brigittines spread widely throughout Europe, and was the only order to survive in England after the Reformation, although much reduced in circumstances. The Order divided into two observances during the seventeenth century, the Brigittines of the Recollection having been founded in Spain by Ven. Marina de Escobar, an ex-Carmelite. The male branch was also discontinued at about this time. St. Catherine of Sweden, Bridget's daughter, was second abbess of the Order and another luminary of Northern mysticism.

Finally, Catherine drew about her a circle of devoted disciples, both men and women, and at last commanded the respect and awe of all those who had most defamed her. At this point in her life she received a revelation of Divine Mysteries culminating in a prolonged trance — a kind of "mystical death" — during which she was directed to go into the world and engage in public life. She at once became active in the most varied kinds of affairs: writing letters and visiting princes, nobles, papal legates, nuns, and men and women of all classes. Through her valiant efforts as mediator between princes and as adviser to two popes, civil and national warfare was quelled or assuaged. At the same time she never ceased to work for the alleviation of the destitute and the afflicted, to write (or dictate) her famous *Dialogues* — a book of meditations and revelations — and to suffer the pain of invisible stigmata. Catherine's books rank among the classics of Italian literature, and her character is one of the most complex and many-sided in hagiography. Almost alone, she held her beloved "Holy Church" on her frail shoulders, out of the mire that might otherwise have engulfed it.

Out of the tremendous influence of the mendicants, the New Devotion, and the great saints of the era came a fresh surge of compassion for suffering humanity. Despite all the attempts of the Holy See — in 1215 and again in 1275 — to limit enthusiasm for the religious life, nothing, it seems, could do so. Like the Mantellate Servites and St. Catherine of Siena, unenclosed Sisters and Brothers flocked out to battle every conceivable social ill. Thousands of tertiaries — who lived at home or in community and were exempt from canon law concerning religious life — worked with heroic patience and fortitude among the sick and destitute in the cities. The uncloistered Sister — those under temporary vows or none at all — distinct from the cloistered nun, here emerges into full view. Attempts were made in the fifteenth century to enclose the Third Orders, but they refused to be denied the work which had called them into being; they simply increased their "extern" members to a majority! Hospitals, refuges, orphanages, schools, founded and served by Third Order Sisters and

Brothers, begin to appear from about the middle of the fourteenth century onward. It is ". . . a movement," says Father Hughes, "that is summed up in the great figure of St. Roch, the patron of the poor and needy sick, whose cult, from the day of his death in 1350, has never ceased."[4] Indeed, St. Roch of Montpellier is the epitome of this amazing development. Said to be a Franciscan tertiary, Roch devoted the full extent of his sanctity to the plague-stricken, curing them by the sign of the cross and completely clearing whole towns of the disease by his miraculous power. With such a tremendous source of inspiration to call upon, it is little wonder that the religious men and women of this last act in the medieval drama so marvelously transcend its mounting horrors.

While the spiritual and scholarly life of the Church on its highest plane continued in the monasteries and nunneries, the uncloistered, active religious completed that full circle which encompasses, in Catholicism, every condition and every need — whether spiritual or temporal. Whereas, in more ancient times, those in need *sought* it in the monasteries and nunneries, in this period just mentioned religious *went out to seek* their suffering brothers in Christ. It was a part of that tremendous innovation in religious life which the friars brought with them when they came. The mendicant was born that the monk might be reborn. In spite of the dire times into which the world and the Church were to plunge, nothing has ever nullified that new miracle brought about by love of God, sought in His creature's needs. And the fervor of the New Devotion, inspired by the great mystics of the thirteenth and fourteenth centuries, still reverberates in Catholic thought and practice — an inestimable treasure, and one[5] undiminished by time.

[4] P. Hughes, *A History of the Church*, Vol. III, p. 213.
[5] A resurgence of the aims of the New Devotion may be noted in Thomas Merton's popular work, *Seeds of Contemplation* (New Directions, 1948).

CHAPTER TEN

GLORY AND SHAME

The New Devotion, for all its good aspects, was no match for the tremendous cultural changes that were taking place in Europe at the same time. The Renaissance was beginning; that last turbulent act in the medieval drama in which beauty and evil, elegance and violence, faith and skepticism, combined without shame. The artistic glory of the Renaissance was accompanied by an incredible decline in manners and morals.

The decline was due to many factors: the rise of capitalism and a bourgeois class, the growth of nationalism, and the rediscovery of Greek and Roman culture. Arts, letters, learning, architecture, all strove to be "classical" and Europe's "latinized" past was despised. The scramble for wealth and prestige, based on these factors, amounted to a veritable passion — to explain and justify which the first *non*religious Western philosophy appeared. This was Humanism, which supported a belief in the self-sufficiency of natural man and purely human values, without reference to God or divine things. And before Western man could assimilate these cultural changes properly, two great catastrophes — one physical, the other spiritual — threw him even further off balance. These catastrophes were the Black Death and the Great Western Schism. Neither could have happened at a worse time in history.[1] In consequence of all these new elements and circumstances, religious life was as adversely affected.

The degree of laxity infecting religious orders during the Renaissance has never been accurately evaluated, owing to the few records kept during the Black Death and their destruction during the Reformation. The highly colored prejudices of the classical cynics and the enmity of Reformation writers have led historians to believe that such laxity as existed has been much exaggerated, although it did indeed exist. Relaxed rules allowed the admission of unsuitable candidates, as well as the acquisition of great wealth and many privileges. This, despite the ravages of the Black Death, swelled the ranks of the religious orders out of all proportion to the spiritual quality of the population. The general relaxation did not mean, however, that there was little interest in religion, or that the era did not abound in sincere and holy men and women of extraordinary spiritual talents. Besides the saint-mystics like Catherine of Siena, Bridget of Sweden, and the orders inspired by the New Devotion, great preacher-reformers of the Renaissance — of which Savonarola was one — are particularly conspicuous.

One of the first great preacher-reformers was St. Vincent Ferrer

[1] The Black Death wiped out a quarter of the population of Europe between 1347 and 1349. The Great Western Schism (1378–1411) was the controversy over succession to the Papacy, during which two and sometimes three popes seemed to be reigning at once.

(1350–1419), a Spanish Dominican theologian. Although Vincent knew no other language than his own, he was imbued with the "gift of tongues" as he traveled from country to country, converting many thousands of Moors and Jews, and followed by an army of about 10,000 disciples. One of these disciples was the Franciscan, St. Bernardine of Siena, who became known as the "Apostle to Italy." He tramped barefoot the length and breadth of that country, on one vast mission of peace and repentance. Towns contended hotly for the favor of hearing him preach, and built great bonfires to consume the "vanities" abandoned by his reconverted listeners. St. John Capistrano, another Franciscan, did much the same thing in Germany, while other missionary mendicants carried the Faith to India, China, and Asia. Although the waves of religious enthusiasm stirred up, first by the mendicants, and then by the New Devotion, continued to sway great masses of the people through such eloquent zealots, that enthusiasm was too often temporary; continued sustenance for it was lacking when such men as Vincent, Bernardine, and John moved on.

Of the established orders, none were so disturbed by the times as the Franciscans. Throughout the fourteenth century, anti-Minor factions, both lay and ecclesiastical, fought for their suppression, and within the Order dissensions split its ranks into many pieces. The main point at issue was the clause concerning poverty in the original Rule. Because of the economic anarchy created by so many thousands of friars having no means, no property or stabilizing sources of income whatever, various steps had been taken to rectify this condition almost from the first; in 1332 the Order was allowed ownership of property and revenues (before that time property and revenues had been held for the Order by the Holy See), together with other privileges and exemptions. This made the Minors wealthy and powerful and encouraged its overgrowth and relaxation — anathema to those within it who believed in a strict observance of Franciscan poverty. Those who desired to live in strict poverty created many "recoil" communities, called by various names (Zelanti, Spirituales, Recollects, Reformati, Discalced) but known, altogether, as Observatines — or Friars of the Strict Observance, as opposed to the Common Observance or Conventuals — those living in owned convents. The rivalry between the Observatines and the Conventuals was intense; the whole population of towns were wont to unceremoniously oust the friars of one observance, in order to install those of another! Internecine quarrels of the Observatine groups became so heated that many communities fell into heresy, to secede finally from the Order and be suppressed later. Obviously, mitigation of the Rule had been no solution.

When Pope Martin V called a general chapter of the Friars Minor in 1438, in an attempt to unify the Order and improve discipline, it was found that a complete reunion of all the factions within it was quite impossible; whereupon a bull of separation was published and St. Bernardine of Siena, the most illustrious Observatine friar, was appointed first Observatine vicar-general. Bernardine worked hard to merge the two branches, but in this he was unsuccessful; however, under his leadership and that of his successor, St. John Capistrano, the Observants, as they were now known, so increased and prospered that when partition of the two branches became complete in 1517, the Observants took precedence over the Conventuals in rank. Only a few Observatine congregations of the First Order — Discalced, Reformati, Recollects — remained outside the main body, and they finally merged with it as late as the nineteenth century. The Franciscans remain thus, in two parts, today, and the rivalries and dissensions of the strife-ridden fifteenth century are forgotten in an observance of the Rule which varies only in detail, reasonably and suitably interpreted to fit the social and economic patterns of the present day.

The Franciscan tree has never ceased to put out new branches. Indeed, so many tertiaries of the Third Order Secular had formed themselves into congregations of Regulars even then, in the thirteenth and fourteenth centuries, that in 1458 they were put under one superior-general. Today they continue to increase in numbers of members as well as numbers of congregations. Also, two other branches of the First Order were added to the Conventuals and Observants in the Renaissance era, both of which are still among the more austere orders of the Church. These were the Minims and the Capuchins — both examples of the dramatic extremes of those times.

St. Francis of Paula (1416–1507), the founder of the Minims, was a man of such great piety that his ascetic nature was hardly satisfied by life in a Conventual community. Leaving it, he first went to an isolated spot on his father's estate to live as a hermit, then to a cave on the seacoast, where he was joined by an increasing number of disciples. The community soon grew so large that Francis was obliged to build a monastery and church. Although he was unswerving in his loyalty to the Franciscan Rule, Francis of Paula's interpretation of it was far more severe than any which prevailed anywhere — Conventual or Observatine. Humility was its distinguishing mark, combined with extreme poverty and complete abstinence. As the community's mode of life was semi-eremitical, the Order received the approval of the Pope in 1436 under the name "The Hermits of St. Francis"; but this title was later changed to one the founder preferred — "Minims," meaning "the least," or lesser than Minor, as it were. By the middle of the sixteenth century the Order had four hundred and fifty monasteries in France, Spain, and Germany. In 1562, fifty-five years after St. Francis of Paula's death, Huguenots broke open his tomb and found his body entirely incorrupt, whereupon they burned it. His Order, which counts two beatified and other distinguished members, suffered such depletion during the French Revolution that it has never recovered; only several houses of it now exist, with a few hundred members.[2]

The now-great Order of Capuchin Franciscans seemed to have a curiously inauspicious beginning, to say the least. The founder, as well as the first two vicar-generals, even deserted its ranks in a drama that was almost as comical as it was regrettable.

About fifteen years after the death of St. Francis of Paula, an Observant friar named Matthew Bassi decided to reform his community in certain respects — including a change of habit to

---

[2] There is only one monastery outside of Italy. The friars are principally engaged in serving the poor through missions and retreats. There are also contemplative nuns and tertiaries.

one which he believed closer to the design of that of St. Francis
of Assisi. This habit had a long pointed hood, or *capuche,* from
which the Order derives its name. Having obtained permission of
the Pope to attempt his reform, Matthew appeared at one of the
chapter meetings so attired. His proposals were not at all welcome, however; he was summarily imprisoned as an apostate.
Through the influence of a duchess at the papal court, Matthew
was released; then, joined by two other dissident friars, he
obtained a brief of permission to found a new hermitage. In the
meantime, however, their provincial superior had obtained a coun-
terbrief against them, so that when the friars appeared before
him he charged them with being apostate fugitives — and imprisoned all three. This time they escaped and fled to a Camaldolese monastery, where they waited until the wrath of the
provincial had cooled sufficiently to allow them to go ahead with
their plans.

The new hermitage, at Albacina in the Marches of Italy, was
a great success. The one community grew to several, while
the Capuchins earned high esteem with their preaching, conver-
sions, and their heroic charity during a raging pestilence. Matthew
Bassi had meanwhile been elected vicar-general, but finding this
office too confining, he resigned. Two of the next four Vicar-
generals ruled prudently enough at first, but they later caused
so much trouble that they were dismissed from the Order.
Moreover, the second of these, Bernadine Ochino, when summoned to Rome fled to Switzerland instead, left the Church,
and married, later perishing with his family during an epidemic
of plague. The scandal thus created caused official censure of
the Capuchins for a few years, but this was finally lifted and
the Order went on to grow and prosper. Matthew Bassi, the
founder, in the meantime had been preaching about the country, oblivious to the authority of his own Order. When the
Pope issued a bull excommunicating all those wearing the habit
of the Capuchins, but refusing to live in their convents or
be subject to their authority, Matthew cut off *half* of his
capuche and continued on his way! As he was buried in an

Observant convent church, some believe that he returned to them; but this point is in doubt. At any rate, the Capuchins flowered into remarkable success; they now number over ten thousand, with many saints and scholars included in their later history.

In the midst of so many thousands of religious of every conceivable kind and degree, true religious asceticism was not nearly so much diminished as historians would have us believe; it was only hidden beneath the flamboyant excesses and ills of Renaissance life. Spontaneous answers to the need for reform sprang up all over Europe during the entire period — until a purified Papacy and the Counter Reformation would bring back that sweeping unity of effort lacking during the time. New Sisterhoods and Brotherhoods continued to take their places beside the old ones, and "primitive" observances of monastic rules, begun by numerous high-minded monks and clerics,[3] developed into many reform congregations — some of which continue to the present.

Of the new active orders of the fourteenth and fifteenth centuries, three are of special note. The first began in Germany, early in the fourteenth century, as a group of young men devoted to nursing — and burying — the victims of bubonic plague. Taking St. Alexius of Edessa as their patron, they formed a society of Brothers, known then as "Cellites" or "Llalorden" (from "to sing softly"; i.e., to chant the Office of the Dead). The society became a religious congregation, the Alexian Brothers, whose many hospitals, retreats, and sanitoria are scattered over the world. Also devoted to charity among the poor and sick were the Oblates of St. Benedict, an order of women founded by St. Frances of Rome in 1433. St. Frances was a matron of the nobility, the mother of three children, and a mystic who enjoyed many unusual graces — such as ecstasy, visions, miracles, and prophecy. In an effort to turn the thoughts of her more worldly

[3] As early as 1334 Pope Benedict XII, himself a saintly Cistercian, did his best to renew and enforce the decrees of the Fourth Lateran Council concerning orders. In the fifteenth century at least six popes were reformers whose efforts were blocked by a worldly Curia (Martin V, Eugene IV, Nicholas V, Calixtus III, Pius II, Paul II). Cardinal Nicolas of Cusa, scholar and patron of classical learning, was the most successful of the prelate reformers of religious life.

friends to God, Frances organized them into an association of Benedictine oblates, or tertiaries, and together they devoted themselves to works of charity. The association of oblates was subsequently approved as an uncloistered Sisterhood without vows. The ladies used their personal fortunes on charitable works and devoted themselves entirely to social service. St. Frances, after being widowed, became the first superior of the Order, which sustained a remarkable degree of regularity throughout the whole era. The other new Order was the first female branch of the Carmelites, the Carmelite Sisters, formed in 1452 out of several communities of Beguines — now much relaxed but very numerous, especially in Spain. It was this Order which was to rise to such glory under St. Teresa of Ávila in the next century.

One of the earliest of the renewed "primitive," or strict, observances of monastic rules, was a most austere form of Benedictine life, instituted by Blessed Bernard Tolomei in 1313, called the Olivetans after their first monastery at Mt. Oliveto, near Siena. An independent Benedictine Order, it is still extant today though not widespread. About a dozen monasteries exist today, all in Europe. There is also a Second Order. It was from the Olivetans that some Black Benedictines — non-Cistercian — took over the monastery of St. Justina of Padua, in 1409, to found the first of many reform congregations of the Benedictine Order. These were associations of houses under an archabbot. Also from the Olivetans, the new community borrowed more efficient and up-to-date constitutions, which were later incorporated into the constitutions of the whole Benedictine Order. The movement was called the Cassinese Congregation in honor of the most distinguished member of it — Monte Cassino — and soon incorporated many celebrated abbeys, to become the major reform observance in the South. The Cassinese Congregation may be called Cluny's successor, for the last remnants of the Cluniac observance — much declined at the time — died when the Cassinese supplanted it. In Germany, the same spirit brought about the Benedictine Bursfield Union, which comprised over a hundred abbeys; and along the Rhine and Moselle rivers, strict discipline was restored in over two hundred convents and monasteries by Nicolas of Cusa. In Holland the Augustinian Windesheim Congregation had much influence in reforming many religious houses there and in Germany, while the English Augustinians — known as the Austin Friars — were the least declined of the orders in that country and were enjoying an especially fruitful period in their history. Also there were many reformed congregations of Cistercians organized after 1425, but without the more lasting and widespread results occasioned by the Black Monks' successes. It was in the fifteenth century also that another saint-mystic, Colette, brought one part of the Poor Clares back to the strict observance of their founder's Rule.

Thus, in a time commonly supposed to have been barren of all but disorder and vice in the Church, we see contemplative life continuing in a really never-ending stream, striving valiantly to balance the scales of divine justice by prayer and penance. It is to these mostly unnamed saints that we perhaps owe the salvaging of so much in the storm that soon will follow.

As the sixteenth century opened, on the very eve of the Protestant Revolt, the reaction to Renaissance evils was growing stronger and stronger. Pope Julius II (1503–1513) was a reformer, bent on purifying the Roman court and reorganizing religious orders;[4] also it was now that the seedbed of the Counter Reformation was being thickly sown by the saints who are among the greatest that the Church has ever produced. Ignatius Loyola, Francis Borgia, and Francis Xavier; Teresa of Ávila, John of God, Philip Neri, John Fisher and Thomas More; Cajetan, Peter of Alcantara, Peter Canisius — these are only a few. And all but one were monks, nuns, friars, and priests whose harvest would come after the storm, to refresh and renew the vitality of Catholic Faith in doctrines miraculously untouched[5] by both the blight of scandal and the fury of the succeeding storm.

It is not within the scope of our story to probe and recount all of the causes of the Reformation, or Protestant Revolt. It is

[4] Julius II was succeeded by Cardinal de'Medici (Leo X), an event which tragically nullified Julius' efforts and coincided with Luther's revolt.

[5] Not one of the "bad popes" was responsible for any additions or alterations in Catholic doctrine.

enough to say that unprecedented and incredibly powerful forces
of history — some already mentioned — coincided, to come to a
more spiritually explosive point of combustion than any other
that the Western world had ever known. Suffice to say also that
the major blame for the revolt is to be laid at the door of the
Church; a fact that no Catholic historian will deny. The failure of
the Church lay entirely in the hierarchy; men so engulfed in the
delusions and complexities of their time that even when a reform
of "head and members" was demanded and attempted, it was
throttled or short-lived — or a real understanding of the conditions behind the demand was lacking. These men put off drastic
measures to engage in the hundreds of economic and political
quarrels raging throughout Europe; the Holy See was making a
last stand against the increasing encroachments of Statism — which,
in itself, created much antipapal feeling among the princes. At
the same time, anticlericalism among the people mounted, whipped
to outlandish proportions by millions of printed pamphlets. The
hierarchy and Pope Leo X refused to take very seriously what
seemed to be only a local reverberation of the minor Wyclif and
Hus heresies.[6] In higher society, Humanism and Classicism had
seriously weakened the roots of faith, as has been mentioned; and
even the popular piety of the New Devotion was overstimulated
by emotion but underfed by Catholic thought — a divorce of doctrine and practice caused by the repudiation of philosophy and
Scholasticism. A lush growth with such shallow roots was the
first to wither in the winds of controversy.

The matter which touched off the Protestant Revolt in Germany
is too well known to be repeated at length: the erroneous preaching, by the friar Tetzel, of a papal indulgence, and the misunderstanding of that doctrine — which was later clarified and
restricted. To plunge into heresy and schism was not Luther's

[6] The followers of John Hus (1369–1415) in Bohemia, called Hussites, professed the errors of the English Wyclif, which subscribed to several extravagant
heresies, many conflicting with one another, such as communism and sexual
promiscuity, and abolition of certain sacraments, doctrines, and the liturgy.
The heresy caused savage religious wars for fifteen years. The more conservative Hussites were reconverted by St. John Capistrano. The present successors
of the extremist Hussites are the Moravians, or Bohemian Brethren.

first intention; he considered himself but one of the "reformers from within," until he realized how willing were the poorly instructed people, disgruntled with ecclesiastical sins, and the German princes — delighted with this ideal weapon in their economic quarrel with the Papacy — to follow him outside the Church. Whereupon he withdrew his support from the peasants and turned his attention to securing the co-operation of the nobles. The masses were thereby forced to follow the religio-political policies of their masters;[7] they could not have turned back had they wished. Thus began the "state religions" of Europe.

Soon after Luther came Calvin and Zwingli in Switzerland and the Low Countries, and a host of other "reformers," all disagreeing violently with one another — to continue that process of division and dilution of Christendom which has not entirely yet ceased. The "Reformation" that was indeed so needed turned into a revolt that but added to the need. Indescribable suffering, bloodshed, and devastation ensued for the next seventy-five years.

In Germany, convents, monasteries, schools, and churches were expropriated by the Lutheran nobles, as well as by apostate prelates, and religious and clerics were turned out, persecuted, and vilified. For Luther's doctrines abhorred asceticism in any form; "justification by faith alone" disavowed the merit of any "work" of virtue and allowed any license without harm to the "justified." As much suffering as the "liberation" of the religious caused, however, it also seared away all the deadwood that cluttered religious houses and which had caused much of the decline. Convents had too often become houses of refuge for unwanted relatives and unmarried daughters; and monasteries were crowded with

[7] The leaders of the Reformation taught that princes were supreme in religious matters as well as secular, a device largely aimed at destroying the authority of the pope; also, by setting up such a powerful counterauthority, the nobles were enabled to seize the property of the Church. Luther's new doctrine swiftly evolved to make the State supreme; the sole agent of God in keeping order, against which there was no appeal. Nor was any deserved by those deemed corrupted by sin and "unjustified" (by faith). "Freedom" was not yet a watchword of Protestantism.

men unsuited to the life for the many reasons already cited.[8] In the other countries to which Protestantism spread — Scandinavia, Poland, the Netherlands, Scotland, parts of Hungary and France — much the same story was repeated. And seventeen years after Luther promulgated his new doctrines in the "Ninety-Five Theses," Henry VIII unwittingly opened the door to Protestantism in Catholic England.

Henry did not intend heresy, but schism only. But as in all schisms, heterodoxy was not long in developing, and the acts and events generated by the break precipitated as much violence as Protestantism on the Continent had caused. For refusing to take the Oath of Supremacy, which would recognize Henry's invalid marriage and make him the supreme head of the church in England, St. Thomas More and St. John Fisher, Bishop of Rochester, were executed, together with a number of monks and clerics. Agents of the King began to close convents and monasteries, and to turn out the religious in them. Henry soon discovered that this was an excellent way to annex their much-coveted wealth, and so proceeded to expropriate monastic property wholesale. Over eight thousand monks, nuns, and canons were dispossessed, the orders finally being suppressed altogether — although Henry professed to uphold the validity of religious vows. The orders' revenues, which had been largely devoted to religion, charity, and education, he now used to secure his cause by lavishing them on his friends. The religious were reduced to penury, education[9] and community life was disrupted, and the indigent left to starve.

The old assumption that pre-Reformation England was an abyss of religious ignorance and indifference is now largely discarded. The dissolution of the orders was not carried out because of the

---

[8] Luther was ordained and took his final vows after only a year in an Augustinian monastery. An extremely moody, overscrupulous religious, he would never have passed modern standards as a candidate.

[9] Universities were nearly emptied, libraries and art treasures were destroyed, and innumerable grammar schools were closed when the orders were dissolved. By the end of the century there were fewer than half the number of schools that there had been at the beginning.

criminal or immoral conduct of monks and nuns, nor was the spiritual life of the people at the scandalously low ebb depicted in the past. It is not denied that many priests were unworthy of their office, and that members of the hierarchy were too often over-powerful and self-indulgent, as on the Continent; but as St. Thomas More remarks with his usual wit: ". . . it would not be very easy, I ween, to find sufficient [laymen] to match the good [churchmen], even though they be as few as some folks would have them be." A Venetian traveler, writing of his visit to England, reported scenes of ardent rural church life, wherein the people supported their religion with the greatest enthusiasm; and Brewer, the noted English historian says: ". . . but that the corruption was either so black or so general as party spirit would have us believe, is contrary to all analogy, and is unsupported by impartial and contemporary evidence."[10] All the same, with the Act of Supremacy and the Suppression, a reign of terror began that persisted intermittently for the next hundred and fifty years.

Protestant ideas and doctrines soon began to infiltrate the Anglican Church, so that by the time of Elizabeth's accession to the throne, England had become definitely Protestant. With the promulgation of her Thirty-Nine Articles and the Second Prayer Book it was entirely so; Roman liturgy, belief in the Real Presence, Transubstantiation and the Mass, and all but two sacraments, were repudiated as "blasphemous fables." All of the bishops except one, and half the clergy, resigned in protest, but they were replaced by political appointees. Every Catholic priest became a traitor and all Catholic worship a disloyalty. Of the two hundred and twenty-one Catholics put to death during Elizabeth's reign, a hundred and twenty-eight were priests (including thirty-two Franciscans) and three were women. The property of all those Catholics who had fled to the Continent was confiscated, the abbeys were sacked and left in ruins, and death or imprisonment was decreed for either saying or hearing Mass. All hope of peace and union dwindled, as even the Catholic princes in Europe hampered every attempt to achieve either by their hostility to

[10] Henry VIII, Vol. II.

one another or the reigning pope. While Protestant rulers made their sects an arm of the State, Catholicism was besieged from within and without.

Not since the time of Arianism had the Roman Catholic Church been in such peril. To the enemies of the Church, the admonition of Christ that "I will be with you all days, even unto the consummation of the world" and that "the gates of Hell shall not prevail against it" was an assumption disproved. The heresiarchs, in their zeal and their bitter contempt, thought the Catholic Church leveled and broken forever.

But even at that moment the cleansing fires of the Counter Reformation had been already set.

CHAPTER ELEVEN

THE SUN AGAIN

From the pulpits of Florence the fiery Savonarola had cried,
"The Church will be chastised and then renewed, and this will
come to pass quickly!" And just as he had prophesied, so it
happened.

When Giovanni de'Medici became Pope Leo X (1513–1521), the
final humility of both scandal and chastisement was reached. Leo X,
whose pontificate was marked by frivolity and extravagance, was the
last of the "bad popes"; his successors were different men,[1] bent on

[1] Leo's successor, Adrian VI, had already spent a lifetime of consecrated
service to the Church when he was elected; Adrian's successor, Clement VII,
was harsh and headstrong, bringing reform to a standstill, but only temporarily.

reform, even though little was achieved, owing to vested interests, generations old. It would take many years and many popes to dislodge them. But the first titan of the new spirit was not long in appearing; the third pope after Leo was Paul III (1534–1549), a Renaissance man himself who was equal to the task through firsthand experience. He was all of fifty before he had been con- verted and received Holy Orders. As Pope, he clearly under- stood the source of all the trouble — indifference to the true teach- ings and doctrines of the Catholic Church. It was Paul who planned and designed the great Council of Trent, to be called to deliberate on reform. For ten years he labored patiently to organize it, while the Protestant Revolt, political pressures, greed, and indifference put every conceivable obstacle in the way. None- theless, Pope Paul managed to marshal a huge corps of reformers from among the hierarchy; men who could deal with the machina- tions of princes with skill and vigor, and who stood ready to enforce reforms with sincerity and zeal. When the Council of Trent finally convened in 1545, it began with theology — not law. Indifference could only be overcome by knowledge; and knowl- edge would make laws self-propelling.

During the eighteen years of these sessions of the Council[2] it never deviated from this pattern conceived by Paul. A new codifica- tion of Catholic doctrine and practice resulted, on which were based the most stringent reform decrees. Education was the starting point of them all: colleges and seminaries for the clergy were founded, a Catholic Confraternity of Christian Doctrine was established in parishes for the instruction of the people, and ele- mentary schools were opened. Everywhere, diocesan and provincial synods met to strengthen the Trent decrees, while a new army of religious orders moved in to teach and to strengthen the new spirit. It was not so much the briefs and sanctions, however, that revived religious life as it was the sanctity of men and women whose heroic virtue was not the result of any decrees or defini- tions. They would have been great saints anyway. But without

---

[2] The Council was prorogued several times, and once suspended for eleven years.

them the Council's decrees might well have become "little more than a solemnity of pious resolutions" — and the Counter Reformation could not have taken place.

Hundreds of briefs were written by Pope Paul, directing the reform of monasteries and convents, and approval was given to several new orders. Among these was the Society of Jesus, which was to be the greatest single weapon of the Counter Reformation, and the Ursulines of St. Angela Merici, whose group of charitable laywomen — formed into an order in Italy — was the first true teaching order of women in the Church. Her example was to be followed shortly in France, where several affiliated congregations of Ursulines were established. The Ursulines were also to be the first order of women to establish themselves permanently in the New World — in Quebec, and then in Louisiana.

Early in the century, before the Protestant Revolt, the first sign of spiritual reform in Rome had shown itself in a confraternity of laymen, priests, and prelates of the Roman court, banded together for the purpose of high morality and strict attention to the practice of the Faith. This confraternity was called the Oratory of Divine Love, and from it Pope Paul III was to recruit six of his most noted reformer-cardinals. Also members of it were two priests named Cajetan and Caraffa — afterward Pope Paul IV. After the outbreak of the Protestant Revolt the two men decided to form a society of priests with the same aims as the confraternity's. Their work would be that of the parochial clergy, but especially in the city's slums. The vow of poverty would be particularly strict; a set income was forbidden, nor was even begging allowed; the order must subsist on voluntary contributions alone, although they were allowed to ring the monastery bell if the community was in too desperate straits. It was called the Theatines, after the town of Theatre, in Italy, of which Caraffa was bishop, and was the first of a new kind of order known as Clerks Regular. The Theatines, approved in 1524, were closely followed by two other orders of Clerks Regular — the Barnabites of St. Anthony Zaccaria, whose origin was a Milanese confraternity like Cajetan's Roman one, and the Somaschi, founded about the same time by

St. Jerome Emiliani, a worldly nobleman-soldier turned penitent. The Barnabites specialized in giving open-air missions, while the Somaschi worked in hospitals and founded orphanages and refuges for abandoned and destitute children. But more important still was another order of Clerks Regular approved in 1540 by Pope Paul, which would prove to be by far the greatest force of the Counter Reformation, as it would prove to be one of the greatest forces of the Catholic Church for all time — the Society of Jesus.

In organization, intent, and method, the Society of Jesus is unique; consequently, from its inception it has always been one of the much-disputed and most colorful elements of Catholic religious life. It is a living distillation of its founder's unique personality and genius.

The earliest description of Ignatius Loyola (1491–1556) is contained in a bill of indictment against him, during his swashbuckling youth in his native Spanish city. He is, it says, "bold, defiant; he wears a leather curass and is armed with a sword and pistol; his long hair flows from under his velvet cap . . ." and he is accused of being "perfidious, brutal, vindictive. . . ." He looked on without shame while others were punished for his misdemeanors; he perpetrated the most vulgar pranks on his fellow soldiers and drank heavily. Ignatius had always been consumed with but one ambition — to gain favor at court by fair means or foul. Yet when this man died he was world-famous as a master of self-discipline, completely above all worldly passion.

During a skirmish in the war between Charles V of Spain and Francis I of France, the knight Ignatius insisted upon defending an untenable position. The result was not fame as a hero, but a shattering leg wound. The French sent the injured knight back to his ancestral castle, where he had to undergo long and painful treatments designed to prevent his being permanently crippled. Ignatius was bored and restless. As his family was not in the least scholarly, there were only two books in the castle to relieve the tedium — one a life of Christ and the other a volume of legends about the saints. These he took up with the utmost distaste; they were better than nothing.

To his surprise, Ignatius discovered that all manner of honor and glory had been showered on these soldiers of Christ. Yet they were without armor or armies, without the favor of kings or great ladies. They had, nonetheless, achieved what he had sought in vain. The thought dogged him bitterly until he decided that there was nothing to do but to try the method of the saints. If his thirst for glory would be assuaged that way — why then, he would be a saint! As soon as Ignatius was up, he set about being a "saint" without delay. He went to the famous sanctuary of Montserrat and wrote out a general confession which took three days, gave his clothes to a beggar, laid his sword and shield at our Lady's feet, and started on his way. Dressed in rags, he proclaimed his intention of going to the Holy Land, to liberate the Christian shrines. Ignatius soon enough found out, however, that there was one drawback; he was *not* a saint, or even close to being one. The remedy for this, he told himself, was obvious; he would start learning to be one at once.

Near the town of Manresa, in Catalonia, Ignatius found a cave. First buying all the instruments of self-mortification he would need, he established himself in it. He let his hair grow, wore a ragged cloak and a huge rosary around his neck, used a stone for a pillow, and began attempting to please God quickly and fully. But as his reeling senses dashed wildly from visions of hope and heavenly images to despair and glimpses of hell, he became feverish and finally desperately ill. Yet he would not give up; he was determined that his body and will, like a platoon of raw recruits, would be disciplined without pity until they could obey his slightest command. He would become the perfect knight and soldier of God — to be fit only then to grasp God's grace as a military prize.

From his experiences in the cave at Manresa, Ignatius discovered by what means the full faculties of the soul might be developed, and what may act upon those faculties to create a desired state of being. In acting in accordance with such knowledge, he could make a deliberate choice between good and evil, a choice so conclusive, deep, and total that the individual learning to obey such laws moved into a sense of reality more actual than in any previous experience. Such a mystical "system" Ignatius plotted out like a tactical exercise in military practice; he knew every rule, stage, and result of it by experience — and through it he at last became the saint he had set out to be. After ten months he was ready to leave his retreat and proceed with his original plans.

With his ambition for a personal crusade in Jerusalem still uppermost, Ignatius made his way to Palestine. When he arrived there, however, he was firmly rebuked for such a presumptuous idea, and so was forced to return to Spain, where he settled down to compose his mystical "system" into the Jesuit military manual of perfection, the now-famous *Spiritual Exercises,* and to make up for his scanty education. Starting in a boy's Latin class, Ignatius studied for the next eleven years — at Barcelona, Alcalá, Salamanca, and Paris. At the same time, he campaigned for disciples and continued to practice his Spiritual Exercises, while practicing all the austerities he had learned at Manresa. This caused him almost ceaseless harassment: he was beaten up, imprisoned, flogged, quizzed by the Inquisition, deserted by his first friends and followers. In Paris he succeeded in converting his roommate and two other students, one of whom was St. Francis Xavier. Here, at last, were his true companions. With youthful zeal they tacked a picture of Christ on the door of their university rooms — and under it some scoffing fellow student printed *Societas Jesu.* Thus was named, and thus began, the organization that was to amaze — and often antagonize — the world.

When the number of his disciples had risen to ten, Ignatius decided again to try out his ambition to go to the Holy Land, but an illness caused delay, which was prolonged still further by the Turkish wars in Palestine. The "Company of Jesus," as they called themselves, decided to wait a year; if they were unable to fulfill their vow to go to Jerusalem at the end of this time they would go to Rome instead and put themselves at the disposal of the Pope. This they did, and Ignatius abandoned his first plan for good. He and his companions were welcomed at Rome, where they were ordained priests, and with the Pope's approval began to attack the multiple evils of the Eternal City. Plague, famine, destitution, prostitution, heresy — all were vigorously attacked in a dozen ways, with an insight and efficiency that was entirely new. Military precision, thoroughness, and authority marked everything they undertook, and with amazing success. When the "Company" decided to become a religious order the plan at first met with some opposition from its own members — as it was contended that they would have to adopt an ancient rule and put aside many of their revolutionary methods — but it was at last approved. Constitutions which would safeguard the principle of their being "all things to all men" as "auxiliaries" of the Holy Father, in a fourth vow of "Special Obedience," were carefully composed by Ignatius. He assumed command of the Society of Jesus, Order of Clerks Regular, from his headquarters in Rome in 1540, from whence his soldiers spread, literally, over the earth.

The history of one major part of the Counter Reformation was made by the Jesuits.[3] Not only were they the most strictly disciplined, efficiently organized, and highly trained "company" — in the military sense — of the pope but their versatility was unprecedented. Unlike other orders, they did not specialize in a few fields of endeavor. They opened colleges, seminaries, and schools, were summoned to universities as teachers, to courts as advisers; and to far countries as missionaries, where their success was prodigious. Everywhere they worked to relieve social ills and promote, as preachers and parish priests, devotion to the sacraments. These diverse activities were carried out not merely by imitators of St. Ignatius but by men who were great saints in their own right — Francis Xavier, Francis Borgia, Peter Canisius, Robert Bellarmine, Aloysius Gonzaga, Peter Claver. The work of Francis Xavier in making many thousands of converts in the Orient is well known; Peter Canisius was a second St. Boniface in Germany; and Robert Bellarmine profoundly influenced Catholic theology for centuries to come by bringing about an organic fusion of medieval

[3] "Jesuit" was, at first, a term of opprobrium, meaning one who masked ulterior motives under a pious assumption of Christ's name. The Society of Jesus, characteristically, seized the appellation and turned it to the opposite account.

and modern thought. In North America, Jesuits underwent hideous tortures and privations to convert the Indians; and in their South American missions, beginning in 1607, they guarded the welfare of the natives against the exploitation of the conquistadors for a hundred and sixty years — until their suppression by Charles III.

It was inevitable that the Jesuits would become involved in all the politico-religious activity of the time, especially as most of it deeply involved the moral and spiritual stand that the Church had to make against the three most serious detriments to Catholic unity, liberty, and reform. These were, first, the encroachments on her authority by the Catholic princes, especially those in Spain and France, who refused to bow to some of the edicts of Trent or to reform their personal lives and courts; then, heresy within the Church — Jansenism and, later, Quietism[4] in the seventeenth century. And last, there was Protestantism itself, allied with the growing nationalism which precipitated the Thirty Years' War. With these and all the other problems confronting a fast-dividing, daily-more-secularized world, the Jesuits wrestled energetically. Whereupon their extremely great influence began to be envied and denounced; all manner of complaints streamed into the Holy See. As the seventeenth century turned into the eighteenth, the complaints mounted, usually contradicting one another. In Portugal, the Order was accused of being irregular, and of having had a hand in the attempted assassination of the king — a charge which was later disproved. In France they incurred the displeasure of Madame de Pompadour, were violently attacked by Pascal in

[4] Cornelius Jansen (1585–1638), Bishop of Ypres, promulgated a work claimed to be based on St. Augustine, wherein was denied the freedom of the will, the impossibility of resisting grace, and that Christ died for all men. The heresy took serious hold in France, to become associated with a convent of Cistercian nuns at Port Royal. It caused a minor schism involving about 10,000 adherents in Holland, which is still extant under the name "Old Catholics." The heresy was officially condemned in 1642.

Quietism was a form of mysticism taught by a Spanish priest, Molinos, which consisted of complete passivity of the soul, in resignation to sin and indifference to either reward or punishment, as the will of God. Such a view denied hope, as a Christian virtue, repentance, or spiritual advancement, confession being considered needless, and fostered all manner of impure acts. It was condemned in 1687. Molinos was tried and sentenced to life imprisonment after confessing his aberrations.

his popular "Letters," and were accused of being too regular and of usurping the power of the local clergy; in Spain they were accused of heresy. Although Pope Clement XIII defended them, the Order was first suppressed in France; four thousand Jesuits were expelled in 1764, although many managed to labor on under assumed names. In 1767 they were then suppressed in Spain; all Jesuits were to quit the country and surrender all their property by a certain date. Six thousand Jesuits — even those who were ill — were herded aboard ships and landed in Corsica, only to be driven off by its hostile ruler. The same story was repeated in Naples, Parma, and Malta. Beset with the apparent enmity toward the Society on all sides, Clement XIV, in July, 1773, issued a decree of total suppression. There were at the time twenty-two and a half thousand members of the Order.

The Society of Jesus was kept alive, strangely enough, by Catherine of Russia, who obtained a brief of exception to the suppression, and by the freethinker King of Prussia, Frederick II. After forty-one years the Order was finally re-established, in 1814, having already gained partial re-establishment in several countries. Although persecution and prejudice continued at intervals, the Society quickly regained its strength and prestige. Decadence or mitigation has never tarnished the Order for an instant — as its worst enemies, including even Voltaire, have admitted. Spiritually and physically, the Jesuits strength derives from the *Spiritual Exercises* of Ignatius; they remain a tightly knit, complex, high-standard organization of teachers and scholars, and the largest single order in the Church — with approximately 29,000 members.

Although Ignatius was a Spaniard, it was not in Spain that the Jesuits' force was felt — being least needed there than in any country in Europe during the Counter Reformation. That Spain was so little affected by the Protestant Revolt was a condition largely due to the reforms of the previous generation by the saintly Franciscan, Cardinal Ximenes. It was here that the renewed spirituality of the Church showed itself most deeply; not as an enforced "answer" to Protestantism, but because Spanish faith was unhampered by controversy. The Iberian Peninsula produced several new orders and many notable theologians during the sixteenth century. Reform observances and a high order of mysticism abounded — away from the busy battlegrounds of middle Europe. Not that Spain was any earthly paradise; "His Most Catholic Majesty," Philip II, was an arrogant absolutist in religious as well as in political matters, whose policies indirectly aided Protestantism elsewhere, seriously strained his relations with the Holy See, and at home made him more feared than loved. But for this there was much compensation. Had not the restless fire of Spanish spirituality produced Ignatius Loyola? And it would produce Teresa of Ávila, John of the Cross, and many other immortal saint-mystics who were also poets, preachers, reformers, founders.

St. Teresa of Ávila (1515–1582) is still known as one of the world's most remarkable and delightful women. Among the greatest of mystics and, unofficially, called a Doctor of the Church, her intensely human charm and adventurous spirit have enchanted generations of admirers of all faiths. As St. Bernard was known as the "perfect monk," so St. Teresa might well be known as the "perfect nun." She combines every virtue — including gaiety — of the nun, while embodying all the eternal qualities of religious asceticism. It is only a happy accident that she is a figure of the Counter Reformation era; actually, she is a product of not one period, but of Catholic sanctity anywhere in time.

The idea of entering the Carmelite convent in Ávila did not occur to Teresa until her life as a belle of the town was interrupted by a mysterious illness which attacked her in a series of violent seizures. In 1536, upon temporary recovery, she entered the convent much against her father's wishes. Life in this Carmelite community was far from arduous; the Sisters spent much time in the parlors chatting with their friends and relations; they were allowed to receive gifts of dainties, and even wore jewelry! The house was comfortably appointed, if not luxurious, and much fond attention was showered on the good ladies who had at least gone thus far in their pursuit of virtue. Teresa enjoyed it too, except for two disturbing elements which intermittently punctuated the serenity of her existence. One was recurrences of her illness, which necessitated her leaving the convent several times; the other was sudden excesses of religious fervor, during which she had celestial visitations. Both occurrences left her disturbed and hesitant. Should she return to the undeniably attractive world because of her health? Or should she give in to the divine graces offered to her in her periods of fervor — and give up the lax and contented life of her sisters in religion? She finally chose the latter course — the life of contemplation; whereupon her illness ceased and she experienced a heretofore unknown joy and resolution.

But now Teresa's sudden piety and mystical transports caused talk, suspicions, enmity. The subject of heated debate, she was examined by learned clerics and given all manner of harsh advice. A vehement majority of her examiners declared her to be either hysterical or possessed of the devil. She was then told to write her own deposition for the Inquisition. This would be the end of her, it was generally concluded, and a great relief to everybody. The document (her *Vida*) was examined by several of the Inquisition's sternest judges — who thereupon issued a brief of recommendation!

No sooner had Teresa settled down to the life of a contemplative than she found herself profoundly shocked by the relaxed mode of life in the convent. Any disposition to austerity, even by those who might be inclined toward it, was virtually impossible. True, the required cycle of devotions was observed by the Sisters; but such a combination of worldliness and piety as existed in the community obviously led to no advancement whatever in their interior lives. Teresa yearned to change all this — to return to the silence that is "the language of heaven," by a return to the original monastic Rule of St. Albert. But the Sisters would not hear of it. Teresa left the community — and then her battle was really to begin. After many more setbacks, opposition, and negotiations, she finally was able, with four other women, to establish her own convent. The group was known as the Discalced Carmelites.

With the tenacious zest of a man — but always with the gracious good humor of a woman — Teresa traveled throughout Spain, founding new houses of her Order. She encountered the severest

hardships along the way, not the least of which was the resentment and hostility of the Calced Carmelites; for although the
Holy Father and the Carmelite General in Rome highly approved,
the Carmelites in Spain regarded her as a fanatical innovator.
They put up every possible obstacle to the reform observance. One
day in Medina, however, she was called upon by two Calced
friars; one named Antonio, a huge man of middle age, the other
a diminutive young man of twenty-four named John. They had
come, they said, to help her establish a branch of her Order for
men. With typical vivacity she exclaimed, "Blessed be the Lord,
for now I have a friar and a half for the foundation of my new
monastery!" And so she had — and more, for the diminutive Friar
John was to become St. John of the Cross, one of the great saint-
mystics of Spain who, as a mystical poet, would also become
one of the immortals of Spanish literature and a Doctor of the
Church.

Hostility continued, however; the papal nuncio was so incited
against Teresa that he forbade her to continue her work, and
virulent pamphlets were circulated against her. Again she was
called before the Inquisition, again to be acquitted. Then Friar
John was kidnaped and hidden by a community of Calced Friars.
Brought to a standstill on all sides and unable to find Friar John,
Teresa wrote King Philip a long letter explaining her predicament,
and then went to see him. To her immense relief, she found him
wholly sympathetic; he simply deported the nuncio and gave her
full permission to continue. St. John, who had been cruelly mis-
treated by his captors, miraculously escaped — more dead than
alive — and made his way (led, it is said, by a mysterious mongrel)
to Teresa's convent, where he was nursed back to health by the
nuns. The worst of Teresa's troubles were over at last; the reform
began to win approval and respect in Spain — and many recruits.

Even when old and ill, Teresa kept at her arduous traveling,
always in an ancient wooden cart without springs, indefatigable
and vivacious to the last. Leading the way, on foot, across a
swift and icy stream, she slipped and almost drowned. "Why,"
she asked of God, "do You put such difficulties in our way?" He

answered, "Thus I treat My friends." Never at a loss, as usual, she quipped back, "Ah, my Lord, that is why You have so few!"

When St. Teresa died at Alba de Tormes, in 1582, so great was her fame that the population of Ávila, her native town, and Alba literally fought over the honor of owning her body; it was transported — and stolen — back and forth several times, in a lamentable comedy of furious rivalry. Alba finally won the contest, and her incorrupt body remains there to this day. This great lady of God, called "one of the most extraordinary women known to history," was not only the instigator of one of the most important and lasting reform observances in religious life, and the saint of prodigious miracles — wrought after her death — but she is hailed as one of the world's greatest mystical writers. Her three volumes of letters and her *Vida* (Life), *Interior Castle,* and *Way of Perfection* amaze and enchant all who read them. So vivid and full of depth is her writing that in it she emerges as a completely rounded individual, ". . . a woman teeming with life, of great determination, humor, and sensitivity." Today, the Order of Discalced Carmelites is as she reconstructed it: monastic, penitential, austere — and just as full of her cheerful vitality.

Throughout her many ordeals and then her triumphs, Teresa was counseled and encouraged by her spiritual director, St. Peter of Alcantara, minister of a Franciscan province of the "Stricter Observance," a branch of the Observants. He gave up his office and with St. John of Ávila — a renowned preacher, called the "Father of Spanish Mysticism" — and another priest went into the mountains to live a semieremitical life. Peter's thirst for austerity was insatiable; his cell was so small that he was unable to stretch to full length in it, nor did he sleep any more than an hour or two in twenty-four. The ground was his bed, he ate only once every three days, and no matter what the weather he never raised his hood or wore sandals. He and his disciples meditated three hours a day and observed, unless ill, perpetual abstinence from fish, meat, and eggs. The hermitage was enlarged into a convent with rooms so small that they were more like tombs; without chapter room or library, the whole house measured only eight by thirty-five feet.

Other such houses following the same constitutions were founded in Spain, Portugal, and Italy, until there were enough to form a separate congregation — called by some historians the "Friars Minor of the Strictest Observance." St. Teresa reported that after Peter's death — at an advanced age — he appeared to her and exclaimed, "Oh happy penance which hath obtained for me so great a reward!" For all the wide-scale "softening" of Western civilization, contemplative asceticism of the same brand as that of the first eremites had not become extinct.

On the active side, Spain and Portugal's contribution to the Counter Reformation was equally outstanding. By the huge army of Jesuits, and an even larger army of intrepid missionaries composed of members of all the great orders, the Faith was, in this "age of colonization," carried to the farthest parts of the earth. More than a dozen theological and mystical writers of lasting importance were contemporaries of St. Teresa; older orders revived and several new ones were founded. The Jeronymites, founded in the previous century (c. 1400), were particularly notable. They had many monasteries and great wealth, with which they were lavish in almsgiving. Of the new orders, the most outstanding was the Hospitallers of St. John of God, founded in 1540. Influenced by the great John of Avila, St. John of God — after being brutally treated in a hospital for the insane — had organized a community of nursing Brothers, to relieve the great suffering of the destitute sick. The Hospitallers spread to other countries in Europe and overseas, and is now one of the outstanding nursing orders in the Church.

In Italy, the powerful forces needed to uphold Trent and to fight the onslaught of Protestantism were exemplified by two remarkable men, backed for thirty years by a vigorous and uniform policy of three great popes. One of these men was St. Charles Borromeo, Archbishop of Milan; the other was St. Philip Neri. Like Pope Paul III, Borromeo had been a spoiled prince of the papal court, but, finally converted, he had made the Spiritual Exercises, received Holy Orders, and then retired from the Roman court to become head of a diocese that had not had a resident bishop in eighty years. Combining the talents of administrator and lawyer with great compassion and personal piety, St. Charles made his diocese a perfect example of the Trent reforms. He set up nearly eight hundred schools of Christian Doctrine, prepared a manual for teachers and one for pupils, and influenced the whole Catholic world through his vast correspondence. The measures of his uncle, Pope Pius IV, were, in fact, largely inspired by Borromeo. His personal holiness was demonstrated most brilliantly during a siege of plague in Milan; he turned his episcopal palace into a hospital, nursed the sick himself, and administered the sacraments to them. Everywhere, the hierarchy did their best to imitate him; for, as one contemporary wrote, "Borromeo does more good by his example than all the decrees of the Council."

Within the Holy See the severe spirit of reform, the bitterness of religious and political wars, and the harsh echoes of Calvinism and Lutheranism might well have cast a depressing pall over the Eternal City, had it not been for St. Philip Neri (1515–1595). He seemed to have been created for the purpose of counterbalancing such a state of gloom. Imperturbably good-natured and light-hearted, a sympathetic friend of children and young people, Philip had devoted himself to the welfare of the orphans of his native Florence while still a layman. In Rome he became a tutor, spending all his free time in shops, markets, and hospitals, endeavoring to convert the roughest characters with his gentle wit, and cheerfully enduring their scorn. On the advice of his confessor, he became a priest and took up residence in a room of the rectory of San Girolamo della Carita — which immediately became the rendezvous of young men of all classes throughout Rome, and the focal point of the city's spiritual revival. An apartment nearby was made into an oratory — a chapel for private prayer — where Philip's young friends met for meditation, spiritual reading, and conferences. They soon overflowed the first oratory and had to move to the Church of Santa Maria, where Philip was assisted by other priests. These formed a community, without vows, which was the origin of the "Congregation of the Oratory of St. Philip

Neri," or Roman Oratory.[5] Just as St. Charles raised the standards of the hierarchy, so St. Philip created "a new race" of priests, based on his example and those of his disciples. The Oratorians used every possible means to save the souls and bodies of their neighbors in Christ, especially the young. The poor were fed and clothed — in secret visits to their homes — the sick attended in hospitals — one of which St. Philip founded in Rome — poor girls were provided with dowries and indigent students with books. Philip's concern for young people and his popularity with them could recognize no affront; when remonstrated with for allowing them to constantly and noisily take up his time, he replied, "They may chop wood on my back, so long as they do not sin." For older friends he often used the same playful methods, with surprising success, as when he restored the good humor of a priest by insisting that they "have a run together!"

Into faith and the care of souls St. Philip put a joyful heart, just as the Jesuits put military efficiency and learning to the same end, and the Theatines put austere regularity. And added to these were the Capuchins, whose preaching and heroic charity fulfilled whatever need remained. Protestantism made little headway in Italy, but the Counter Reformation made a great deal.

With the beginning of the English Reformation about three thousand Catholics fled to Europe. The exile scholars among the refugees set up seminaries and schools of English Catholicism in Europe from which intrepid priests emanated, to return to England and secretly work there.[6] One of these was Blessed Edmund Campion, Jesuit and martyr, whom the Anglicans — including Elizabeth herself — offered every blandishment to persuade him to

[5] Here originated the *oratorio*, a kind of musical religious drama, which was one of the means of engaging the attention of the young people of Rome, as were sermons, novenas, and various other services conducted by the priests of the Oratory.

[6] Cardinal William Allen's English College at Douay, in France, was the most notable. Other noted English scholars and missionaries were Nicholas Sander, Thomas Stapleton, Robert Parsons, Robert Southwell, Edward Rushton, William Watson, Richard Bristow, and others. By the end of the sixteenth century there were 366 priests in England, including 16 Jesuits.

return to their side. It is estimated that almost half of the population of England was won back to the Church, but owing to Mary
Tudor's tragic mistakes, the blunders of Charles I and Charles II,
and the machinations of Cromwell, they were lost again. By the
time of the Act of Toleration in 1689, under William and Mary,
only a small minority was left. Nor was the Act of Toleration a
show of greater sympathy for Catholicism, or a lessening of hatred
for "popery"; it was, rather, a lessening of fervor and orthodoxy
on the part of the Anglicans, already diluted by Calvinism, deism,
atheism, and the stultifying effects of a politico-religious statism
which was by then almost universal. Deprived of the example and
the teaching — on either side — of religious scholars and ascetics
in England, the font of spiritual vitality which the religious orders
had provided for sixteen hundred years was almost dry. Only with
the return of the orders in England would that vitality also return
— to sweep into its flow the great Cardinal Newman. The real
Counter Reformation in England had to wait until Newman's
time. Meanwhile, it struggled out of the Thirty Years' War in
France to a difficult triumph.

Chapter Twelve

ROYALTY, REASON, AND REVOLUTION

The enforced aridity which temporarily dried up the springs of faith in England did not, fortunately, exist on the Continent. Everywhere, Jesuits, Capuchins, and papal legates heroically strove to recover lost ground. By the end of the sixteenth century, half of Switzerland and most of Poland had been won back to Catholicism; and in southern Germany the people only needed competent men like the Jesuit Peter Canisius to have their faith rekindled. However, national rivalries were now further complicated by religious disunion. Political wars were also religious wars, and vice versa. Catholicism and Protestantism were irrevocably divided into two camps, defended and protected by princes who were religious as well as secular despots. The result was royal absolutism on a grand scale, a condition, in religion, far more acceptable to Protestantism than Catholicism — whose doctrines and moral law emanated from the Holy See, not the king.

The Counter Reformation started late in France, owing to the "Wars of Religion" there, which wracked the country for the last forty years of the sixteenth century. The same interplay of religion and politics locked Huguenot and Catholic forces in a degrading struggle, in which endless treachery and murder engaged the ruling families of France, and wholesale massacres and destruction mounted, unchecked, among the people. Huguenots murdered thousands of nuns, priests, and monks, and the same mass madness provoked the St. Bartholomew's Eve Massacre of the Huguenots by the Catholics. Added to such savagery and intrigue was a French nationalism already so advanced that publication of the decisions of Trent was forbidden by the French kings, who feared the strength of the reconstructed papacy. The bishops had to issue their own form of the Trent decisions in a document called the Tridentine Decrees. Nonetheless, when internal peace was finally established by the Edict of Nantes, in 1598, France saw a religious renaissance that has been called ". . . in some respects the most brilliant passage of the whole Counter Reformation epic."

With peace restored, the clerical aristocracy of France immediately put their brilliance — as statesmen, scholars, and saints — into the cause of reform. Their first thought was for the improvement of the clergy, whose ignorance and indifference in the lower ranks was reflected in the people. This entailed far more than a return to the theology and culture of the ancient Church; the secularized world of the humanist must be met and dealt with as a reality, yet without compromising or denying one doctrine of the traditional faith. The cleavage between Humanism and Christianity, between spirituality and the normal materialism of free men, must now be repaired. But the astuteness of the Jesuits and of these great French priests made them well aware of the problem faced — and they were well equipped to deal with it.

St. Philip Neri's society of Oratorians for secular priests inspired many of the same type in France; it was an ideal force for the reform of the clergy, together with the Jesuit colleges. The most important early congregation of French Oratorians was Cardinal Pierre de Bérulle's French Oratory, founded in 1611, in Paris. Warmly supported by Richelieu, the French Oratory was to school and develop almost every great name in the forthcoming renaissance of Catholicism in France. Two of its first members, St. John Eudes and Jean Jacques Olier, went on to found their own societies of priests — the "Eudists" and the Society of St. Sulpice — both of which also became famous arms of the revival of faith. Still another friend of Cardinal de Berulle was St. Francis de Sales, Bishop of Geneva and a future Doctor of the Church. With Vincent de Paul, he represents the zenith of the French Counter Reformation.

St. Francis de Sales was the perfect prelate who, as Bishop of Protestant Geneva, was responsible for the reconversion of much of Switzerland. De Sales was an eloquent preacher, tireless as a confessor and adviser, and a scholarly writer. His books, letters, and treatises are masterpieces of practical piety. In his enormously popular *Introduction to a Devout Life,* de Sales achieved the solution of the problem of Catholic Humanism in simple, unscholastic terms which could be comprehended by all; and in his *Treatise on the Love of God,* in twelve books, his genius and sanctity is presented in a manner that is credited with having brought the refinement of the French language to its highest point. The French king, Henry IV, who "wished to make a third in this fair friendship" (with de Bérulle) kept Bishop de Sales in Paris as long as he could, making him preach a course of Lenten sermons at court and encouraging all his efforts. The Bishop of Geneva was too conscientious a pastor, however, to remain long. With tireless energy he visited all the parishes of his diocese, reformed communities, organized catechetical instruction, directed and advised his priests, and personally succored those who were too proud to ask alms. Bishop de Sales, as a spiritual director of both religious and laymen, continued to win fame after his death in 1622. Innumerable associations of priests and laymen, and several later orders, took him as their patron. His *Introduction to a Devout Life* is a classic that stands beside the *Imitation of Christ* in universal acclaim.

In his great charity, Bishop de Sales envisioned an order of women who would devote themselves to the service of the poor, uncloistered and unhampered by the restrictions of an austere rule. At first, this was the mode of life he established in 1610 for his "Visitandines," conjointly founded with Madame de Chantal, a widow whose spiritual director he was. Rather against his will, however, he was later persuaded to change the constitutions of the congregation to make it an enclosed order of nuns, but retaining the principle of a mild regimen. As this precluded work outside the convent, the Order shifted its object to the education of girls, with a contemplative branch. The Visitation Order was immediately successful, well suited as it was to devout women of the upper and middle classes; within the founder's lifetime eighty-seven houses were established in France and Savoy alone, and today it ranks among the most notable of the world-wide orders of women.

As Bishop de Sales was bringing the higher levels of society and his clergy into active participation in the Counter Reformation, another friend of Cardinal de Bérulle was busy effecting the same end in an entirely different sphere and by entirely different methods. St. Francis de Sales and St. Vincent de Paul were contemporaries whose individuality contrasted as sharply as that of Francis of Assisi and Dominic — existing to complement one another in the same way. The scope of Vincent's accomplishments would be even wider than Francis de Sales's, for the unassuming little Gascon priest was to realize that which the Bishop of Geneva had begun, or hoped for. This was charity — on an undreamed-of scale — and the raising of standards of the country parish, an accomplishment which was to reach into the most obscure corners of the war-broken provinces. Moreover, the lowly "Monsieur Vincent" was to be the confessor and confidant of royalty. All France, including the government, would respond to the challenge of his wishes.

After half a century of internal war — both spiritual and physical — the "Third Estate" — the common man — of France was thoroughly demoralized; year after year of grinding poverty, habitual ignorance, and unchecked disease, including frequent outbreaks of plague, were endured with bitter resignation. Much good was being achieved by a lay confraternity called the Confraternity of the Blessed Sacrament — one of whose directors was the great Fénelon — but this effort was only a small beginning in a world of such widespread misery. Nor was the ordinary country pastor much help; he was, likely as not, as burdened with ignorance and penury as his parishioners, a state of affairs taken very much for granted even by good, devout priests. Young Vincent de Paul was no great exception to this condition. True, he was virtuous and intelligent, and wished to become a good priest — but also in the forefront of his ambitions was the thought of a parish, or benefice, which would provide an adequate living, preferably near home. From the age of twelve he was provided with schooling by a gentleman-neighbor who had been attracted to the amiable youngster, and who later had given him a job as tutor to his sons to help pay for Vincent's education. But the struggle for money was a constant worry; he had to run a little school of his own at Dax to make ends meet, and was often in debt. After his ordination in 1600, the problem of finding himself a benefice further strained Vincent's meager resources; he must travel about — as was then the custom — trying to find an opening. Before he had found one, however, he suddenly met with a bizarre adventure.

Evidently aware of the young priest's penniless state, a kind lady of Toulouse — where Vincent had been studying and teaching — willed him a little money. However, most of it was owed to her estate; Vincent must collect the debt or lose it. As he knew the debtor was well able to pay, he dashed off to Marseilles, found the debtor, collected the money, and started back to Toulouse by sea. On the way, the ship was attacked by Turkish pirates. Enraged by the fierce resistance put up by the passengers and crew, the pirates took the lot of them, in chains, to Tunis. Here they were paraded in the slave market and sold to the highest bidder. Vincent was bought and sold as a slave several times within two years, the last time by a renegade Catholic from Savoy, whom he reconverted and with whom he escaped back to France. The now ex-renegade eventually became a Franciscan friar. It was not the end of Vincent's adventures, but it was the end of a thoroughly provincial young cleric; his experience had matured his soul and sharpened his mind. He was now a truly adult son of the Church, a boy-priest no longer. He did not return to Gascony, but went to the papal legate in Avignon, who took him to Rome.

Vincent seems to have been well appreciated in Rome, where he spent three months, for he was entrusted with a secret mission to Henry IV and dispatched to the court in Paris. Queen Marguerite also seemed to value him, for she made him one of her chaplains and gave him a small benefice which at least kept him in Paris — although in as wretched circumstances as ever. Here he began to serve the poor in the Charity Hospital, distribute the Queen's alms, and give away any money which she, or others, happened to give him. Here, also, he met Cardinal de Berulle and was completely awed by a man of such deep piety, yet who was a diplomatist, scholar, and energetic administrator as well. Vincent joined the Oratory, and de Bérulle became his spiritual director.

As Cardinal de Berulle wished to replace him by a priest whom he considered more indispensable in Paris, Vincent became a country pastor in Clichy, a village outside of the city. However, he had no sooner settled down to learning how to be a good pastor before the Cardinal ordered him to another post, as tutor to the three sons of a high government official named de Gondi. Vincent was dismayed but obedient; it sounded like the end of his pastoral hopes, which had been so aroused in Clichy. The de Gondi children were small devils, while their mother was all too "saintly"; Vincent was pressed into being her spiritual director, confessor, and friend, as well as tutor to her almost unmanageable progeny. He soon found himself quite exhausted by Madame's spiritual hypochondria and the boys' misbehavior.

The devout Madame de Gondi was very charitable; she visited the sick tenants on the estate and was most solicitous for their spiritual welfare. When she began to take "Monsieur Vincent" with her on her errands of mercy, he became fully aware, for the first time, of the spiritual destitution into which so many of the country parishes had sunk. Many of the people had not confessed in years, rather than go to unworthy priests; or if they had, many priests did not know the correct form of absolution — so the confessions were worthless. Madame was horrified by the discovery and persuaded Vincent to preach a mission, the results of which so crowded the confessional and the altar that the Jesuits, who had refused Madame de Gondi's request before, were finally persuaded to help out. It was at this moment that Vincent conceived the idea of the Congregation of the Mission, to train clergy for country districts.

Hearing that de Bérulle needed a priest for a poor parish at Châtillon, Vincent volunteered for the post and without notifying the Gondis, or even saying farewell — escaped! Once again he was able to revivify parochial life in an amazingly short time; his calm and practical way took everything into account and set it right within a space of weeks. To remedy the destitution in his parish, Vincent organized what he called "Conferences of Charity," a women's confraternity designed to seek out and minister to all the prevalent ills of society. The women who participated in the "Conferences" became known as Vincent's Ladies of Charity. Well-to-do and nobly born, they were able not only to raise the necessary funds for his projects but to carry them out with a devotion and zeal almost equal to that of a religious congregation. Up to this time, no such powerfully equipped body had existed to carry out these aims on such a scale.

Vincent's work in Châtillon had hardly begun before the de Gondis, distracted by his escape from them, began a siege of entreaties and plots designed to make him return. Madame de Gondi went into an hysterical "decline" and swore that she would die in despair and that Vincent would therefore be responsible for her damnation! She made her boys and her husband write to him, pleading, arguing, begging; but to no avail. Their plotting then turned to using their influence with the hierarchy, which was considerable; a tactic which proved highly successful. Vincent was ordered to go back.

In jubilation the de Gondis welcomed Vincent by rewarding him with a new status in their household. He was to be no longer just their children's tutor, but chaplain of all their estates, and also chaplain-general in the Comte de Gondi's Ministry of the French Galleys. This would give him a scope for his pastoral work and for his compassion for the suffering which they hoped would make him satisfied to remain with them permanently. It must have mollified Vincent considerably, for he threw himself into both activities with great energy. Missions which included the whole countryside were given on the estates, and Conferences of Charity were set up all along the way. Indeed, so impressive was Vincent's success that several other priests were inspired to join him, and together they worked out plans for a society of rural clergy such as Vincent had envisioned in the very beginning. The plan grew fast, enthusiastically sponsored by Vincent's patrons, who contributed a large sum for the purchase and the launching of a headquarters in Paris, at St. Lazare.[1] The priests of the new congregation became known, therefore, as Lazarists. By this, Vincent was again a part of the center of European civilization and, moreover, a power in it. He had been well rewarded for his obedience.

With the spread of the Conferences of Charity to Paris, the scope of the Ladies' work became immense. The municipal hospitals, set up by the French government, were at this time only huge pesthouses; the municipal refuges for the indigent and orphans were brutally inadequate and prisons were cesspools of human degradation. The Ladies attacked them all, under the direct supervision of Vincent. Tremendous sums were raised by the Ladies, by

[1] Madame de Gondi died the same year, 1625, and M. de Gondi became a priest of the French Oratory.

Vincent at court, and through the influence of the growing Congregation of the Mission. In the country, seeds were distributed to the poverty-stricken farmers and other charities organized. Vincent thought of everything; never had such a wide-scale assault on misery in every form been made. If "Monsieur Vincent" had been well liked and well befriended before, he was now beloved as few men had been since St. Francis of Assisi. He had the confidence of Louis XIII, Cardinal Richelieu backed his projects, and the Cardinal's unscrupulous successor, Mazarin, was completely non-plused by the simple, threadbare little priest who was his Queen's confessor. Queen Anne made him a member of the "Council of Conscience," as minister of all appointments to clerical benefices. As such, he was able to prevent unworthy clerical appointments and block other efforts to use the Church as a political tool.

Despite the tremendous accomplishments of the Ladies of Charity, their director's shrewdness observed a probable drawback: the movement was fashionable. When, perhaps, the fashion passed and the Ladies grew tired of their work — what then? Already he noticed that some of them were wont to send their maids in their stead, ashamed or afraid to be seen in the shocking mires of indigence, disease, and crime. It was understandable, certainly. What was really needed was a dedicated company of religious, to carry on the work, and in whom such sensibilities would be trained out. He broached the idea to a widow whose spiritual director he had been for some years, Madame Le Gras, and with the two first recruits, a congregation first known as the Confraternity of Charity of the Servants of the Sick Poor was formed. These were the first Sisters of Charity, founded in 1634. No modern order in the Church is more well known, revered, and imitated.

Monsieur Vincent was active in every aspect of the Counter Reformation, in the most personal way possible. He helped to concoct and ladle-out thousands of gallons of soup to the poor, to English refugees, and to the victims of a siege of Paris. He gave retreats to young clerics called the "Tuesday Conferences for Ordinands," which resulted in the modern custom of thirty-day retreats in seminaries, and added degrees after ordination to the requirements; and as chaplain-general and almoner to the galley prisoners he relieved their terrible lot with untiring energy and tenderest sympathy. He built a great hospital in Paris and an old people's home where elderly couples could remain together. His friend, St. Francis de Sales, made him spiritual director to the Visitation Order, and he was responsible for the introduction into France of several other religious orders, and for their support. Cardinal de Rochefoucault, in charge of the reorganization of all the older religious orders in France, called Vincent his "right hand." Vincent saw to the ransoming of Christian slaves, such as he had once been, and sent his priests of the Mission to alleviate the suffering of these slaves in every possible way. Refuges for girls, orphans, and for refugees from England, Ireland, and Lorraine were set up, as were free schools and training centers for young people; Lazarist missionaries were sent to the center of Protestant countries. There was no need to which he was indifferent, or to which he did not contribute.

The middle of the seventeenth century was the climax of the brief golden age of both Catholicism and the monarchy in France. The work and influence of such men as de Bérulle, de Paul, de Sales, produced glorious results. Brilliant theologians, historians,[2] an able and zealous hierarchy; saints, missionaries, and founders of remarkable holiness dominate a society which was genuinely devout — even though it was often devoutness of an overly mystical cast which led to Jansenism and Quietism. Education, the keynote of Trent, became modern in concept and method, gradually worked out in the schools of the many new teaching orders such as the Ursuline Sisters of the Blessed Virgin founded by Blessed Anne de Xainctonge in 1606, the Sisters of Charity, the Visitandines, the Congregation of Notre Dame, and the "Jesuitesses" of Mary Ward, in England. Yet theirs was only a beginning compared to the progress made, a little later, by St. John Baptiste de la Salle (1651–1719) in the field of Catholic education.

[2] Among many such writers and scholars were the Bollandists, Fénelon, Bossuet, Bourdaloue, Masillon, and a vast array of mystics of both sexes — a veritable "dust-cloud of saints," as the historian Bremond expresses it.

Distressed by both the widespread illiteracy and the low-standard teaching in the few poorly attended free schools of the time, Father de la Salle resigned his office as canon of the Cathedral of Rheims to organize a brotherhood of primary school teachers, soundly trained in a method which he himself devised. His system, laid down in a comprehensive handbook, was a revolution in pedagogy called the "Simultaneous Method" — a method so revolutionary, in fact, that it met with a great deal of official opposition. St. John fought for it for over thirty years before he was sure of its successful establishment. Nonetheless, by the time he died, his Brothers of the Christian Schools numbered two hundred teachers, having taught over 9000 pupils. Called the "Father of Modern Pedagogy," St. John Baptiste de la Salle may be ranked in the field of education beside Vincent de Paul in the field of welfare. Also like St. Vincent, he worked from the desire to create, in charity and justice, a perfect Christian — truer and better for the knowledge and skill which sound education imparts, but never separated from the moral virtue inculcated at the same time. The extensively expanded Catholic school system which we know today is the realization and the continuation of St. John's ideals.

Besides the Capuchins, many of the older orders were revived and reorganized in France at this time, assisted by Cardinal de Rochefoucault and Vincent. There was no lack of material with which to work: there were, in 1630, 37,000 Colettines and Urbanist Poor Clares in France alone (70,000 in all Europe), and the Teresan Carmelites, introduced into France in the latter sixteenth century, were numerous. A reform observance of the Black Benedictines, begun in the Abbey of St. Vann, spread to so many monasteries that in 1618 they were incorporated into one congregation called St. Maur, after St. Benedict's disciple-missionary to Gaul, with six provinces and one hundred and eighty houses by the end of the century. The scholars of St. Maur lent the Congregation great intellectual prestige all the way up to the French Revolution; their work in ecclesiastical and literary history, patrology, and liturgy is still of immense critical value — considered the "touchstone of truth for medieval history." The Cistercians were, so far, not so fortunate. The Order was now in two branches, the Common and the Strict Observance — rivals whose jealousies and dissensions held off most of the attempts at reorganization. Some of the abbots of the Common Observance made a show of compliance with these attempts, but it was insincere; nor was the so-called Strict Observance branch in any better condition. Half ruined by war, and impoverished by commendatory abbots, their abbeys struggled on in proud and bitter discouragement, their number few and their adherence to the Rule declining steadily. It was not until 1660 that Cistercian life was at last electrified by the last revolution in it which has ever been necessary. This was the Reform of La Trappe, a French abbey whose commendatory, *in absentia,* abbot was Jean-Armand le Boutillier de Rancé.

The Abbey of La Trappe was one of the many benefices which belonged to members of the French nobility, inheritable only if the families provided sons to fill such offices. This was a custom claimed by France as one of her "Gallican Liberties" since the time of Clovis and a weak spot in the French hierarchy which would prove disastrous, although — owing to men like Vincent and de Bérulle — there was not too much damage done by it at this time. Such an hereditary scion of the Church was de Rancé, the member of his family designated to hold its valuable benefices intact. In spite of being a canon of Notre Dame, coadjutor of his uncle, the Archbishop of Tours, member of the General Assembly of the French Clergy, and abbot — *in absentia* — of several monasteries, de Rancé was an indifferent priest. Wealthy, handsome, and extremely sophisticated, he divided his time between the pleasures of the chase, society, and his sacerdotal duties. Although his conscience vaguely troubled him for several years, he did nothing about it — until several strange and disquieting incidents occurred during the deathbed rites of a number of noble personages whom de Rancé attended. These incidents at last led him to change; he disposed of all his benefices but one, the Cistercian Abbey of La Trappe, where he went and took up his privilege of abbot. The monastery was half destitute and almost deserted

— a dismal remnant of its Cistercian heritage. However, the Abbot's penitential zeal soon changed all this.

De Rancé appears as a somewhat enigmatic figure, lacking the very human qualities which are to be seen in even the most austere reformer-religious — such as the star of his own Order, St. Bernard of Clairvaux. De Rancé was not lovable; perhaps it is one of the reasons why he has not been canonized. Yet his severity brought to the spirit of Citeaux an astringent vigor when it most needed such a tonic. At the same time the principle of study was retained by de Rancé, a Benedictine tradition which the Cistercian's founder, St. Robert, had tried to do without. To the Charter of Charity was added other new austerities, making the community a kind of cenobitical Chartreuse. The success of the "Trappists" is well known: the Order's unmodified observance — the strict enclosure, total abstinence, silence, night Offices, manual labor — are one of the wonders of our own time. Inspired by de Rancé's success, other communities of the Strict Observance followed him in it; the abbot of Sept-Fons sent the first of his new generation of monks to be trained at La Trappe, with the result that Sept-Fons became the second outstanding example of Cistercian reform up until the French Revolution. It was later re-established as an abbey of one of the two congregations of La Trappe. The Cistercians of the Strict Observance of La Trappe, their correct title, were to emerge the true heirs of Robert, Stephen, and Bernard, after the Revolution had burned away every other, lesser, branch of that illustrious Order. [3]

Although the seventeenth century held many such contrasts as the life of de Rancé depicts, the balance remained in favor of a high degree of religious fervor and a continuation of the Counter Reformation, although its geographical spread was halted by the Treaty of Westphalia in 1648. The conditions of the treaty were disastrous, based as they were on the principle that civil government may interpret both divine and natural law. This was a Protestant principle, fought in vain by the Holy See, and in

[3] A female branch, called Trappistines, was founded in France, in 1786, by Dom Augustine with the co-operation of his sister. There is also a Third Order, devoted to teaching.

France it was the signal for antipapal Gallicanism on a scale never dared before. As long as the great figures of the Counter Reformation were on the scene, the danger was successfully checked; but as soon as they were gone, "Court Religion" began to reign supreme in France, just as it did in all the other countries of Europe.[4] Appointments to all important offices and benefices were made by the crown, with virtue or faith having little consideration. A great gulf began to form between the upper clergy and the lower, and the wide gulf between the Third Estate and the first two became wider still.

Since the basic principle of Protestantism was individual interpretation of Scripture, it was inevitable that a myriad of divergent sects would soon crop up which, in turn, led to skepticism and unbelief in revealed religion, abetted by the poor examples of orthodoxy — Catholic and Protestant — to be seen in "Court Religion." Science was claimed as the new "religion" of the "Age of Enlightenment"; it became fashionable to be a "freethinker" or "rationalist," and at court the label was an excuse for immorality. Freemasonry spread anti-orthodoxy, especially anti-Catholicism, throughout the Continent and to the spokesmen of Rationalism — Voltaire, Rousseau, Kant, Locke, Hobbes — the Church was "an infamy, not to be endured." Only the Jesuits presented a real threat, with their unswerving loyalty, their highly disciplined learning, and their tremendous influence. The Society of Jesus must be destroyed first; whereupon the Rationalists and the Jansenists combined forces in a common hatred of the Jesuits, determined to see them suppressed, as had happened five years before in Portugal and which would soon after happen in Spain. The maneuver was highly successful; in 1764 the Jesuit schools, missions, and all their other major influences were wiped out at one stroke. The parochial clergy and the congregations, ruled by an indifferent "Court" hierarchy, were

[4] Antipapal feeling spread in Spain, under the first Bourbon king, Philip V (1700–1746), causing the closing of the papal nunciature in Madrid and quarrels with the Holy See over the royal right to appointment of benefices. In Germany, Maria Teresa and Joseph II began to control all religious affairs, independently of the Pope; and in Sardinia, Venice, Naples, and Austria the "reform" of Joseph began to be copied. In England and other Protestant countries such State control of religion was taken for granted.

cut off from every side — left to share the miserable lot of the Third Estate.

When the French monarchy was finally declared bankrupt, the National Assembly decided that the First and Second Estates (the nobility and the hierarchy) must surrender their holdings. Confiscation of all immovable Church property was agreed to in exchange for the maintenance of its ministers from public funds. The possibilities inherent in this capitulation were soon realized; within a year *all* Church property was placed under State control; all religious orders not connected with welfare and instruction were ordered suppressed,[5] and every ecclesiastical office not directly concerned with parochial affairs was abolished. Bishoprics were cut down and redesigned according to the Assembly's dictates, and bishops were to be elected by the people — non-Catholics included. Thus was the Church to be completely severed from Rome and made a paid servant of the State. All of these new laws were compiled in the "Constitution of the French Clergy," and an oath to uphold it was required. The Pope quite naturally condemned the Constitution of the Clergy, from which there arose a fresh complication: a schism by those who took the oath anyway, and the banishment by the government of those who refused to do so. Three hundred and eighty priests were deported to French Guiana, thousands fled to England[6] and Germany, and some found refuge in the newly independent United States. Nonetheless, nationalizing the Church, selling its holdings, and stripping the churches solved nothing. The State was bankrupt anyway. In January, 1793, the monarchy fell and the Reign of Terror began.

One of the first acts of the rationalist revolutionaries was to declare Christianity entirely swept away and a new deistic national

---

[5] About half of the monks left their monasteries, but all of the nuns refused to do so.

[6] The eighteenth-century rulers of England (Anne, George I, and George II) were indifferent to all religion, as the Church of England and the court was in the same condition as that of France. Although the penal laws were still in effect, toleration of all minority religious groups was beginning to be grudgingly given by England, as well as a majority of other countries. The Second Relief Act (1791) in England was the beginning there of this new tendency.

religion was set up. When Napoleon completed the catastrophe
by carrying off the Pope to exile, where he died, how the Rationalists rejoiced! The last Pope of Rome, they declared, had reigned;
Catholicism was finished.

A French historian has written: "God now saved the Church by
sending the French Revolution to destroy princely absolutism."
Certainly it was the last great crisis of feudalism, breaking forever
the fatal relation of pope to prince which had resulted in the
almost total enslavement of the Church in every Catholic country
of Europe. It was need of the absolutist ruler's patronage which
had caused the suppression of the Jesuits; humiliating capitulation
to royal exploiters and impotence by a quiescent Papacy in the face
of insult after insult. But the captivity of Pius VI and Pius VII
proved to be the starting point of the modern Papacy, achieved at
tremendous cost — and paid for in great part by the sufferings of
priests and religious. The annals of every community tell of a prolonged agony of suppression, escapes, martyrdom, and decimation.
Although Napoleon finally realized that it would be impossible to
stamp out Catholicism in France, and so made peace with Rome in
the Concordat of 1801, allowing the practice of religion again, he
maintained a firm hold on the confiscated property and continued
the nationalization of the Church. Elsewhere in Europe the Revolution spread, with his help; in Germany, he authorized the expropria-
tion of abbeys and churches, which were sold to the highest bidders;
bishoprics were vacant, parishes left without priests, and religious
scattered. While other German princes secularized and suppressed
the orders and constantly interfered in ecclesiastical affairs, Protestant rulers renewed their war on Catholicism. Such wholesale despo-
liation had not taken place since the time of Diocletian. By the time
of the downfall of Napoleon, the Church had been entirely stripped
of every vestige of her temporal power and her medieval splendor.
Still another fresh start must be made; this time as the Poor
Bride of Christ, in the new climate of Liberty, Equality, and
Fraternity — the watchwords of the Revolution.

CHAPTER THIRTEEN

NEW LIFE, NEW WORLDS

The demigods of the Age of Reason proclaimed the Catholic Church to be dying, completely defeated by the innovations of the Enlightenment. To render the Church impotent, docile — and finally dead — became the chief aim of all the intellectuals and politicians of Europe. Since nationalization and secularization of the Church was the only means of severing her from the authority of Rome, every government began to pursue such a course of "legalized strangulation." To hamper, curtail, and suppress everything Catholic became a civic duty. Anticlericalism, promoted by

185

Liberals and Freemasonry, found a special target in the monastic orders. Impoverished and depleted, many shrank to near-extermination. The Benedictine abbeys were reduced to about thirty by the beginning of the nineteenth century; the Trappists were driven out of France; the Carthusians were suppressed; and the Cistercian reform of Sept-Fons was all but extinguished. It was believed that, except in Russia, the Society of Jesus had been annihilated.

In Italy the scene was especially chaotic. The whole peninsula was riddled with secret societies, revolutionary conspiracies, overrun by foreign armies — all equally bent on the destruction of the Papacy. The common people were caught in conditions much resembling those of France during the Revolution; excruciating poverty — from which the country has not yet recovered — famine and disease were even heavier yokes than alien rulers. Despite losses, the Faith held, however, sustained by the wake of a religious revival stirred up the Observant friar, St. Leonard of Porto Maurizio, who had preached throughout Italy from about 1710. After him, the revival was sustained still further by the creation of two orders — the Passionists, founded in 1720, by St. Paul of the Cross, and the Redemptorists, founded in 1732, by St. Alphonsus Liguori. Both orders helped to bridge the gap left by the suppression of the Jesuits and the shrinkage of the monastic orders. They also helped to perpetuate monastic asceticism — contemplative and penitential — as well as Jesuitical devotion to discipline and Benedictine scholarship. While scores of "active" communities would soon emerge to battle the more elemental tides of evil, the Passionist's and the Redemptorist's ideals soared into the highest realm of Catholic spirituality.

St. Paul of the Cross, founder of the Passionists, was primarily a great mystic and ascetic, in the tradition of the Celtic and Eastern saints — "a man of incredible penances and of ceaseless prayer, whose whole life is marked by visions and special revelations that center around devotion to the Passion of our Lord." With his brother he became a hermit on Mount Argentaro, to soon be joined by several disciples. A cenobitical community was formed and began to grow under St. Paul's own Rule. Although a congregation under simple vows, the horarium is highly monastic in its austerity. The Passionists spend five hours a day in choir or meditation, and an hour and a half at night Office, besides practicing severe mortifications prescribed by the Rule. On the other hand, the sanctification of others, as well as themselves, is also the object of the Passionists; any duties that lead to this end are undertaken, especially the giving of missions and retreats.[1] Although suppressed during Napoleon's conquest of Italy, the Society was restored in 1814, after which it spread throughout the Continent, England,[2] and then to the United States, where it has enjoyed its greatest success.

St. Alphonsus Liguori, the founder of the Redemptorists, was of the Neapolitan nobility and a brilliant member of the bar. He was reputed to have never lost a case — but lose one he finally did, owing to his own error. Taking this humiliation as a chastisement from God, he immediately abandoned his practice for the priesthood. As a cleric, Alphonsus found the people of Naples spiritually starved, a condition which he planned to improve by organizing a lay confraternity called the Association of the Chapels, in which thousands were enrolled. St. Alphonsus then conceived a plan to expand the object of this society by also founding an order devoted to giving missions and retreats in urban and rural areas, but in this he met with nothing but opposition from both secular and ecclesiastical authorities. Suppressed and resurrected many times, the Redemptorists finally won permanent recognition, entirely owing to Alphonsus' administrative talents and great spiritual gifts. The "Society of the Most Holy Redeemer," as it is officially known, became "a veritable fountain of grace to the people," spreading throughout the Continent and then to America during the next one hundred years. It was largely due to the efforts of

[1] A Second Order was cofounded, with St. Paul, by Faustina Constantini (Mother Mary of Jesus Crucified) in 1771, and is contemplative. Another order of Passionist nuns was founded in 1850, in England; these teach and run hostelries and refuges for workingwomen.

[2] After the Catholic Emancipation in Great Britain in 1829, there were only about 500 priests in England. The Passionists were among the first orders to establish themselves there, as were the Redemptorists, and to re-establish public devotions, processions, missions, community life, etc.

the Redemptorist, St. Clement Hofbauer, that the Church in
Germany was prevented from becoming nationalized after the
treaty with Napoleon in 1815.

When St. Alphonsus was canonized in 1839, and declared a
Doctor of the Church, it was proved that he was endowed with
the gifts of healing, levitation, clairvoyance, and bilocation (the
ability to be in two places at once). Prodigiously active in spite
of severe ill-health, St. Alphonsus was a prolific writer, poet, and
musician; his works of spiritual direction and popular devotion,
his hymns and poems, are still in constant use; and his monu-
mental *Moral Theology* is considered the foundation of the Catholic
intellectual revival that was to follow him. His intense spirituality
gave a distinctive quality to his Society which it has never lost;
missions and retreats are conducted with an imaginative and rather
fiery zeal, as unforgettable as it is effective.

While the Passionists and Redemptorists were holding high the
cross of Christ's passion, death, and His resurrection, in an indifferent and hostile world, the "practical" side of Catholic fervor
responded in equal measure to the temporal plight of the people.
One of the most beloved figures of the modern Church, as well
as in the development of modern welfare work, was St. John Bosco,
the founder of the Salesians. He was born in 1815, the son of
poor Piedmontese peasants, and achieved Holy Orders after the
severest hardships. While visiting the prisons of his neighborhood,
he was struck with the miserable condition of the children of
crime and poverty. Dragged within prison walls, or into their
shadow, they lived in filth, want, and complete ignorance. Beginning with one such ragged urchin, Don Bosco started an "oratory"
for children — meeting with them to play, hear Mass, and to be
fed and instructed. His personality was ideally suited to befriending
the wildest, most abandoned, boys; indeed, his insight into their
needs and characters bordered on the miraculous. It was not long
before his "oratory" numbered seven hundred waifs. For those who
worked in factories he started a night school — and then a refuge
for all of them to live in. So revolutionary was Don Bosco's interest
in these half-wild "delinquents" that at one time he was considered

insane and attempts were made to commit him to an asylum! After innumerable setbacks and discouragements he established his first Salesian home, dedicated to St. Francis de Sales. It grew to house as many as one thousand boys, with a technical school, workshops, and a church. Other such homes followed as he was joined by a number of teachers and priests who had become interested in his projects. The result was the formation of a community, under his direction, called the Salesian Society. At Don Bosco's death in 1888 there were over two hundred and fifty homes housing one hundred and thirty thousand boys, in Europe and South America; and over six thousand priests had come from his Salesian institutions. The Society still follows its original ideal and also conducts hospitals and asylums, nurses the sick, and does rural pastoral work.

Several congregations of women carried on the same work among girls in Italy at this time, while in Ireland Katherine McAuley's Sisters of Mercy were to grow into one of the largest and most widespread congregations of women in the world. It was in France, however, that the spirit of boundless charity was most evident. No sooner had Napoleon concluded a concordat (1801) with the Vatican than new communities began to spring up in France at a remarkable rate. The annihilating fury of the Revolution had only served to increase the fervor of Catholicism and the need to alleviate the terrible social conditions left in its wake. As France teetered violently back and forth between kingdom and republic, the new ideals of Liberty, Fraternity, and Equality had little opportunity to function; the state of the commoners was worse than ever. It was active mercy, not theory, that now came to their aid. New orders devoted to welfare, nursing, teaching, and missionary work sprang up almost overnight, and older ones revived, under the guidance of priests and women who were themselves members of the Third Estate. In the first eight years after the Concordat, sixteen new congregations came into being, and by the end of the century there were many more.[3]

[3] Among the most notable orders founded in France at this time were: the Little Sisters of the Poor, Sisters of St. Joseph of Cluny, Daughters of Wisdom, Brothers of St. Gabriel, Brothers of the Holy Ghost, Little Brothers of Mary,

French refugee clergy and religious, driven into exile by the Revolution, had a large share in reawakening English Catholicism, consolidating and organizing the overwhelming growth of the Church in America, and sending vast armies of missionary workers into even more distant fields. Lay societies, such as the "Propaganda of Lyons," the "Conferences of St. Vincent de Paul" and the Society of the Holy Childhood, began to raise huge sums for relief and missionary work, at home and all over the world. By 1900 about 17,000 men and women of all nationalities, belonging to over two hundred orders, mostly French in origin, were scattered throughout the world. However, in France, the end of the Concordat in 1901 would see the beginning of a new enslavement. The true spirit of France's ages-old Catholicism would take root and grow elsewhere, especially in America.

Religious, priests, and Brothers share with the *conquistadores* the glory of the discovery and conquest of the New World. Supported and encouraged by the crown, armies of Franciscans, Dominicans, and Augustinians accompanied the explorers, a "burden" willingly accepted by these otherwise ruthless adventurers. Following the friars came thousands of Jesuit "Black Robes" of New France; together they stood between the conquerors and the conquered, as mediators, fathers, and friends, converting many thousands of Indians, enduring endless hardships, and often torture and death. Nine-tenths of the vast continent of North America might well have become Latin and Catholic had not the European balance of power then shifted to the British.

The subsequent history of religious life in the Americas during the eighteenth century is one of disaster, as the early glories of the first friars and Jesuits were all but completely vitiated by anti-Catholic England. The suppression of more than three thousand Jesuits was, of course, a major blow to the Church on both American continents. Their vast mission territories, the Reductions

---

Religious of the Sacred Heart, Sisters of St. Chretienne de Metz, Sisters of Notre Dame de Bon Secours. Others of the same era are: Marist Fathers, Oblates of Mary Immaculate, Pallottines, White Fathers and Sisters of Africa, Franciscan Missionaries of Mary.

of Paraguay, were leveled, and in North America the greatest
spiritual sustenance of the huge numbers of Indian converts
was dried up at its source, especially in Canada and New York.
To imported Rationalism and Freemasonry, to racial antagonisms
and conflicting colonial policies, was added the intense enmity
of the various Protestant sects toward Catholics, whose only
haven, Maryland, was short-lived. In 1654, the religious liberty
which had been granted Lord Baltimore — and which he extended
to others — was denied, and the penal code became as stringent
there, if not more stringent, as in the other English colonies. In
Canada the suppression of orders and confiscation of Church
property was begun as soon as Canada was ceded to England by
France in 1763 — to be mitigated only just before the Revolution.
To the credit of William Penn, religious freedom for Catholics
was at this time only to be found in Pennsylvania.

In the still Spanish territories of the West and South, the missions
suffered from the neglect of the crown, Indian uprisings, and the
moral laxity of adventurer-settlers. Only in California was the
saintly Franciscan, Junipero Serra, able to carry on the Jesuit's
activities, to build twenty-one prosperous missions with a population of thirty thousand Indian converts. In Louisiana[4] and Florida
the Faith barely survived through the emigration of Acadians and
Spaniards from San Domingo. Altogether, the prospects of the
Church in America before the American Revolution looked dim
indeed. And even after the Revolution, the immediate prospects
were far from bright, as long social ostracism, persecution, and
insufficient instruction had taken a heavy toll. Only Rhode Island,
among the states, provided complete religious equality; five states
established a Protestant church, and four discriminated against
non-Protestants. Within five years, however, the constitutional ideal
of the First Amendment began to take effect in the various states;
the first bishop and former Jesuit, John Carroll of Baltimore, was
able at last to establish a permanent organization of the Church in

---

[4] The first teaching nuns in the future United States, the French Ursulines,
opened a hospital and school in Louisiana in 1727.

the new country. All the same, it looked as though Catholicism was to be only a minority.

Then, quite suddenly, there was a change. Persecution, war, and famine drove millions of refugee Catholics to the new country. As the resources of the newly organized American Church were strained to the limit, appeals for help to the clergy of Europe brought boatloads of priests of every nationality — with the advantage that they could serve the hordes of immigrants in their own language and revive the beloved customs of the old countries. Immediately, a deep Catholicism began to take root.

At this the Protestant population took alarm; distrust of "papists" arose once more. Catholics were viewed as "foreigners" with strange ways, "run" by foreign priests who could barely speak English, and who undoubtedly wanted to "put the Pope in the White House." Nor were matters improved by the quarrels of the Catholics among themselves; in many communities ill feeling, for instance, arose against French priests put in charge of predominantly German parishes, or vice versa. The Trusteeism[5] controversy also caused disloyalty and division in several quarters. Tension and prejudice mounted as current literature, education, and politics became violently anti-Catholic. Riots broke out in several states; some convents and churches were burned, at least one priest tarred and feathered, and some Catholics were killed. Bigotry at home and freemasonry from abroad met to defeat all the tolerance and democracy which the country was supposed to stand for.

In the meantime, Europe's concerted effort to strangle the Catholic Church to death was admitting defeat; a series of compromise concordats was effected, which allowed the Faith more latitude and to fit itself into the new political and ideological climate produced by the French Revolution. Everywhere — but especially in Germany — Catholic life and scholarship began to attain an impressive status, and the older religious orders began

[5] Trusteeism was a system of church property administration, by a board of laymen and/or priests, attempted by Bishop Carroll. Encroachment upon the Bishop's jurisdiction caused serious quarrels and even schisms. The difficulty was eventually settled by court decision and the plan was satisfactorily altered by the Holy See in 1911.

to pick up the pieces of their ruined and looted monasteries and start anew. The Benedictines entered into a new chapter of their life of contemplation and liturgical tradition; the Franciscans — about 35,000 strong — were reorganized with the absorbing of the Discalced, Reformed and Recollects into the three main branches (Conventual, Observant, Capuchin); the Cistercians reopened many of their ancient houses and established new ones; and the Dominicans acquired fresh vigor as they threw themselves into the work of reviving the philosophy of St. Thomas. With the restoration of the Jesuits in 1814, Catholic higher education began to thrive once more — even under the limitations of secularization. The heroism of the rapidly multiplying congregations was proving again that religious asceticism was not the imposed and outdated custom that the Rationalists believed it to be. When reaction to the supercilious premises of the Enlightenment set in, the Church was ready for it.

That reaction took a number of forms, but the most important was the "Romantic Movement." The value and beauty of Tradition was suddenly rediscovered, and religious mystery, mysticism, symbolism, emotion began to have a renewed appeal. The Middle Ages, especially the classic age of the Church, found new appreciation. Art and literature began to emulate its forms, attempts were made to shape political and social life on the past, and Protestantism took a turn toward mystical piety. Such a turnabout created an ideal atmosphere for a reconstruction of Christian, and Catholic, values. Internally and culturally, a true Restoration began. Although the Church was never to regain its stolen property or lost privileges, this was much to the good, for what she lost, temporally, would be gained spiritually. The world was now to see how essentially fluid is her ancient content of faith; how Catholic doctrines remain intact, yet adjust to the requirements of every age.

The Romantic Movement and the Restoration (of the hierarchy) in England in 1850 brought many thousands into the Church, especially in England and America. With the abolition of the anti-Catholic laws in England, in 1829, the dread of all things "popish" began to subside. Certain intellectual and religious minds turned

again to the traditions which the rigidly Protestant Church of
England had abandoned, to create the Tractarian Movement, or
High Church Party. A group of scholars and churchmen, originating at Oxford University, urged a return to at least some aspects
of Catholicism. This partial return to tradition brought many of
the Tractarians to Rome, among them its two geniuses, Manning
and Newman. The Catholic aristocracy — about five hundred families — were no longer ostracized, and a half million Irish, fleeing
the terrible famine in Ireland, were absorbed into English life
without resentment.

The result of these occurrences in England was a renaissance of
religious life akin to that which France was experiencing; for the
first time since the Reformation, English names of founders and
scholarly religious appear in the annals of community life. The
monastic orders, particularly the Benedictines, resume their life
in the few abbeys not ruined or requisitioned; the Jesuits, hidden
under various interim orders and names ("The Gentlemen of
Stoneyhurst" was one) return to view as vigorous and astute as
ever; and orders from the Continent rush to the aid of reviving
Catholicism. In view of the former enmity toward religious life
on the part of the Church of England the effect on that Church
was somewhat surprising: it began to produce its own orders!
Welfare societies laboring among industrial workers and the poor
were organized into Sisterhoods and lay societies, or communities
modeled on that of St. Jean Baptiste de la Salle. Some of the
ancient abbeys were revived to house communities of Anglicans,
in the Benedictine and Canon Regular tradition. Several of these
came into the Roman Catholic Church later, such as the Angli-
can-Franciscan Order of the Atonement (both male and female
branches) in this country in 1909. In the Church of England there
are at present about twenty Sisterhoods, several Brotherhoods, and
societies of lay deaconesses, some with vows.[6] This link between
the Catholic and the English Church is still the "gateway to
Rome," bringing thousands within the fold every year.

[6] Lutheran lay canonesses, in Germany, are the only other form of religious
life to be found in the Protestant Church.

The Restoration in England and the Romantic Movement soon had repercussions in America; converts began to come into the Church from among some of the most prominent intellectuals of the country. These included the writer, Orestes Brownson; the former Episcopalian bishop, Levi Ives, and the president of Hobart College, James Kent Stone, who later became provincial of the Passionists. Hostility flared up occasionally, and members of religious orders were still distrusted as "minions of a foreign potentate," but refutation of this charge was not long forthcoming. Although native orders had already begun with Mother Seton, the founding of the first American order for men was an especially apt retort to such charges, for its founder, Isaac Hecker, was a man who could dispel such apprehension with the kind of vigor Americans understood.

Isaac Hecker (1819–1888) was a typical American "rugged individualist." With little formal schooling and less talent for it, he was nonetheless of an "inquiring mind." He was energetic, forthright, and intelligent, a friend of Orestes Brownson, and familiar with all the currents of American intellectual life. After becoming a Catholic, he went on to become a Redemptorist priest of the German community established in this country to give missions and retreats to the German-American population. Father Hecker and four other convert-priests — who had become friends in the seminary in Europe — entered upon the work in America with zest, traveling together to all the principal cities in the East and South. During this time they observed the population as a whole, and concluded that their Order should establish an American, English-speaking foundation, and so be better fitted to evangelize *all* Americans, instead of one segment of them. With this object in mind, Father Hecker set out for Rome to put the idea before the Superior-General of the Redemptorists.

The Superior-General so promptly and completely disapproved of Hecker's plan that in only three days he found himself dismissed from the Order as a disobedient and disloyal renegade! He remained in Rome for seven months, impressing his novel American personality on Vatican society at the same time. Indeed, he created quite a sensation when he wrote an article on conditions in America for a Vatican publication, and another when he converted a well-known artist of the English colony. Ecclesiastical society was even more amazed when he was finally able to obtain consent from the Holy Father to establish a new order altogether — as this seemed to be the only solution to his dilemma. He and his four friends were dispensed from their vows as Redemptorists, and the Missionary Society of St. Paul the Apostle — the Paulists — was established in 1858. Father Hecker then returned to America.

The five new Paulists began their work with an idea that was entirely unique to American Catholicism — the conversion of Protestants. The Paulists held to their idea and from it developed a brand of Catholic Action exactly suited to the new avenues of thought and communication that were developing so fast in this country. Some of these new American ways were popular "shows" made up of lectures and debates at "Lyceums" and at the Chautauqua, as well as discussions in the popular press. Father Hecker entered into the current of such media with all his forthright vigor. Though never a great orator or preacher in the classical sense, he became an immediate success as a lecturer and the author of several books. His simple, winning style, his keen wit and incisive thinking, won him a huge audience, hundreds of converts and made him the subject of much controversy — even within the Church. Complaints had been made to Rome that Hecker was promoting "Americanism,"[7] and possibly nationalism in the Church. When he was vigorously defended by several prominent members of the American hierarchy, however, the brief furor subsided; the Holy Father was persuaded that the charge was only "the figment of the imagination of three or four Frenchmen."

It is thought by some that Father Hecker coined the now famous phrase "the apostolate of the press" but however that may be, the Paulists soon led this very important movement. The Society

[7] "Americanism" was the advocation of certain modifications of faith and conduct, on the theory that they would increase conversion among the people of the United States, charged to Hecker and other American Catholics by several members of the French hierarchy. Cardinal Gibbons and Archbishop Riordan maintained that the charge was entirely baseless.

organized a Catholic publishing company — taking over a bankrupt firm — to publish two highly successful magazines, as well as all kinds of Catholic apologia in the form of books, pamphlets, and tracts. One of these magazines, *The Catholic World*, is considered one of the foremost Catholic publications in this country today. Although a relatively small and select body of men, the Paulist Fathers are nationally famed for the erudite zeal with which they pursue the aims of the first five members of the Order. It is one of the very few congregations of priests who do not take religious vows, but solemn promises only.

Throughout the eighteenth century, bishops had sent urgent calls to Europe for women religious. The response was generous, but with the prodigious growth of Catholicism in America, by the nineteenth, it became increasingly inadequate. American vocations had been few, as young men and women wishing to become religious were required to travel to Europe or Canada to enter the novitiates. It was inevitable that native congregations of women should soon appear. The first order of women was founded by a lady as typically American, in her way, as Father Hecker was in his. She was also a convert.

Elizabeth Bayley had been a debutante belle of New York society before her fashionable marriage to Mr. Seton in 1794. When Mr. Seton died suddenly, on a European trip, his widow and five small children were not left entirely destitute; both she and her husband belonged to well-to-do Protestant families and provision for her and her family was made by her relatives. After a visit to some friends in Italy, Mrs. Seton was converted and returned home a Catholic. As beloved as she was by all her relatives, their sorrow and indignation over her new faith was so extreme that the young widow was all but ostracized by family and friends. Rather than endure it, she decided to make her own way in the world, and provide as best she could for herself and children.

Mrs. Seton's first two ventures ended in failure — first, a boardinghouse for schoolboys, and then a position in a small school run by a Catholic couple, which had to be given up when anti-

Catholic feeling forced its closing. At the suggestion of a Baltimore priest Mrs. Seton then opened a school there, in a building next door to St. Mary's Seminary chapel, where she became a familiar sight to the seminarians during their hours in the church. One of them, a convert like herself, wishing to dispose of his worldly goods, bought for her a tract of land at Emmitsburg, Maryland, and provided for the building of a school, to be used for poor boys.

At about this same time, several young women of Baltimore, aspiring to the religious life but loath, for financial and other reasons, to make the long journey to foreign novitiates, were advised by their confessor to join Mrs. Seton instead. It was a happy suggestion; the arrangement worked out so well that Bishop Carroll urged them to incorporate themselves into a religious community. As a preliminary to this plan, Mrs. Seton took her vows privately, before the bishop. Soon after, the little community was joined by several other women, including her two sisters-in-law — who had been converted through their respect and affection for her — and later by two of her own daughters. By the time the community had grown to eighteen members the house in Emmitsburg was ready, and in 1808 the new Congregation moved into it.

At this time, the structure of the new Congregation had not been fully developed, but it was finally decided that St. Vincent de Paul's French Daughters of Charity would be their model. The bishop therefore requested that three members of the French Order should come to Emmitsburg to instruct the community in the observance of their Rule, with a view to becoming affiliated with the Daughters of Charity. However, Napoleon refused to allow the three Sisters to leave France. This led to the decision to become a separate congregation of the same type, with its own habit — which was Mrs. Seton's own widow's cap and dress — and its own rule and constitutions, but modeled on the original Daughters of St. Vincent as closely as possible. The community at Emmitsburg then took their public vows in a body, and the Sisters of Charity of Emmitsburg became an autonomous religious society.

Mother Seton's initiative and success in founding an independent congregation inspired many others, either to originate here or to cut their European ties, so difficult and expensive to maintain. Small communities, serving many different needs, sprang up all over America. By 1860 the number of native congregations had increased to twenty for Sisters and eight for Brothers. In the meantime, the Catholic school system in this country was growing prodigiously. Many thousands of teachers would soon be needed — to be supplied through these and yet many more new communities. The result was little short of a mass miracle.

Throughout the nineteenth century, sectarian schools of all denominations carried a large share of the burden of education in America, aided by the Federal Government. Beginning with the French Ursulines, in 1727, in New Orleans, the Jesuits' "Georgetown Academy" in 1789, and the Visitandines, in 1799, also in Georgetown, Catholic private schools had steadily grown in number, and parish schools had multiplied to such an extent that by 1884 about 40 per cent of the Catholic parishes in the United States had their own schools. It soon was decided that this type of education would have to be greatly extended, with the burden of expense assumed almost entirely by the Church. In 1883, the Plenary Council of Baltimore decreed that all parishes, with necessary exceptions, were to have their own schools within two years. This meant that a truly enormous number of teaching religious would be required in the immediate future, for the Catholic population was fast approaching twelve million — from 50,000 in 1800. At the same time, the corporal works of mercy needed the dedicated zeal of religious as much as ever, as the growing slums of our large cities were producing the usual evils of destitution, neglected children, and old people. So great was the need, in fact, that Mother Seton's congregation very soon added nursing and the care of orphans, the insane, and elderly to its works of charity, and technical, normal, and nursing schools to its work of teaching.[8]

---

[8] The Sisters of Charity now number about 9000. The Sisters of Charity of Nazareth, Kentucky, founded in 1812 by Father J. B. David and Catherine Spalding, was the next major congregation to be formed in this country.

Not only did the native congregations and branch foundations of European orders continue to increase, but the need for religious was further met by a new flow from abroad, precipitated by renewed persecution in several countries.

In Germany the effort of the State to control the Church was greatly intensified with the rise of Prussia under Prince Bismarck. By 1872, anti-Catholic laws, called the *Kulturkampf,* or "culture war," banished the Jesuits and several other orders from the German Empire; and in Prussia all communities were expelled or suppressed except nursing orders. When the May Laws, a year later, put all education, appointment, and discipline of the clergy under State control, many bishops, refusing to obey, were imprisoned or exiled, or their salaries were suspended. In 1879 over a thousand parishes were without priests; seminaries, monasteries, and charitable establishments were closed; punishments for administering the sacraments were imposed; and attempts were made to set up "official" parish priests and form schismatical churches, in much the same manner as that now being attempted in Communist countries. The effect was quite the opposite to that intended: "they succeeded in sending Catholics of every political shade and color pell-mell into the arms of Rome." A powerful Catholic political party grew up whose efforts resulted in the abrogation of the May Laws and eventual liberty for the Church. In the interim, however, many hundreds of religious and priests had fled to America, to be replaced soon enough in Germany by those whose fervor had only been increased by persecution. The *Kulturkampf* was a victory in reverse.

In France, the Catholic revival that had started after Napoleon's Concordat with the Vatican began to be slowly snuffed out. After the establishment of the Third Republic in 1879, the State became increasingly anti-Catholic in spite of the Concordat. Ultimate victory for Catholicism might have been accomplished, as in Germany, had not the several Catholic political parties made so many disastrous mistakes — thereby completely defeating their own cause. In vain the Pope and the Papal Legate urged them to co-operate with the Republic, but just as some measure of success seemed imminent, government power fell to the Radical bloc. Severe new laws were passed against the congregations, including taxes so exorbitantly high that the smaller, poorer communities were threatened with extinction. However, most of them struggled on, managing to keep their free schools going — with far more success than the government's new program of neutral, lay, and gratuitous education. As this situation posed a threat to the Radical party, even more drastic attempts were then made to crush the orders.

The first move of these attempts was directed against the Augustinians of the Assumption; the premises of their newspaper *La Croix* were invaded by the police, all papers and documents seized, twelve members of the Society were imprisoned, tried and fined, and the Order was declared dissolved. Rumors were spread that an immense amount of money to be used for overthrowing the government had been found. The new move went on to damage the orders by wildly exaggerated estimates of their assets, with a promise to reduce the country's taxes by confiscation of the orders' property. This led to the final move — the notorious Associations Bill of 1901 which provided that no congregation could be formed without legal authorization, which would, in turn, determine its functions. All congregations must each year draw up an inventory of their goods and expenses. Nullification or refusal of authorization could be arbitrarily decreed at any time, and confiscation leveled. All congregations were also to be heavily taxed. As a result of charges of infractions of the Associations Bill, 2635 free schools were closed, 110 congregations and orders devoted to teaching and 28 devoted to preaching were suppressed. By 1904, over 17,000 congregational schools had been suppressed, and Catholic primary education in France was practically extinguished. In 1905 the Concordat was dissolved, separation of Church and State declared, and Church property was declared "laicized," that is, handed over to lay associations, but owned by the State. When the Pope and the bishops of France would not accept the Law of Associations, *all* ecclesiastical property passed into the hands of the government where it remains to this day. Its use is

"allowed" by the State, under various restrictive conditions, with
no security of tenure whatever.

In the suppression of the orders and congregations in France,
America benefited immeasurably. At a time when we needed them
most, French religious emigrated to the country in large numbers, to establish permanent foundations here, many of which
transferred their mother houses to the United States or Canada.
Thus, by such a great infusion of religious life — bringing with
it all the highest traditions of Catholic culture and spirituality —
American Catholicism has risen far above the status of "just
another denomination" among hundreds.

In our own generation, begun in a state of complacent optimism,
the century was still new when we became appalled at the
reversal of our hopes for it. Two world wars, the breakdown of
Christian tradition, and the rise of industrialism have assailed
modern civilization with ruthless and cynical ideologies, materialism, and fear. Democracy, scientific progress, and economic justice
— the great accomplishments of our age — are overshadowed by
ominous new forces which seriously endanger them.

Although there are more than 575,000 Sisters, 30,000 Brothers,
and 300,000 priests in the world today, many thousands are being
suppressed, persecuted, and martyred. Even Christian countries
still enforce suppressive laws against them; notably France, the
Scandinavian countries, and several in Central and South America.
Demand yet exceeds supply for all the work there is for religious
to do, particularly teaching; and apostolic zeal is as imperative now
as it was when the first monks and canons set out to evangelize
barbarian Europe in the fifth century, for new and greater need
of it continues to appear. But new and greater sources of that
zeal also appear; in the Americas, there grows a veritable army of
missionary religious to push forward the frontiers of faith in every
hemisphere. Beginning with the Maryknoll Fathers in 1911, and
the Maryknoll Sisters in 1912, American missionary orders have
spread over the world, to command the respect and admiration of
all, especially in the present time of trial in the East. Nor has the
highest plane of ascetical life — the contemplative — shown any

signs of diminishing, in spite of the materialistic tone of our civilization. The growth of the Trappist Order in this country is phenomenal; readers of Thomas Merton's best-selling autobiography, *Seven Storey Mountain* see how intact and attractive still is the Cistercian way of Robert of Molesme, Stephen Harding, and Bernard of Clairvaux. New foundations are rising so fast that some Trappist communities have been obliged to lodge in tents! The Carthusians, whose present life is not in any detail different from the horarium of St. Bruno, are busy building their first foundation in this country; and the Trappistine's first monastery here is a large and beautiful one built a few years ago in Massachusetts. The Orders of Passionists, Redemptorists, Carmelites, and many congregations dedicated to monastic austerity and the contemplative, mystical, life of prayer — both male and female — are prospering. The century is but half over, yet the "odor of sanctity" envelops many latter-day Catholics who are, or soon may be, beatified or canonized. The first American-citizen saint is one of these: St. Frances Cabrini, foundress of the Missionary Sisters of the Sacred Heart, who emigrated to this country from Italy with her new Order early in the century. Owing to the unmistakable heroism of her life, and the miracles proved to have been attributed to her intercession, Frances Cabrini was canonized in 1947, only thirty years after her death. Other well-known saintly figures of our generation include Matt Talbot, the Dublin laborer; Charles de Foucauld, the French hermit-martyr; Brother André of Montreal; and St. Maria Goretti.

It might well be said that modern religious life, in general, is rather more ascetic in certain ways than in medieval times. In these days of "two-camp" Christianity (Catholic and Protestant) and of continual expansion, the orders must expend every effort and resource in the achievement of their ideals. There is little room for laxity anywhere.

The landed and wealthy classes, which in other ages included the orders, are now largely abolished; religious are workers, dependent on their own abilities for maintenance. No material resources whatever are left over from their constantly progressing endeavors, in teaching, welfare, nursing, missions, etc. The contemplative orders manufacture cheese, wine, books for their living, and women religious of the same type must bake altar bread, sew, or do handcraft and art. In this country, without the inheritance of beautiful and ancient monastic buildings, communities are often meagerly housed and hard pressed to make ends meet. In the United States there are ninety orders and congregations of men and over three hundred orders (congregations, institutes, Orders, etc.) of women. The number of religious teaching in the secondary and primary schools alone is 86,000. From the twenty-nine Catholic colleges in 1866, the number has increased to 236, with a personnel of about 9000 priests and Brothers besides the lay faculty members.

During the three preceding centuries, various combined religious and social experiments — such as the Mormons, Shakers, Mennonites, Brook Farm — tried to make use of organized religious asceticism. But most of them failed, for various reasons, and have been forgotten except as historical curiosities. The only outstanding, world-wide form of organized religious asceticism in the West remains Roman Catholic. Once more the world is becoming aware of this fact. An ever deep, always growing Catholic Faith is the proof of this eternal union of love with Love; of sacrifice with joy; of practical activity with the stillness of contemplation. Just as God's grace and His love shall never fail, so will there never be a lack of those who leave all lesser loves to enter the household of His counsels.

Chapter Fourteen

THE VOWS

In the foregoing account of religious orders, the inner content of the life has been little touched upon. Yet the chief reason why "organized religious asceticism" in the Catholic Church has persisted so long and so successfully is to be found only in its inner content. Community life may not be understood without at least some knowledge of that side of the story. The essence of that inner content is in the vows, the rule, and the Office.

Of first importance are the three vows of religion, because they contain all of the principles concerning that state in life. We will consider here only why they are taken, what they embody, and within what limits they are bound, as their subtle relationship to mystical theology and natural psychology is almost limitless.

A vow is a promise made only to God, of *something better than its opposite*. The vows of poverty, chastity, and obedience bind the individual to follow the Evangelical Counsels of the Gospel, which counsels surpass in importance and extent all the others of Scripture. The counsels are distinct from Scripture's precepts, which are the laws binding upon every Christian and necessary to a good life. The Ten Commandments are precepts, but the counsels are not; they are *suggestions* of ways of devotion to God above and beyond the moral law, both natural and revealed. St. Thomas explains the difference thus: "A precept implies obligation, a counsel is left optional to the person to whom it is given. Thus in the new law, which is the law of liberty, counsels are given in addition to precepts. This is not so in the old law, which is the law of servitude. It is necessary, therefore, to understand that the precepts of the law refer to such things as are necessary for the attainment of eternal beatitude; whereas the counsels have to do with the things by which man better and more swiftly achieves that end."

Whereas obedience to the "precepts of the law" is good and necessary, obedience to the precepts *and* the counsels is better — creating two levels of Christian life. Through the vows the individual "tends to perfection" in the exercise of complete and selfless charity — in love of God and neighbor — and tends away from the imperfection and self-interest to which man's fallen nature is inclined. The way of the Evangelical Counsels is but a higher and more direct road to heaven. This is not to say that the Church or those who choose to vow themselves to the practice of the counsels impugn the lesser way; indeed, quite the contrary. That lesser way — which includes the privileges of private ownership, love of family, and the right of free choice — is essential to human life in the supernatural as well as in the natural order; for the Divine Plan wills us to His grace and to heaven by that way also. But those who voluntarily dedicate their whole lives to God are assisted to a higher level of the supernatural order in sacrificing the lesser rights for the greater ones of following the Evangelical Counsels in their purest possible form. We say "their purest possible form" because it is quite possible to follow the counsels in the world — to be voluntarily poor in Christ, to be continent and in every manner chaste, and to consider always the will of God and that of our natural superiors. But how very difficult! Religious life is designed to make great supernatural virtue *easier* for mortals.

Though closer union with God, greater perfection of soul, and surer achievement of heaven are the foremost reasons for entering the religious state, there are other general benefits as well, such as the spiritual and corporeal good achieved in the name of the Church, the example set by ascetic living, the graces obtained for others, and the satisfaction of God's justice by prayer and penance. These achievements provide a bulwark against the temptations and evils which might prey upon the Church and the faithful were it not for this constant defense against them.

The origin of the three religious vows, publicly professed, is indefinite. The ancient monks of the Thebaid renounced all impediments to the practice of the counsels, but there is no evidence of their having made true religious vows in these earliest times. A dedication to the ascetical life required only a promise of "conversion of life" to all that the "way of perfection" demanded. It is not certain that St. Augustine required his Canons and "Canonesses" Regular to take true vows, though there was probably an act of consecration made to God, publicly or privately. The most concrete evidence of Canons Regular taking public vows is found after their reorganization by St. Chrodegang, during the reign of Charlemagne. For this reason many historians date the establishment of Canons Regular from that time. St. Benedict required three vows of his monks, but they were obedience, conversion of life, and stability. Poverty and chastity came under the first two; exactly when they became separate vows is not known. History shows, however, that poverty, chastity, and obedience were definitely regarded as the essential elements of the religious life throughout the Middle Ages. St. Thomas Aquinas so set them forth in his *Summa;* and in St. Bonaventure's Constitutions of Norbonne, written for the Friars Minor in 1260, they appeared for the first time, historically speaking, as three separate vows.

Secular institutes of women (not canonically classed as Orders or congregations but as religious societies) do not always take vows. Instead, they make a solemn promise of conversion of life or an oath of consecration, as do a few societies of religious priests.[1]

Before the profession of the first, or temporary, vows, the aspirant goes through two periods of probation, the postulancy and the noviceship. The first period is short, about six months, during which the general fitness and inclination of the aspirant is determined. The second period — the noviceship — must be for at least a year to be canonically valid. In it the novice is formally trained in the religious life. At any time during these two periods the candidate may leave or be dismissed. There is no onus attached to withdrawal from the community; it is very common and as much expected as not. After the postulancy and noviceship are successfully over, the novice then takes temporary vows, usually for three years, and called triennial. In some orders the religious renews temporary vows two or three times before taking the perpetual, or final, vows which are for life. The religious may also withdraw from the order after the expiration of temporary vows.

There are two kinds of perpetual vows — simple and solemn. Simple vows are less difficult of dispensation than solemn, and when in simple vows the religious has certain legal and canonical rights which, under solemn vows, are abrogated. Thus, in simple vows, the religious may own and acquire property — though not administer it — and marriage is illicit, but valid. In solemn vows all ownership of property is forbidden, and marriage is invalid as well as illicit. Women under simple vows are members of congregations, and are called Sisters; while those under solemn vows are members of true orders and are called nuns. In orders of women, solemn vows entail an obligation to the cloistered, contemplative life, though certain activities may be engaged in — such as teaching — which do not conflict with this obligation. In

---

[1] All priests take the vow of chastity and promise obedience, but these are not the *vows of religion* in the technical sense of the term.

men's orders, under solemn vows, there are many types of religious, with varied activities, such as monks — who are members of the ancient orders — and mendicants, canons regular, and clerks regular.

Those under either simple or solemn vows may be dispensed from them for sufficiently serious reasons; also, they may transfer to another order. However, this dispensation is not common, and is only mentioned to show that those under vows are not arbitrarily "clapped" into immediate and stringent servitude to them, as some seem to believe, but are subject to canonical laws which may legitimately alter or rescind these vows when, after careful consideration, it is deemed advisable.

Poverty

To be poor in Christ is one of the most insistent of the counsels in Scripture. Jesus again and again stressed the virtue of not only being "poor in spirit" but in actuality. This is not to say that He condemned the possession of goods or even great riches. However, He repeatedly pointed out the danger of wealth and required that His disciples renounce all temporal goods before they could become His disciples at all. "Every one of you that doth not renounce all that he possesseth, cannot be my disciple" (Lk. 14:33). Christ highly praised the very rich young man who asked what more he could do for His sake, yet He also said to him: "If thou wilt be perfect, go sell all thou hast and give to the poor, and thou shalt have great treasure in heaven, and come follow me" (Mt. 19:22). So all-important was this counsel that the early Christians divided their goods among themselves, sharing equally.

Poverty, of itself, is not a virtue, even as an ascetic exercise. It is only through its *motive* that it derives any value. Virtue accrues to its practice when motivated by love of God and conformity to His will; conversely, unwilling poverty without motive is of no value whatever. Only when it truly inclines the heart to detachment from all affection for material things does it become an evangelical virtue. Because of its external nature, theologians consider the vow of poverty to be the least of the three, as it concerns exterior acts only, and therefore only exterior acts may violate it — such as disposal, destruction, possession, or administration of any goods without due permission. With chastity and obedience, interior acts may violate the vow as seriously as exterior ones.

In all rules, from earliest times, personal poverty was explicitly commanded. All of the property of the religious was given to the monastery, to be shared by all. Because group poverty relaxed to such an extent during succeeding centuries, it was restressed by St. Francis in the twelfth century, when he made it one of the pillars of his Rule for his new brotherhood of friars. No personal possessions whatever were permitted them. The Order as a whole was forbidden to own immovable property, receive assured income, or hold any capital assets of any kind. However, when the resulting destitution created more chaos and scandal than it removed, the Council of Trent permitted certain common properties to the friars, technically owned and held for them by the Holy See. Assured income is still forbidden, as it is to Carmelites and Jesuits also. The licit use of common property, used according to the judgment and with the consent of the superior, and to the rule and constitutions of the institute, is but a necessity of that ideal of St. Benedict, of the community as a family. It is also necessary to the work and well-being of the individual religious and the order as a whole.

In liberating the soul from materialism, religious poverty promotes that humility and interior detachment which is being "poor in spirit" according to the Gospels. Earthly goods, voluntarily renounced, are given back a hundredfold in the coin of grace, to verify the promise, "Amen I say to you, there is no one who hath left house, or brethren, or lands for my sake, who shall not receive a hundred times as much *now in this time,* and, in the world to come, life everlasting" (Mk. 10:29–30).

Chastity

Although usually listed second in order, the vow of chastity is, in a chronological sense, the first. Women were, as we have seen, the first to embrace the religious life in the Church as consecrated virgins. In the liturgy of the early Church the public consecration of a virgin was an impressive ceremony, conducted during the Mass and only by a bishop. When women ascetics — including the consecrated virgins — dedicated to God and the Church formed themselves into communities of nuns, the public ceremony was dispensed with, except for abbesses. The vow of virginity was widened in scope to include widows and those repentant of lost virginity, and so evolved into meaning a state of perpetual continence.

As with poverty, chastity has been practiced in accordance with the Evangelical Counsels from the time of Christ. The Apostles left their wives to follow Him. The earliest historians and Fathers of the Church, Tertullian, Origen, St. Jerome, and others, speak of the celibate clergy and the honor accruing to that state. Secular priests *could* marry but many did not. The counsel of chastity is expressly given in the New Testament in the words, ". . . there are eunuchs for the kingdom of heaven. He that can take it, let him take it" (Mt. 19:12). St. Paul says, "Now concerning virgins, I have no commandment of the Lord, but I give counsel as having obtained mercy of the Lord, to be faithful" (1 Cor. 7:25). He also spoke at length upon the "better" state of continency and the virtues accruing to it (cf. 1 Cor. 7:32–34, 38, 40). No ascetical practice is spoken of more explicitly or frequently in Scripture than virginity and continence, both of which the vow of chastity includes, in addition to *chaste behavior,* both physical and mental.

Within the meaning of the vow, chastity forbids marriage and any act already forbidden by the sixth and ninth commandments. There are two equal conditions of the vow, however: it is a *virtue* as well as a vow, and therefore to be observed interiorly as well as exteriorly. Any interior acts contrary to the virtue of chastity — that is, all impure and illicit thoughts and emotions, deliberately entertained — are also contrary to the vow. Adherence to the mere "letter of the law" of the vow is not enough, as it is with poverty. There are, on the other hand, many ways in which the vow may be protected and the virtue increased, such as avoidance of idleness and occasions of sin, prompt rejection of temptations, and by temperance, dignity, and simplicity. Avoidance of sin is not growth in virtue, however. The religious makes use of the vow to grow in its virtue — through singleness of purpose and the cultivation of unworldliness so that the thoughts and actions of almost every moment bring added grace, and to make God's love and eternal beatitude an ever present reality.

To renounce the natural desire for a mate and family is a far more difficult sacrifice than the vow of poverty requires. The religious, however, substitutes love of God for love of another human being, and God's perfect love in place of imperfect mortal love. Once this state is accomplished, those who choose such a course for His sake are abundantly strengthened and consoled by the graces promised by God Himself.

The modern abhorrence of celibacy is a prejudice inherited from Luther's denunciation of it, a prejudice which spread during the Reformation. Although many other religions and cultures regard continence with honor, practically all Christians outside the Catholic Church consider celibacy incomprehensible, wrong, impossible, or unnecessary. Yet its practical advantages and widely successful attainment are most evident. It is essential to the religious ideal of continuous prayer and acts of charity, while priestly duties are facilitated without the inherent responsibilities of family life. The wisdom of St. Paul's insistence upon that "better" state, exceptional though it is, has had over nineteen hundred years of proof.

Obedience

The third vow, obedience, is regarded as the most necessary and the most difficult one because, by it, the religious offers to God, as a sacrifice, that most precious of all human faculties — his own will. Obedience also entails more obligation and requires more virtue than either of the other two vows, which concern one element only. Yet obedience is the indispensable bond that makes religious life all that it should be, under its rule and constitutions. It is also a perfect sacrifice to God in the observance of the counsels.

Whether he realizes it or not, every person wants his "own

way." Subjugating oneself to another's will, deferring to another's ideas, working always under a fixed set of rules for the good of all is to sacrifice the strongest of all the human instincts. Yet the reasons for a religious so doing are manifold.

The first reason is that the Evangelical Counsels may be carried out to the letter. In obeying just and lawful authority, a religious is acting on Jesus' affirmation that "He that heareth you, heareth me," and is following His example who said, "I do always the things that please my Father." Second, obedience ranks as one of the highest virtues, theologically, coming only after faith, hope, and charity. Poverty and chastity are virtues through motive only; obedience is a pure manifestation of humility, an act of the will alone; in essence, self-renunciation. In obeying the rule, through his superior as the representative of God, the religious immolates all pride, which is the greatest enemy of virtue, and accepts fully the discipline necessary to "holy harmony," perfect charity, and the full observance of all the vows. Religious obedience is a chain which ends only in heaven: a superior obeys the general of the order, the general obeys the pope, who represents God's law on earth, and who is himself the "first servant of the servants of God."

In these times the very word "obedience" is too often suspect, if not abhorred, as leading to mindless servility. But religious obedience is definitely limited; otherwise it would indeed be mindless servility. Obedience is confined to those things that pertain to the vows, the rule, and the constitutions — insofar as they relate to the laws of God, of the Church, and the object of the vows. It may not include anything outside of, or foreign to, these conditions. The commands of a superior are not canonically valid, in any case, unless he manifests his intention of immediate compliance with them, expressly under obedience, by virtue of the vow and under penalty of sin. Nor do any commands extend to what concerns the *inward motion of the will.* In general, the religious owes obedience in all ways which, if not obeyed, would offend against the law of charity — that is, bring discord to the community in any way, disrupt or interfere with its work, or disregard the objects of the rule and constitutions. Appeal from the obligation of obedience may be made to a higher authority within the order or to the Holy See.

The most obvious and exterior (not spiritual) reason for the practice of religious obedience is merely practicability. It channels the faculties of every member of the community into his or her best use; it organizes that community into efficient working order, according to its particular rules and constitutions and the labor to which it is dedicated. Far from stifling any creative initiative or special aptitudes, obedience prudently fosters and directs these aptitudes in true charity and the best interests of the individual, and the institute as a whole. When, on occasion, it is not so used, or a superior misunderstands or misuses that authority — owing to imperfections from which no human institution is free — those who submit with humility are so much farther along the road to inner perfection.

Just as military organization and operation is dependent for its success on obedience to orders and military law, so a religious community best furthers its objectives by a union of effort, correlated and directed by the superior. These practical reasons for the vow are secondary, however, and are, moreover, a *result* of its observance — not its prime purpose, which is self-perfection. So also does obedience maintain the religious community in its founders' ideals for it — a true family in Christ, obeying the head of that family as its father, and loving one another in filial charity.

CHAPTER FIFTEEN

THE DIVINE OFFICE

The Divine Office is a great public prayer of the Church, which must be recited every day by both the secular and religious clergy. Historically and theologically, the Office is of immense importance; no one may understand the full scope of Catholic practice, or even of Christianity, without some knowledge of this great design of prayer which contains every aspect of the Mystical Body of Christ, which is the Church, and its Head, which is Christ. Carried on in a never ending cycle, it encircles the liturgy's highest point, the Mass, as a setting surrounds its jewel, in an intricate and ancient spiral of the whole liturgical year, with its seasons, months, days, and hours. As prayer and rubric[1] it is the connecting link between the Old Testament and the New, between the Promise and the Fulfillment.

The word *liturgy* is Greek in origin, meaning "public service." At first, it meant those public services paid for by the wealthy and offered for the benefit of all; its secondary meaning is, specifically, divine service, rendered for and by the public. The word "office" derives from *officium* in Latin meaning "a duty"; in this case, a duty performed for God. Thus the Divine Office is the complete public prayer of the whole Church, recited by all those wishing to do so, but especially by those who are dedicated to that duty.

For twelve hundred years before Christ the Jewish people followed the classic custom of praying at certain times, privately and in the temples. The main content of their chanted liturgy was the psalms — interspersed with the Law and the Prophets — just as are the psalms in the Office or Canonical Hours, which are *a part* of the Old Testament, not a derivation of it. References to these hours of prayer may be found in abundance in the Old Testament: "I will meditate on thee in the morning . . ."; "I rise at midnight to give praise to thee . . ."; "Evening and morning, and at noon, I will speak and declare: and he shall hear my voice"; "Seven times a day I have given praise to thee . . ."; etc. The Oriental custom of regular times for prayer still prevails in the Mohammedan religion. In the East, where the Church was born, this ancient custom was naturally carried on by the Christians, especially as they continued to go to the Temple. Evidence of the Apostles continuing to pray in the Temple at such appointed times is to be found in the New Testament (Acts 10:39; 15:125; etc.) and it is known that St. Paul preached there at these times until opposition forced him to desist.

In the Jewish liturgy the hours of prayer were based on the

---

[1] Rubrics are the rules laid down for the conduct and carrying out of liturgical rites.

Roman divisions of the day into portions of three hours each, beginning at dawn and ending at sundown. These divisions varied according to the seasonal course of the sun and were, approximately: *tertia,* from 6 to 9 a.m.; *sexta,* to noon; *nona,* until 3; and *lucinalis,* until sundown, called thus because candles were lighted, and later changed by the Christians to *Vespera,* meaning "eventide." A predawn prayertime inaugurated by the Christians, from 3 to 6 a.m., was at first called *matutina hora,* but was later changed to *prima,* meaning the first daylight hour. All of these day divisions were public prayer times in the Temple. The night was divided into two periods of private prayer, which were called nocturnes, or vigils. There were Matins, from 9 p.m. until 3 a.m., and Lauds, from 3 until dawn. Thus is the Divine Office divided into "Hours" of the same name: Matins, Lauds, Prime, Tierce, Sext, None, Vespers — and Compline, added in the sixth century.

At the same time that the Christians were continuing the Jewish liturgy as their own, they were also celebrating the Eucharistic Sacrifice — the Mass — in a house, on Sundays. As a prelude to the Mass, their first and foremost "mystery," they held the night vigils together at the same place, beginning at Vespers, continuing throughout the night, and ending with the Mass at dawn. While the Mass was the very first Christian liturgical rite, the prayers remained the same as those of the Jews — the chanting of the psalms and reading of the Old Testament — with, at first, only a few additions, made up of Acts and Epistles of the Apostles, legends of the saints and martyrs, and homilies of the earliest Fathers which had been collected together. As these accumulated and were added, the reading of the Law and the Prophets was gradually discontinued. The Mass began to be celebrated oftener, in commemoration of the growing list of saints, although there was as yet no liturgical year as we know it. The life, passion, death, and resurrection of Christ were celebrated in each Mass. Lent and Easter were the first divisions of the year into special times; then Christmas with its preceding "vigil" and continuing "octave" until the full liturgical year emerged with appropriate choices in the Hours for each time space.

In about the year A.D. 65, the Christians withdrew from the Temple to continue the liturgy independently, although its form remained the same. The psalms were chanted by two choirs answering each other, and by a cantor (called precentor by the Christians) who chanted alone and who was answered by one choir. Short hymns, collects (prayers), and versicles were also presented in this way, the legends, lessons, and homilies being read by the precentor. The bishop, if present, or the "choir president" would choose the parts of the Office to be recited, until custom, and later written versions, decided its content. As the numbers of Christians increased, the long night vigils were discontinued and the two nocturnal Hours, Matins and Lauds, were performed together at midnight.

With the various Christian additions to the Hours, as Christianity spread among many peoples, it became impractical for all Christians to perfectly and completely carry on the Hours of the Divine Office. This duty then devolved upon the chief representatives of the laity — the priests of the basilicas, the virgins, and the monks and nuns of the Eastern deserts. In the third century, St. John Chrysostom wrote of the virgins and ascetics who recited the Hours faithfully, and an abbess pilgrim from Spain reported at length upon the manner in which the Desert Fathers chanted the Hours in the fourth century. Also, by this time, many great saints and scholars — including SS. Jerome, Pachomius, and Martin of Tours — had labored at arranging the Divine Office for some particular set of monks. Because of these diversified arrangements and many individual variations, some unification was needed. The first official pronouncement regarding the Hours was made by the Council of Laodicea in 387, regarding its recitation by monks. Also, the liturgical calendar had now fully emerged; a more concise ordo, or schedule, was demanded. By this decree, the psalms were distributed among the various Hours so that all would be included within a week, and each section of the liturgical year and day was appropriately placed. Thus the design of the "Great Office" — or all of the offices contained in the Canonical Hours — was set. Although there was no truly official version of the Great Office as yet, none used thereafter diverged from this general form.

The most important of these arrangements, or "versions," of the Office was St. Benedict's in the sixth century. Like his Holy Rule, his Office was a marvel of skill, taste, and exactitude. He considered it "the first and most glorious duty of the monk" and brought every effort of his genius to bear upon making the *Opus Dei*, as he called it, as beautiful and complete — in ritual, rubric, and content — as it should be, a rite of majestically high order, the highest point of which is the Sacrifice of the Mass. Matins and Lauds were moved up from midnight to 2 a.m. in order that the monks might have more uninterrupted sleep, and all eight Hours were obligatory. Following the night offices were Prime, at 6 a.m.; Tierce, at 9 a.m.; Sext, at noon; None, at 3 p.m.; Vespers, at about 6 p.m. or before supper; and Compline, after supper, but now generally sung immediately following Vespers in the late afternoon. These times for chanting the Hours of the Office varied according to the season; the intervals lengthened or shortened depending upon the daylight available for reading them. This variation still exists in some orders, such as the Carthusian and Trappist. The Benedictines have never altered their founder's arrangement of the Hours, nor has his ideal of its solemnity been permitted to dim.

The official Roman Office, emanating from the Holy See rather than from the East, came so close to the time of St. Benedict's version, in the sixth century, that there is some speculation as to which preceded the other. At any rate, with each succeeding century, the Divine Office continued to develop, drawing into it every vital part of the growing Church; the principal saints, martyrs, Fathers, traditions, feasts, fasts, and commemorations swelled it into many sections. Nothing that added to the glory of God and His Church was lost or left out.

The Divine Office is in four parts, one for each season, and each part is made up of the psalms and canticles, the Proper of the season, the Proper of the saints, the Common and the special Offices. Each Hour is composed of these five elements, arranged in a complex sequence that commemorates every detail of the liturgical cycle. As in the Jewish liturgy, the one hundred and fifty psalms are its main structure, with their accompanying antiphons, responsories, versicles, and lessons. Christian hymns, such as the *Veni Creator,* are included, with Collects, or prayers, for the faithful. These are composed in the ancient and stately rhythms of "ecclesiastical language," dating from about the fifth century. The Proper of the seasons celebrates the liturgical calendar of feasts and fasts, such as Lent, Passiontide, Easter and its octave, the Ascension, Pentecost, etc. The Proper of the saints are the offices in honor of all the saints having a special feast day, and the Common is the office of all saints without special feasts, such as Apostles, Evangelists, martyrs, pontiffs, virgins, confessors, etc., many dating from the third and fourth centuries. The special Offices are made up of the Little Office of the Blessed Virgin, the Office of the Dead, the Litany of the Saints, and the Dedication of Churches. Included in all the offices are other formularies, blessings, Paters, Glorias, homilies, and absolutions.

During the first several centuries of the Church, additions to the Great Office were so numerous that it filled many books. For a monastery this offered no great hardship, but often priests could not own all of these books nor find the time to recite the whole Office. A simplification and abridgment became imperative, so a briefer form, or "Breviary," was then devised.

The word "breviary" first appears in the eighth century when Alcuin, the great English scholar-monk, composed a briefer form of the Office for the laity, but containing no lessons or homilies. A breviary, in the contemporary sense of the word, did not appear until 1099, when one was composed, under the direction of Gregory VII, for monks and clerics. It was in four volumes, one for each season. This first edition was used only by members of the Roman court, until the advent of the Franciscans, in the thirteenth century, when a second edition in one volume was brought out. In their active, nomadic life, the friars needed one book that they might carry about in their wanderings. They spread appreciation and use of the Breviary all over the world and it was soon approved for the Universal Church.

During the many centuries of its growth, the Divine Office was added to and revised many times — sometimes resulting in inappropriate insertions and changes. For this reason a major reform of the Office was undertaken by the Council of Trent in the sixteenth century. This labor of many years, under several popes, aimed at preserving the ancient prayers and verse forms in the best tradition and simplest arrangement for practical use, without destroying the excellent revision of the eleventh century which had resulted in the first Breviary. A few other minor changes have been made since, the last in 1955.

The recitation of the Office by the laity did not completely die out, as may seem to have been implied. The Hours were recited privately by many of the laity for the first five centuries of Christianity, and Alcuin's "Breviary" for them in the eighth indicates that the custom still existed even then. There is also evidence that in the seventh and eighth centuries, Benedictine monks — where their monasteries were near the towns — taught the people to recite the Hours as a public prayer. During this time, a simpler and shorter office in honor of the Virgin was also beginning to be used. Its origin is obscure, though mention of it is found as early as the sixth century, and by the seventh it was made obligatory in some monasteries. It was, however, a private, unofficial devotion. As veneration of the Virgin grew, and the impracticability of the private recitation of the full Divine Office increased, the Little Office supplanted the Great Office as a lay devotion. It is a faithful reflection of its longer and more majestic model, containing psalms, ancient collects, little chapters, and lessons. The approach to God through His Mother, made Co-Redemtrix by her will and by participation in the Redemption, began with Christianity itself and has never lessened.

The Little Office became popular by the tenth century and until the period of decline, in the sixteenth, when it was added to the Roman Breviary as a special Office, to be said on certain occasions. However, the decline did not obliterate its use; a visitor to England during the pre-Reformation era reported that he saw many devout persons reciting it together in churches all over that country. Up to the Reformation and the enactment of the penal laws, it was included in almost every layman's prayer book. The Anglican services of Matins and Vespers, still a part of the liturgy of the Church of England, are a residual evidence of the popularity of the Little Office with the people of the British Isles.

At present, there is a resurgence of liturgical devotion, resulting in renewed interest in the recitation of the Little Office. Also, because of the advent of so many active orders during the past two hundred years, the duty of chanting the Great Office has again devolved upon the contemplative religious of the Church, while the active orders say the Little Office instead. Although neither true orders nor congregations are bound by canon law to recite any Office, their rules and constitutions usually call for one. Some active societies of religious say only one of the smaller Offices of the Breviary, or certain special prayers daily, weekly, monthly, or on special occasions; and a few say no Office. All priests, of course, are obliged to say the full Office of the Breviary daily, and for the contemplative and monastic orders the Great Office is considered an integral part and first duty of the religious life.

Priests and religious whose Rule does not bind them to recite the Office in choir are not required to say it at any set time. The whole Office, however, must be said between midnight and midnight. Except in the more austere orders, the nocturnal Hours are recited about 8:30 p.m. or early in the morning. For those who recite any Office privately, the rule of "vocal prayer" is still binding; the words must be formed by the organs of speech — the lips or tongue — even though not audible. For lay religious (Brothers, lay Sisters, externs) in all orders, the "Office" consists of so many Paters and Aves a day, not said in common. Thus the terms "choir monk" and "choir nun" mean those who recite the Office in choir, that is, together.

That the Great Office must be the special province of the religious and cleric is right and proper; in no other way can the full liturgy of the Church be carried on for all the faithful, in their name. Thus the Catholic Faith continues undiminished in its ancient splendor. To shorten the Canonical Hours into vestigial remnants would reduce our prayers and the content of our religion to a thin stream, and deprive God of the full homage due Him. The Mass is the same Sacrifice as it has always been; the sacraments are unchanged; the full "communion of saints," together with all the wisdom of the Fathers and of Scripture, remains commemorated and revered each day and in every Canonical Hour of the Divine Office.

CHAPTER SIXTEEN

THE RULE

The rule under which a religious lives is an obvious need and consequence of the life. It is a "plan of life according to the Gospels," as old as monasticism itself. A spiritual aid in observing the vows and a practical means to insure mutual harmony, stability, and peace in community life, the rule is the great instrument of perfection, or means to it.

In the deserts of the Thebaid, the eremite sought holiness by apprenticing himself to an older, wiser one, well versed in the practice of discipline and virtue. The disciple sought to learn, the master to teach, the way of perfection; thus, the master's advice to his pupil was the first rule. As we have seen in the earliest history of monasticism, the most renowned and holy master hermits drew around them many disciples; these lived near him in order to profit by his example and counsels, with which they soon became familiar and which they followed faithfully as an unwritten rule. Thus evolved the first religious "communities" of eremitical monks.

There is no record of a written rule of St. Antony, but the "conferences" of St. Basil, explaining the monastic life and answering questions concerning it, were recorded by scholar-disciples. All the ancient founders of the monastic life composed their own rules — Augustine, Pachomius, Caesarius, Cassian, Columba, Columbanus, Benedict, Chrodegang. Although St. Basil's Rule has been adapted to some Western religious orders, St. Caesarius' is used in a few women's orders, and the Carmelites observe the Rule of St. Albert, the Rules of SS. Augustine and Benedict are really the only ancient ones that have retained an important place in modern religious life.

The oldest written Rule, St. Augustine's, dates from the fourth century; yet it is the most widely used in the Church today. Not a relic, or merely the foundation point of the present Rule, it is exactly as Augustine wrote it for the nuns and Canons Regular in his native diocese of Hippo. As we have seen, this Rule originated as a letter to some nuns in a nearby convent. Religious life was then in a period of transition from the eremitical to the cenobitical type, and many details had yet to be organized. Nuns who had enjoyed wealth and high social standing often provided themselves with finer habits and better food than their humbler sisters could afford, and considered the government of the nunnery as their special prerogative. One may imagine that discord had arisen on some such count and the great Bishop had been asked to mediate. The three distinct vows were not then true canonical vows — that is, "public" vows — or as binding as they later became; they therefore could be, regrettably enough, somewhat lost to the customs prevailing at the time. Religious

might be as austere or relaxed as suited their individual con-
sciences; rules, though not binding, could also be austere to the
point of impracticability. Bishop Augustine sought to remedy
these ills so contrary to charity and the religious state, and so
his counsel to the nuns and to his priests living in the episcopal
residence was combined to make a rule which was mild, humane,
and fair, but which would at the same time cover all points of
religious observance in community life. For the priesthood, this
was an innovation. Many priests had practiced the Evangelical
Counsels from the time of Christ, but very few had lived directly
under a rule or in a community. This idea and practice of a
monastic priesthood was most successful, as it is at present.

The Rule of St. Augustine is in twelve chapters, of only one
or two small paragraphs each. Chapter I on the "Love of God
and Our Neighbor, Unity of Heart and Common Life" begins:

"Before all else, most dearly beloved brethren, love God, then
your fellow men; for these are the chief commandments given to
us. Accordingly, we order you who live in the monastery to
observe the following precepts."

The eleven other chapters are:
      II. On Humility
     III. On Prayer and the Divine Office
     IV. On Fasting and Reflection of Body and Soul
      V. On Care of the Sick
     VI. On Dress and External Comportment
    VII. On Fraternal Counsel and Correction
   VIII. On Care of the Goods of the Community
     IX. On the Care of Clothing, Cleanliness, and Other
         Temporal Needs of the Brethren
      X. On Asking Pardon and Forgiving Offenses
     XI. On Obedience
    XII. On Regular Observance and the Frequent Reading
         of the Rule

Chapter XII concludes: "The Lord grant that you may observe
the precepts in the spirit of charity, as lovers of spiritual beauty,
giving forth the odor of Christ in the holiness of your lives; not

as slaves under the yoke of the law, but as free men living under the dominion of grace.

"But that you may look into this Rule as a mirror, that you may neglect no point through forgetfulness, let it be read once a week. And if you find that you have observed its precepts with fidelity, give Thanks to God, from Whom all good things proceed. But if a brother sees that he has failed in any point, let him be sorry for the fault, guard against it for the future, praying that he may be forgiven and may not be led into the way of temptation. Amen."

St. Augustine's Rule, while covering all essential points on the manner in which religious should live and act in accordance with the Evangelical Counsels, is at the same time general enough to allow for variations in degree and for added laws (constitutions) to suit a particular community, so that it may be followed by religious of many types — austere, mitigated, active, or contemplative.

St. Benedict, in the sixth century, wrote a far more detailed Rule. This was — and is — different from all others in that it is most specific in every way. St. Benedict's genius of insight into the human heart and soul shines forth nowhere so nobly as in his Holy Rule. Indeed it penetrates the ego of man so fully, with such a perfect blend of lightness and depth that it may even be called, in spots, amusing. In spite of its exacting penetration, it is obvious that Father Benedict was both happy and kind, and wished only that his sons should be the same. It is not mystical, but practical, implying the attainment of that spiritual state, according to the degree in which the Rule is inwardly and outwardly followed. Herein lies its elasticity: it may be perfectly followed in the mystical, or contemplative, way, or in the active, or apostolic, way by any of the different types of Benedictine Orders from the Trappists (Cistercians of the Strict Observance) to the Third Orders Regular.

In the Holy Rule's seventy-three chapters, St. Benedict presents his "school in the science of salvation" for "beginners in the spiritual life." Like St. Augustine, his foremost aim was to correct similar, but more complex, prevailing ills in the life of his time. Based on his experience, observation, and understanding of the needs of his own countrymen, it was not purely idealistic or arbitrary but entirely suited to the times and the temperament of his generation. The Rule begins:

"Listen, my son, to your master's precepts,
And incline the ear of your heart.
Receive willingly and carry out efficiently
Your loving father's advice
That, by the labor of obedience
You may return to Him
From whom you had departed by the sloth of disobedience."

The following is a brief statement of the theme of each of the 48 chapters of the Holy Rule, including the Prologue and Epilogue.

1. The Prologue. The main principles of religious life: renunciation of one's own will; taking up arms under the banner of Christ; the establishment of a "school" in which the science of salvation shall be taught.
2. The types of monks extant — Cenobites, Anchorites, Sarabaites, and Gyrovagi, and points out that the Rule is for Cenobites and condemns the Sarabaites and Gyrovagi.
3. Qualifications for an abbot. He is to be chosen without class distinctions and only on merit, and is answerable for the salvation of souls in his care.
4. Ordains calling brethren together in council to decide important affairs of the community.
5. Seventy-two precepts called "instruments of good works" on the duties of Christian life, mainly scriptural.
6. On obedience, the "first law of humility."
7. On silence and moderation of speech.
8. Twelve degrees of humility: the "steps leading to heaven."
9. The regulation of the Divine Office: seven Hours for the day and one for night; with detailed instructions on arrangement of the Psalms, the days and seasons for their recitation.
10. On reverence.
11. Prayer in common to be short.

12. Appointment of deans: one over every ten monks. Manner in which they are to be chosen.
13. Regulation of dormitory: monks to sleep in habit, in separate beds, to rise without delay, to have one light throughout the night, etc.
14. Offenses against the Rule: scale of penalties beginning with reproof, ending in expulsion, after all other efforts have failed; offender may return three times before expulsion is permanent.
15. Appointment of cellarer and other officials in charge of goods of the monastery.
16. Forbids private possession but allows use of all necessities.
17. Distribution of goods for use.
18. Kitchen duties; to be assumed by all in turn.
19. Care of the sick, old, and very young.
20. Rules covering the reading aloud at meals.
21. Hours for meals; variations according to season.
22. Reading in the evening before Compline, and observing the "Great Silence."
23. Minor faults and various penalties.
24. The appointing (by abbot) of those to read and chant in choir, and to call the brethren to "work of God" (the Divine Office).
25. On manual labor.
26. Observance of Lent; individual self-denial only with abbot's sanction.
27. Rules for field workers and traveling monks not able to pray in common.
28. Use of the Oratory — for prayer only.
29. Treatment of guests, who are to be received as "Christ Himself"; appointment of host-monk.
30. Reception of gifts and letters.
31. On the quantity and quality of clothing.
32. Abbots to take meals with his guests.
33. Humility of craftsmen; to sell below rather than above the current trade price.

34. Rules on admission of new members. (These rules were later adopted by the Holy See.)
35. Provisions under which boys are admitted.
36. Position of priests desiring to enter the monastery.
37. Stranger-monks desiring to enter the monastery.
38. Choice of monks for ordination.
39. Order of seniority in the monastery.
40. Election and qualifications of an abbot.
41. Appointment of priors, or provosts.
42. Appointment of porter. The self-sufficiency of the monastery.
43. Behavior of monks sent on a journey.
44. Cheerful obedience.
45. Defending oneself or striking one another forbidden.
46. Obedience to one another as well as superiors.
47. On zeal and fraternal charity.
48. Epilogue. The Rule not offered as an ideal of perfection but as a means toward godliness, chiefly for beginners in the spiritual life.

Although for several centuries the Benedictine Rule was by papal decree the most widely adopted, in the course of time, as other orders were founded, each had its own rule. When, in the thirteenth century, this custom of each order adopting its own Rule threatened the general uniformity of monastic observance, the Fourth Lateran Council, in 1215, decreed that no new orders might be founded. It directed all latter-day orders either to merge with the older ones, be suppressed, or assume one of the ancient rules — the Basilian, Augustinian, or Benedictine. When all existing orders had to adopt one of these rules, certain additional prescriptions adapted to the different aims and conditions of each individual order became necessary. These were called "constitutions" — an extension and addition to the rule much like those of St. Benedict of Aniane, of Cluny, and St. Stephen Harding's "Charter of Charity" for the Cistercians. All of these were Benedictine but had their separate characteristics of government and mode of life explicitly set forth.

Besides the Carmelites, whose Rule was allowed but not formally approved, an exception to the decree of the Fourth Lateran Council was the Friars Minor, because of demand and practicability. St. Francis did not intend to found a monastic order to seek formal approbation for his simple counsel to his brotherhood of friars; the verbal approval he obtained was, to his mind, all that was necessary. Because St. Francis was an idealist — far more so than St. Augustine or St. Benedict — he saw little reason why the majority of men could not follow Christ according to the Gospels — without rules and regulations, book learning, equipment, or any direction except example. Poverty and joy were the only specific means by which men were to "mirror God"; their spiritual wellspring would be love of God, neighbor, and nature. Obedience to God, Church, and superiors was to be entirely attained by being poor, without possessions of any kind, and preaching the Gospel wherever sent. His first Rule was specific only in regard to how *little* a friar must possess and how *much* he must love God, the brethren, and the Church.

Confidently Francis set about to make the whole world into Minors as completely selfless as himself. He did not take into account that unchecked, untrained enthusiasm could endanger — even wreck — such an ideal. It was like a torch set to dry brush, firing a whole forest and almost consuming it. Homeless and penniless friars streamed over all Europe. Many were unable, even though willing, to work only for their food and shelter, or to preach without error or excess of zeal. Bishops began to protest and to forbid the friars in their provinces, and people were duped by beggars posing as friars. Factions arose within the Order, each claiming to observe the Franciscan way of life and disclaiming its abuse.

When St. Francis returned from his missionary journey to the East he found endless confusion and complaints, and so was prevailed upon to write a more detailed rule and to obtain its formal approval. This Rule required friars to have credentials and official permission to preach, and to submit the content of their preaching to examination for orthodoxy. This long Rule was to be presented to the next General Chapter for ratification; but

before the Chapter convened, Francis' Minister General, Brother
Elias, "mislaid" the Rule. Francis again retired to a mountain
hermitage and rewrote it, this time in a shorter form.

It is over this point that historians are in controversy. Did Elias
deliberately lose the Rule or not? Was it he who persuaded
Francis to shorten and modify the third one? Or did Francis shorten
it as a compromise between the ministers at the General Chapter
and himself? Were the last two Rules really the same in essence,
one being merely shorter than the other, or did Elias (or the
General Chapter) influence Francis to be less idealistic than in
the one that was "lost"? Only scholars are equipped to debate
these points, but whatever the truth of the matter, the third Rule
was ratified by the General Chapter and approved by the Pope
in a formal bull in 1223.

In spite of the Rule's ratification, factionalism continued within
the Order. Some Minors repudiated the later Rule and claimed to
remember only the first; separate branches emerged and warred
with one another — all claiming to exemplify the Rule in its best
interpretation. This division was largely due to the impracticability
of the clauses on poverty. It is unfortunate that the keynote of
Francis' ideal was its greatest source of misunderstanding, but
the natural law and the necessities of civilization demanded amend-
ments on this point. It took generations, several true divisions,
and much firm handling by the Holy See finally to restore the
Minors to peaceful stability. That the combined orders of Minors
exist as the largest group of religious in the world, and has been
the cradle of hundreds of great saints and scholars, seems to justify
Francis' ideal nonetheless.

The Rule of St. Francis is in twelve short chapters, containing
three main elements — precepts, exhortations, and privileges. The
precepts are the most numerous; they are the laws binding on
every friar, and range from simple to serious matters, but all
very necessary to his status as a Minor. The exhortations are
counsels in behavior, but are not so strictly obligatory. The
privileges concern those things which a friar or a minister may

or may not choose to do, and are not obligatory at all. The subjects of each chapter are stated thus:

1. In the Name of the Lord begins the Life of a Minor Brother.
2. Of Those who wish to Embrace this Life and how they are to be received.
3. Of the Divine Office, and of Fasting; and how the Brothers must go through the world.
4. That the Brothers must not receive Money.
5. Of the Manner of Working.
6. That the Brothers shall appropriate nothing to Themselves; of seeking Alms, and of Sick Brothers.
7. Of the Penance to be imposed on the Brothers who sin.
8. Of the Election of the Minister General of this Brotherhood, and of the Whitsun Chapter.
9. Of Preachers.
10. Of the Admonition and Correction of the Brothers.
11. That the Brothers must not enter Monasteries of Nuns.
12. Of those who go among the Saracens and Other Infidels.

In the matter of handling money and community property, each order of Minors has designed its constitutions with a view to Francis' ever willing obedience to the will of the Holy Father. Proprietorship of all property of the Capuchins and Observants is vested in the Holy See and used by permission. Other Franciscan institutes may own property in common, as do other orders in the Church, though individual poverty is still a strict requirement. In the matter of learning, St. Francis himself soon saw the necessity of enough study and knowledge to preserve orthodoxy, and appointed ministers of education in doctrine — rather than in scholarship for its own sake, of which he strictly disapproved. However, scholarship naturally developed, as great minds among the Franciscans were called upon to contend with necessary and edifying vigor in the philosophical controversies that raged in the late medieval schools. However, with the Franciscans, unlike their fellow mendicants, the Dominicans, learning is not a guiding principle, but rather an outgrowth of the Order's inherent quality and many activities.

Although prohibiting new orders and new rules, the Fourth Lateran Council did not intend to stifle or obstruct religious life, but to regulate it. Its aim was to weed out excesses, relaxations, and imperfections in this highest type of organized asceticism in the Church. Some exceptions were permitted and several orders were later authorized, but only after the most careful scrutiny and for very exceptional reasons. All of these orders are under one of the four great Rules, except the Carmelites, Franciscans, and the Jesuits, who have their own rules. Certain classes of religious communities not coming under the decrees — such as societies under simple vows — continued to multiply, especially from the eighteenth century onward. Although the majority of such societies live under one of the authorized Rules, particularly the Augustinian Rule, some have constitutions only, which, today, are most important, for they particularize the distinctive differences between each society, assure that each conforms to Canon Law, and dictate the management, conduct, dress, economy, training, etc., of the community. The degrees of cloister — that is, the rules concerning the coming and going of members and non-members of the community — are set forth; stipulated is even such minutiae as the kind of eyeglasses a Sister may wear, or whether she may or may not disembark during the course of a journey or partake of any refreshment other than a meal while outside the cloister. Nothing so safeguards a community against faults which could subject it to the criticism from the outside, or the laxity within, which so often occurred during the centuries of formation and growth. By harmonizing every temporal aspect of the religious life, in the constitutions, with its every spiritual aspect, in the rule, a double link to the divine law and the counsels is unerringly forged and made well-nigh unbreakable.

The rule, in its ascetic wisdom, is a source of inspiration and tradition which anchors the religious life to the ancient Church and at the same time ever renews itself by its use throughout the centuries. For this it is mainly valuable: to keep always alive the main principles of community life — as they were, are, and always should be. By observance 'of the rule, the vows are preserved and exemplified in their most perfect spirit. It is "an exercise in perfection," an authentic expression of the Divine Will and a means of arriving at holiness — rather than merely avoiding sin. For a religious, fidelity to the rule should be "universal,' continual, and generous, based on supernatural motives." The rewards of such fidelity are rapid advancement in sanctity, spiritual riches, perfect security, and great peace of soul. Hence it is stated in the Code of Canon Law that each religious should order his life according to the rule and constitutions of his institute and thus *"tend to the perfection of his state."*

GLOSSARY

Canonesses Regular: The "Second Order" (q.v.) so to speak, of Canons Regular, having developed as a female order of the same category. They are nuns dedicated to the recitation of the Divine Office in choir and are strictly cloistered.

Canons Secular: As distinct from Canons Regular, Canons Secular are clerics attached to collegiate and cathedral churches.

Clerks and *Canons Regular:* Clerics in Holy Orders, under vows and a rule, dedicated to apostolic work. They may be attached to the service of a church, and are also dedicated to the greater dignity and splendor of divine worship. Commonly, Canons Regular are designated as monks, but not Clerks Regular, as the objectives of the latter are entirely active rather than contemplative-active.

Cloister: The word is the anglicized version of the Latin *claudere*, meaning "to shut up." It now means not only "a place of religious retirement," but also the laws and rules governing the egress of the religious from the community, and the ingress of all persons to that part of the house reserved to the work and living quarters of the religious. All religious houses, of men or women must have cloister. There are different kinds of cloister, depending on the type and classification of a religious society. These kinds are: *Papal Cloister, Major* or *Minor,* for orders under solemn vows; and

Common Cloister, which is minimal, for congregations, which may vary in degree according to the constitutions of each.

Constitutions: The detailed regulations of a religious institute, usually supplementing or modifying the rule. Each institute has its own constitution whereas many follow the same rule.

Contemplative Order: One devoted primarily to mental prayer, meditation, and penance, to the exclusion of external works of the active life and all that is a hindrance to divine contemplation.

Divine Office: The service of prayer and praise, psalms, hymns, lessons, which all priests, and some other clerics, are required to say daily; and which is chanted in choir (or recited) by monks, nuns, friars, and some other religious. Also may be recited by laymen.

Evangelical Counsels: The counsels of the Gospel which advocate voluntary poverty, perpetual chastity, and entire obedience as instruments of perfection, but not necessary to salvation or perfection in itself. As distinct from the precepts of the Gospel (the Ten Commandments) which are binding upon all.

Extern or *Out-Sister:* Member of a contemplative community who is not bound by the rules of enclosure or solemn vows.

Lay Brother — Lay Sister: Lay Brothers and lay Sisters are members of those religious institutes

236

which consist of two classes of members: those that are priests or destined for the priesthood, and those (lay Brothers) not so destined, but who attend to the manual labor and material affairs of the order; the lay Sister serves in the same capacity in a woman's order. Neither have any part in the government of the order, nor is either required to recite the Office of the order.

Mendicant Order: "Mendicant" means "begging." The mendicant friars were to beg and work their way in their active life of apostolic preaching and works of charity, with special emphasis on the vow of poverty. Thus their main principles are very different from those of the monastic orders, though friars are commonly regarded as being monks also.

Monastic Congregation: A monastic order of many monasteries united under a common head, forming a complete, autonomous organization, with its superior subject only to the Pope (with exceptions in some women's orders). The Cistercians, for instance, are grouped into "congregations" of houses, each with its own head, with no interrelation of government except when General Chapters of the Order are called, which are held in Rome.

Monk: A member of one of the ancient orders, whose first principles are contemplative, rather than apostolic, even though they may be both active and contemplative now. These are the Benedictines, Cistercians, Camaldolese, Vallombrosans, Sylvestrines, Olivetans, and Carthusians.

Nun: A religious woman under solemn vows, or whose vows are normally solemn, but which are simple in certain regions, by dispensation of the Holy See. However, the term has come to be often inter-

changeable with "Sister," as many congregations with simple vows have used the term in their title — such as the "Grey Nuns." Nuns, strictly so called, must be members of true religious orders, and be cloistered and contemplative, though some are contemplative *and* active today, as in the case of monks.

Oblate: (1) Not a member of a Third Order Secular but very similar. A lay person is enrolled as such in a particular monastery, partaking of tertiary privileges and wearing a scapular. Obligations vary: they usually include daily vocal prayers and conversion of manners; some live in the monastery by special arrangement. Of Benedictine origin; a lay Benedictine is an oblate, not a tertiary.

(2) A priest of a congregation not under the three vows but dedicated to undertake any work for which he is called upon by the bishop of the diocese.

(3) Several communities of priests and Brothers, under simple vows, are called oblates.

Penitential Order: A congregation whose members are bound to perform extraordinary works of penance.

Province: A union of several houses presided over by one authority or superior.

Recollets: Implies a reform order.

Regulars: In the strict sense, professed members, male or female, of any religious institute having solemn vows. Commonly, clerics bound by vows and living in community under a rule.

Religious: Member or members of a canonically erected community, living under vows (or oath or solemn promise) and a fixed rule of life.

Religious Congregation: A religious institute in which members take only simple vows, either temporary or perpetual, publicly professed (received by the superior in the name of the Church) and to be renewed (if temporary) except for unforeseen obstacles. Those under diocesan approval, not papal, come under this category.

Religious Institute: A society of men or women approved by ecclesiastical superiors (bishops or the Holy See) whose members are under vows, either temporary (to be renewed) or perpetual. An institute must have its own constitutions to determine the mode of government, rights, and duties of each. There are two types of religious institute, clerical and lay. Those whose members are predominantly priests are clerical; where the majority are Brothers with only a few priests, the institute is lay.

Religious Order: Canonically (technically), institutes taking solemn vows, which vows may be taken only by orders directly approved by the Holy See. The superior-general of a religious order is under the jurisdiction of the pope alone. All orders of men are "exempt institutes" but some orders of women are subject to the bishop of the diocese in which they reside. Commonly, however, the word "order" has become a generic one, denoting any society recognized by Canon Law as a "religious institute," and therefore may be so designated.

Religious Vocation: The fitness of the subject to undertake religious life, bear its burdens, and have a right intention for serving God in this manner. No "call" or divine inspiration is necessary, as such a fitness and inclination, though natural, is God-given and the work of grace. "It is better to go into religion with a view to testing oneself than not to go in at all, since this is the first step to stopping in it altogether," says St. Thomas Aquinas.

Rule: The general principles of daily life and discipline under which a religious lives. Although, generally speaking, the rule is not binding under sin, deliberate and serious infractions may be a grave offense against the vow of obedience.

Second Order: In general, a women's order corresponding to the men's order of the same name, but with a modified rule when the original rule is not compatible with the female sex. However, there are orders equal in status that have the same rules and constitutions. Not all women's orders of the same name are "Second Orders," although the majority are.

Secular Institute: A relatively new (1926) type of religious life not a congregation or order and therefore not subject to the canonical regulations governing either — much like the secular or "lay" canonesses of the Middle Ages. They vary in their forms. The members of some do not live in community or wear habits; others wear habits, either privately or publicly, and live in community or in the world. Members bind themselves to the Evangelical Counsels by vow, promise, solemn consecration, or oath, depending on the institute. Approved by papal bull in 1947.

Simple Vows: Vows not recognized as solemn. They render contrary acts unlawful but not invalid. Ownership of property may be retained and the contracting of marriage, though valid, is illicit. Dispensation from simple vows may be obtained from the superior-general of the congregation.

Sister: Member of a religious society designated as a "congregation," whose rule and constitutions require only simple vows.

Solemn Vows: Public vows rendering contrary acts not only illicit, but invalid. Thus ownership of property and the contracting of marriage is both invalid and illicit. Dispensation from solemn vows may be obtained only from the Holy See.

Tertiary: A member of a Third Order Secular.

Tertiary Regular: A member of a Third Order Regular.

Third Orders, Secular and *Regular:* Third Orders Regular are those under simple vows, rather than solemn, whose members live in community (a diocesan congregation or of papal status). "Third" means of the same order as a first and second of the same name. Third Orders Secular are for those in the world. They are true orders, however, with a noviceship and rule (not binding under sin) but no vows. The habit may not be worn in public without permission; instead, a scapular is worn under the clothing. Members may also be buried in the habit. They share in the spiritual life and benefits of the first orders of which they are a part. The order may be left at will and another joined. Their object is to bring the spirit of the cloister into the world and to sanctify its members in the striving for greater perfection, in union with the members of the first and second orders. Third orders take precedence over all lay societies and confraternities and are organized into chapters, under a priest of the order. The Franciscans, Carmelites, Augustinians, Minims, Premonstratensians, Servites, and Trinitarians have Third Orders Secular.

BIBLIOGRAPHY

Adams, H., *Mont St. Michel and Chartres* (Boston: Houghton Mifflin, 1930).
Alzorg, J. B., *A Manual of Church History* (N. P. Clark, 1903).
Attwater, D., *A Catholic Dictionary* (New York: Macmillan, 1952).
Ayd, J., *A Brief Introduction to the Divine Office* (New York: Devin-Adair, 1918).

Batiffol, P-H., *History of the Roman Breviary* (London: Longmans, 1929).
———— *Primitive Catholicism* (London: Longmans, 1911).
Baudot, J. L., *The Breviary, Its History and Contents* (London: Sands, 1929).
Belloc, H., *A Shorter History of England* (London: Harap, 1934).
Brémond, H., *A Literary History of Religious Thought in France*, 3 vols. (London: Macmillan, 1928–1936).

Calvert, J., *St. Vincent de Paul* (London: Burns, Oates, 1952).
Chesterton, G. K., *St. Francis of Assisi* (Garden City, N. Y.: Doubleday, 1924).
———— *St. Thomas Aquinas* (New York: Sheed & Ward, 1938).
Cotel, P., *Catechism for Those in the Religious Life* (Westminster, Md.: Newman, 1952).
Coulton, G. B., *Five Centuries of Religion* (Cambridge: Cambridge University Press, 1923).
Cram, R. A., *The Great Thousand Years* (Boston: Marshall Jones, 1918).
Currier, W., *History of Religious Orders* (New York: Murphy, McCarthy, 1909).

Dawson, C., *Religion and the Rise of Western Culture* (New York: Sheed & Ward, 1950).
Dehey, E. T., *Religious Orders of Women in the United States* (Hammond, Ind.: Consey, 1930).
De Montalembert, *The Monks of the West*, 6 vols. (New York: Appleton, 1907).
Dunney, J., *Church History in the Light of the Saints* (New York: Macmillan, 1944).

Eckenstien, L., *Women Under Monasticism* (Cambridge: Cambridge University Press, 1896).

Feaney, L., *Mother Seton, American Woman* (New York: America Press, 1938).
Feasey, H. J., *Monasticism, What Is It?* (London: Sands, 1898).
Ferguson, W. K., *The Renaissance* (New York: Henry Holt, 1950).
Fullop-Miller, *Saints That Moved the World* (New York: Crowell, 1947).

Gardener, E. G., *The Dialogues of St. Gregory the Great* (London: Warner, 1911).

Garrigou-Lagrange, *The Three Ways of the Spiritual Life* (Westminster, Md.: Newman, 1950).

Gasquet, F. A., *Monastic Life in the Middle Ages* (London: Bell, 1922).

Goodier, Alban, *The Jesuits* (New York: Macmillan, 1830).

Harnack, *Monasticism, Its Ideals and History* (New York: Christian Literature, 1895).

Herkless, J., *Francis and Dominic and the Mendicant Orders* (New York: Scribner's, 1901).

Housmann, B. A., *Learning the Breviary* (London: N. N., 1933).

Huber, R., O.F.M.Conv., *A Documented History of the Franciscan Order* (Milwaukee: Nowiny, 1944).

Hughes, P., *History of the Church*, 3 vols. (New York: Sheed & Ward, 1947).

―――― *A Popular History of the Catholic Church* (Garden City, N. Y.: Image Books, 1947).

―――― *A Popular History of the Reformation* (New York: Hanover House, 1957).

Hulme, E. M., *The Renaissance, the Protestant Revolt and the Catholic Reformation* (New York: Century, 1923).

Jameson, A. B., *Legends of the Monastic Orders* (London: Longmans, 1880).

Janelle, P., *The Catholic Reformation* (Milwaukee: Bruce, 1949).

Knowles, Dom D., *The Benedictines* (New York: Macmillan, 1930).

―――― *The Religious Orders of England* (Cambridge: Cambridge University Press, 1947).

Littlefield, H. W., *History of Europe 1500–1848* (digest) (New York: Barnes & Noble, 1954).

Lortz-Kaiser, *A History of the Church* (Milwaukee: Bruce, 1938).

Mac Caffrey, J., *History of the Church from the Renaissance to the French Revolution*, 2 vols. (St. Louis: Herder, 1917).

―――― *History of the Church in the Nineteenth Century*, 2 vols. (St. Louis: Herder, 1910).

Masse, V., *A Short Explanation of the Rule of St. Francis* (Montreal: Franciscan Friary, 1943).

Maynard, T., *Apostle of Charity* (St. Vincent de Paul) (New York: Dial, 1939).

―――― *The Story of American Catholicism* (New York: Macmillan, 1951).

McCarthy, T., *Guide to the Sisterhoods of the United States* (Washington, D. C.: Catholic University Press, 1952).

McSorley, J., *Father Hecker and His Friends* (St. Louis: Herder, 1952).

―――― *An Outline History of the Church by Centuries* (St. Louis: Herder, 1949).

Meehan, A. B., *A Practical Guide to the Divine Office* (Rochester, N. Y.: Smith, 1912).

Merrick, D. A., *Saints of the Society of Jesus* (New York: Macmillan, 1930).

Merton, Thomas, *Seeds of Contemplation* (New York: New Directions, 1949).

―――― *Seven Storey Mountain* (New York: Harcourt, Brace, 1948).

―――― *The Waters of Siloe* (New York: Harcourt, Brace, 1949).

———— *The Sign of Jonas* (New York: Harcourt, Brace, 1953).
O'Farrell, *St. Patrick* (New York: Kenedy, n.d.).

Poulet-Reamers, *A History of the Church*, Vol. II (St. Louis: Herder, 1935).
Putnam, G. H., *Putnam's Handbook of Universal History* (New York: Putnam, 1914).

Ratisbonne, M., *The Life and Times of St. Bernard of Clairvaux* (New York: Sadlier, n.d.).
Reeves, J. B., *The Dominicans* (New York: Macmillan, 1930).
Robinson, Breasted, and Beard, *Outlines of European History* (Boston: Ginn & Co., 1914).
Roche, A., *The First Monks & Nuns* (London: Burns, Oates, 1942).
Ryan, M., *Our Lady's Hours; Out of the Depths* (New York: Spiritual Book Associates, 1941).

Shea, J. Gilmary, *History of the Catholic Church in the United States* (New York: Shea, 1886–1892).
Smith, I. G., *Christian Monasticism From the Fourth to the Ninth Centuries* (London: Innes, 1892).

Tourcherosa, F. E. (trans.), *Rule of St. Augustine* (Villanova, Pa.: St. Thomas of Villanova, 1942).

Verheyen, Dom B., *The Holy Rule* (Collegeville, Minn.: St. John's Abbey Press, 1935).

Ward, Maisie, *Saint Catherine of Siena* (New York: Sheed & Ward, 1950).
White, C. I., *Life of Mrs. Seton* (Baltimore: Kelly-Piet, 1879).
Wishart, A. W., *A Short History of Monks and Monasteries* (London: Longmans, 1880).
Woodhouse, F. C., *Monasticism Ancient & Modern* (London: Gardiner Dayton, 1896).
Workman, H. B., *Evolution of the Monastic Ideal* (London: Kelly, 1913).

General

Butler's Lives of the Saints, 4 vols. (New York: P. J. Kenedy & Sons, 1956).
The Catholic Encyclopedia (New York: Appleton, 1907).
The Guidepost; A Vocation Manual for Young Men (Washington, D. C.: Catholic University Press, 1948).
Sponsa Christi (Apostolic Constitutions) (Derby, N. Y.: Daughters of St. Paul, 1952).
The Roman Breviary in English (New York: Benziger, 1936).

INDEX